Schizophrenia and Human Value

For Joseph and the rest

Schizophrenia and Human Value

Chronic Schizophrenia, Science and Society

Peter Barham

Basil Blackwell

© Peter Barham 1984

First published 1984

Basil Blackwell Publisher Ltd
108 Cowley Road, Oxford OX4 1JF, UK

Basil Blackwell Inc.
432 Park Avenue South, Suite 1505,
New York, NY 10016, USA

British Library Cataloguing in Publication Data

Barham, Peter
Schizophrenia and Human Value
1. Schizophrenia
I. Title
616.89'82   RC514

ISBN—631—13474—3

Library of Congress Cataloging in Publication Data

Barham, Peter
Schizophrenia and human value
Bibliography: p. 212
Includes index.
1. Schizophrenia. 2. Schizophrenia — Social aspects
I. Title
RC514.B366 1985   616.89'82   84—14565

ISBN 0—631—13474—3

Typeset by Cambrian Typesetters, Frimley, Surrey
Printed in Great Britain by The Pitman Press, Bath

Contents

Preface

If things get worse I won't be able to cope with my direction gear. I see myself heading for the life of a recluse, being valued at 7 and ½ pounds per calendar month.

Joseph, chronic schizophrenic

I have attempted in this book to make the whole problem of chronic schizophrenia historical, and to seek to enhance our grasp of the nature of the problem with some insights from recent discussions in the philosophy of the social sciences about how human action and the enterprise of human understanding are to be framed. This necessarily involves a considerable trespass across disciplinary boundaries. There is, I believe, nothing to apologize for in this, and such an incursion is perhaps a precondition for taking the problem at all seriously. But in trying to carry through such a project I have perhaps been more than usually dependent on the work of scholars in different fields and on the support and guidance that have been given to me directly.

I have tried to acknowledge in the text all those intellectual debts of which I am aware. For different forms of help at different times I should like to thank Nick Beacock, Professor Neil Bolton, Stephen Collins, Geoff Griffiths, Maurice Hindle, Professor Liam Hudson, Barry Richards, Dr Eric Sutherland, Dr Morton Schatzman and the music of Dingle Spike. Professors Manfred Bleuler, Luc Ciompi and J.K. Wing have readily responded to my inquiries about their work. Geoffrey Pearson, Dr Arthur Still and Irving Velody have over a number of years provided seemingly unflagging intellectual and practical support and encouragement. Ruth Taylor has not only managed to tolerate this project over a long period but also, through agreement and disagreement, contributed directly to the life of the argument. But perhaps my greatest debt is to the willing collaboration of the schizophrenic people with whom I have worked, some of whom appear in these pages. To preserve the anonymity of those whom I discuss, I have to the best of my ability altered all identifying details.

It needs to be said finally that this book is introductory. I have attempted to sketch out a view and to bring various issues into a fertile relation with each other, but a number of questions surface in the text which space and incapacity have prevented me from taking further at present; no doubt there are still others of which I am not aware. Needless to say none of the people mentioned above has any responsibility for what follows, and I am only conscious that this must seem such an unfinished product to offer in return for so much kindness extended over the last years.

Peter Barham

Introduction:
The labours of schizophrenia

*Men make their own history but they do not make it just as
they please; they do not make it under circumstances chosen
by themselves, but under circumstances directly encountered,
given and transmitted from the past.*
> Karl Marx, The 18th Brumaire of Louis Bonaparte

*While we recognize the hereditary factor in schizophrenia and
while we are willing to see the contributions made in individual
cases by physical disorders, we look with suspicion on any
theory of schizophrenia that divorces the subject from the
problems of ordinary living and the universals of individual
development in a given environment.*
> D.W. Winnicott, Playing and Reality

*What we hope for from social scientists is that they will act
as interpreters for those with whom we are not sure how to
talk.*
> Richard Rorty, Consequences of Pragmatism

This book is about the historical problem of chronic schizophrenia
— the problem, that is, of the transformation of a characteristic
crisis of participation within social life, and arguably within human
life, into permanent incapacity and chronic demoralization. Put in
other terms, it is the problem of the transformation of a potentially manageable illness not only into chronic illness but into
chronic illness with chronic status — into all that the ungainly
word 'chronicity' conveys.

The identification of the chronic schizophrenic took place at
the end of the nineteenth century. Represented in the psychiatric
literature of the period is a newly discovered social type who is
deemed to have forfeited any legitimate claim on human worth

and value, to have passed beyond the reach of comprehension as a social being — an abject figure of utter uselessness, locked in a remorseless spiral of chronic deterioration. For most (though not all) psychiatrists of the late nineteenth and early twentieth centuries, and for many of their successors, the decline into chronicity was not any kind of problem, least of all a historical problem, but served rather to indicate the operations of a natural and inexorable disease process.

The type of the chronic schizophrenic that we have inherited from the last century has weighed heavily on our own thinking, not to say on our own practices, in relation to schizophrenic people. Yet if we contrast the type of the chronic schizophrenic with what emerges from a scrutiny of the actual histories of schizophrenic lives, it is apparent that the chronic schizophrenic does not exist (and never has existed) in the 'pure' or 'natural' form in which he has been represented. That it is possible to make such an assertion today is largely due to the effort and dedication of a small group of (mainly Swiss) workers, who have helped us to recognize not only the astonishing variability of schizophrenic lives but also the crucial role played by the individual's sense of his own value in the outcome of a schizophrenic illness.

What the traditional conception conflated into a unitary disease process turns out to be no such thing, and from the point of view from which I am discussing it, therefore, the problem of chronic schizophrenia is the problem of schizophrenia and history. For to speak not only of the variability but also of the unpredictability in the enterprise of schizophrenic lives, and of individuals' assessments of where they find themselves placed in relation to moral community, is to see that it is social (and therefore moral) agents with whom we have to contend in talking about the 'course' of a schizophrenic illness, and not with a plurality of unfortunates who have absented themselves from history and therefore only merit discussion in the language of 'patienthood'.

Now whilst these developments have been welcomed in certain quarters, it has also to be said that they have given rise to a good deal of embarrassment and resistance. It has been difficult to find the words, against the currents of our customary and culturally deeply rooted habits of response and relation, in which to reconceive the whole problem of the enterprise of schizophrenic lives. And as a consequence the implications of the knowledge that we now have before us, not only for our immediate practices but also for our sense of where the historical project of schizophrenia has brought us to, and as I shall try to show for our own self-understanding in entertaining claims about other human beings, have very largely still to be absorbed. Not only do we have to grasp the origins and perpetuation of a legacy, and its permeation into our thinking, but we have also in the widest terms to put serious questions to the sorts of vocabularies we need to discuss the enterprise of human lives in general. For, if the history of the scientific project of schizophrenia is in considerable part one of a devastating set of follies, these follies are hardly — the exhibitionism and self-aggrandizement of a section of the psychiatric fraternity notwithstanding — of its own singular devising. And beyond (but in close connection with) the question of intellectual frames, there is the difficult (and perhaps intractable) problem of how any morally less disingenuous view of schizophrenic people could feasibly be negotiated and sustained in our type of social order.

The aim of this book is to contribute to the process of reconceptualization on these several fronts, and in particular to give some substance to the idea (contrary to what late nineteenth and early twentieth century scientists thought it was, and some contemporary scientists still think it is) of the project of schizophrenia as historically constructed. Perhaps more ambitiously, the aim is to present chronic (in the sense of long term, not of progressively degenerate) working-class schizophrenics as in the full sense social beings — as, within the terms of Marx's suggestive but elusive dictum, makers of history within the constraints and pressures of their situations. I have introduced the notion of the *labours* of schizophrenia in the title of this Introduction to convey the sense of the actions of lives within the labours of history — in one aspect a history of scientific effort, in a second the historical actions and sufferings of schizophrenic people — and to present these two aspects in their conflictual relation within a history of the enforced definitions of the 'productive' as against the 'unproductive', the 'useful' as against the 'useless'.[1]

There is no better way to understand the force of the legacy with which we still have to contend than to look at the identity type furbished by Emil Kraepelin in his account of the victims of dementia praecox, the precursor of what we now know as schizophrenia.[2] Thus Kraepelin describes how:

In work the patients soon become negligent, they get bad certificates, pass no examinations, are turned off everywhere as useless, and easily fall into the condition of beggars and vagabonds. They sit about idle and the most they do is to turn over the pages of an old calendar or to stare at the advertisements in a newspaper. Others develop great diligence, 'study all night long', but accomplish nothing at all, take up trifling or aimless occupations, begin to compose bombastic, incomprehensible rhymes, to copy a foreign dictionary, or they lock themselves up to learn poems off by heart.

The patient appears, moreover, unconcerned by what befalls him:

> Hopes and wishes, cares and anxieties are silent; the patient accepts without emotion dismissal from his post, being brought to the institution, sinking to the life of a vagrant, the management of his own affairs being taken from him; he remains without more ado where he is put 'till he is dismissed', begs that he may be taken care of in an institution, feels no humiliation, no satisfaction; he lives one day at a time in a state of apathy. The background of his disposition is either a meaningless hilarity or a morose and shy irritability. One of the most characteristic features of the disease is a frequent, causeless, sudden outburst of *laughter*.

At one extreme we find a pointless form of withdrawal from social life, as where patients 'lock themselves up to learn poems off by heart', at the other the disappearance of delicacy of feelings, a marked disdain for the norms of public behaviour and comportment:

> The patients have no longer any regard for their surroundings; they do not suit their behaviour to the situation in which they are, they conduct themselves in a free and easy way, laugh on serious occasions, are rude and impertinent towards their superiors, challenge them to duels, lose their deportment and personal dignity; they go about in untidy and dirty clothes, unwashed, unkempt, go with a lighted cigar into church, speak familiarly to strangers, decorate themselves with gay ribbons. The feeling of disgust and shame is also lost. The patients do not preserve control of the sphincters. They pass their excreta under them, they ease themselves under the bed, in the spittoon, in their hat, in the dishes, they make little balls of faeces, collect their evacuations in handkerchiefs or cigar-boxes, smear themselves with urine, wash their handkerchief in the full chamber; they take their

food with their fingers, they spit in their bed or in their hand, or on their bread, they devour beetles and worms, sip dirty bath-water, or empty at one draught the full spittoon. The want of a feeling of shame expresses itself in regardless uncovering of their persons, in making sexual experiences public, in obscene talk, in improper advances, and in shameless masturbation.

But perhaps what taxes Kraepelin the most, in a still informing Augustan conception of madness as a mob, is that these people are prone to run with the crowd:

As the inner activity of volition fails, the resistance which outside influences meet within us is also easily lost. The patients therefore are usually docile, let themselves be driven as a herd, so that they form the necessary nucleus of those crowds which conform willingly to the monotonous daily round in large institutions. A not inconsiderable number join without resistance the crowd of vagabonds which chance leads today hither, tomorrow thither.

Along with the loss of volition goes the loss of the need to express oneself:

The patients become monosyllabic, sparing of their words, speak hesitatingly, suddenly become mute, never relate anything on their own initiative, let all answers be laboriously pressed out of them. They enter into no relations with other people, never begin a conversation with anyone, ask no questions, make no complaints, give their relatives no news. They write no letters, or only those with almost nothing in them, stop writing after a few lines.

But quite in contrast sometimes:

In place of taciturnity a prodigious flow of talk may appear which does not correspond to a need for expression, but usually unburdens itself without any reference to the surroundings. Often it consists of outbursts of filthy abuse, piercing shrieks or singing; a patient whistled tunes all day on a water-bottle; many patients carry on monologues or answer voices out loud, often cursing and abusing, especially in the night.

One way to characterize Kraepelin's achievement (and it is, as we shall see, also the source of his attraction) is to say that he succeeded

very cleverly in transforming a perplexing set of actions within
the calendar of historical time into a set of behaviours within the
time of a disease process, a form of participation in the social into
a set of happenings within the ecology of an individual brain. My
claim will be that in order to contend with this legacy (and it is, as
I remarked, a legacy that Kraepelin furbished but did not invent),
and to help us bring the problem into historical focus, we will do
well to take some guidance from those theorists who have advanced forceful arguments in recent years to demonstrate that social
phenomena can only be defined in the medium of time, and that
the generic framework of the social sciences — and psychiatry,
whatever it may sometimes think it does, is such a science — is
that of a historical sociology. To reintroduce time into social
theory is, among other things, to abandon the traditional anti-
nomies between action and structure and between the individual
and society in favour of conceptions of social structure and
identity formation as interacting constituents in a historical process of 'becoming'. As Philip Abrams frames it for the historical
construction of individuals:

> The knowledge we have accumulated about the making of
> individuals, and about the thoroughly historical nature of
> that process, seems to me to make the case for thinking our-
> selves out of our conventional ways of describing and living
> the relationship of individual and society altogether com-
> pelling.[3]

Just what this might mean in its application to schizophrenic
people, and in the clarification of the historical problem of chronic
schizophrenia, we shall have to explore. However, the sorts of
conceptions proposed by sociologists like Abrams and in particular, as we shall see, by historically minded philosophers like Alasdair MacIntyre, do at the very least put us on the road we need to
travel down.

The scheme of the book is now described. In part I I shall explore the context of emergence of the type of the chronic schizophrenic in the social circumstances of England in the late nineteenth century, and the reception accorded to Kraepelin's theory
of dementia praecox in the early part of the present century. The
inherited wisdom from the last century has been devastated by
discoveries about the life histories of schizophrenic people, and
in chapter 2 I try to situate the problem of schizophrenia and his-

tory in the context of recent discussions in the philosophy of the social sciences, in particular Alasdair MacIntyre's exploration of the role of narrative in human action and understanding. In part II we shall engage directly with the action of schizophrenic lives, and I prepare for this in chapter 3 by describing a narrative concept of selfhood. Chapters 4 and 5 explore the interconnections between personal, social and historical aspects of identity among a group of contemporary hospitalized working-class schizophrenics against the background of the inherited identity type of the chronic schizophrenic. In chapter 6 I examine the implications of the previous discussion for the sorts of conceptions that we need for thinking about the enterprise of human lives in general and that of schizophrenic lives in particular, and bring out the importance of Manfred Bleuler's contribution to the field. And finally in part III I take up again some of the themes from chapter 1, this time in the contemporary context of the welfare state, and identify some of the ambiguity and mischief in policies of community care.

It need hardly be said that any entry into the debate about schizophrenia is a hazardous affair, and I make no claim for any kind of grand theory of schizophrenia or even to tackle directly all of the issues that are implicit in some of my arguments. However, given the confusions that abound in this field, it may be useful to make explicit at this stage some of the assumptions that (for present purposes) I have taken for granted. So, for example, in my concern with the relationship between schizophrenia and history, there is no suggestion that the problem of schizophrenic illness as such (and even of chronic, in the sense of long term, schizophrenic illness) will necessarily be eliminated by any amount of transformation in the social order. (The question of the historical origins of schizophrenic forms of illness in Western societies is, I believe, still an open one.[4]) Similarly — and this is a matter to which I shall return in the text — I take for granted the application of concepts of 'illness' to the sorts of human predicament that we term schizophrenic, not because I think they can be grounded in nature's realm but because (as we shall see later), for reasons that run deep in our sense of what is involved in sustaining community, they are concepts that we cannot do without in coping with such states of affairs. And thirdly, though I shall not discuss it here, I take for granted the evidence of a genetic contribution to schizophrenic conditions in a large proportion of instances, so long as we appreciate that such evidence neither licenses any kind of sharp division between the biological inheritance of the schizophrenic person and the inherited natures that the rest of us have to contend with, nor renders the trajectory of any particular life history in any way determinate. Furthermore, as Oliver Sacks so clearly shows, it is only through learning to think historically that we can learn to think biologically.[5]

Lastly, this is a book about the sort of person illustrated in this characteristic vignette:

> *James Brown* (age 30): Single. Duration of illness: seven years. Previous treatment: one course of electro-shock therapy. He had been employed as a clerk before his break- down. His clothing was usually untidy as he repeatedly tied and untied his boots and tie, and buttoned and unbuttoned his jacket and waistcoat. He was timorous, and made no spontaneous comments, his speech being restricted to 'Yes', 'No', and 'I couldn't say'.[6]

The representative male chronic schizophrenic is a man who, in his late teens or early twenties, at the point of culmination of the long period of socialization which has prepared him to take up his role in the workplace or wherever real manhood is supposed to declare itself, shows himself inadequate. It is as if, as one of the schizophrenic people whom we shall meet later described, one were to spend years constructing a vehicle only to watch it fall to pieces a hundred yards along the road on its first run.

But if the male schizophrenic breaks down a hundred yards into manhood, there is also another kind of person:

> Girls throw themselves away on anybody who wants inter- course with disastrous consequences — one hebephrenic student, daughter of a respectable family, waited behind a hedge on the roadside determined to give herself to the first passer-by. She had been unable to concentrate on her studies for several months and had spent her days in bed, while drinking and dancing by night in low taverns.[7]

Generally female schizophrenics have travelled as much as ten years further into adulthood before breaking down. In addi- tion, as brought out by the above quotation (which describes a 'flare-up' of sexuality, as the authors term it in this well-known textbook), where schizophrenic men have traditionally been repre- sented as passive and withdrawn, schizophrenic women have been pictured as active, domineering and highly sexed.[8] The fate of women in the history of schizophrenia over the past hundred years deserves intensive study in its own right, and the suggestion that the sex difference in the age of onset is to be accounted for on the basis of brain maturation could perhaps be improved upon.[9] But for these questions, alas, there is no space here, and I suspect that in any case I am not adequately qualified to embark upon them.

Part I

Progressive Deterioration and the Progress of Science

1

The making of
the chronic schizophrenic

For the last 40 years it has been the persistent effort of our legislators, under the co-ordinated stimulus of science and philanthropy (chiefly administered by our own noble profession), to bring under observation the loose and scattered madness of the country, and provide for its subjects fitting homes and refuges.
Edgar Sheppard, Professor of Psychological Medicine, King's College, London: *Journal of Mental Science* 17 (1872)

Traditionally, the history of psychiatry has been conceived as the story of how, in a circuitous but none the less impressive series of developments, the rationality of science has been brought to bear on the phenomena of insanity and the mentally ill have been ushered into the light of a more progressive epoch. Whereas in our own period morals and science work in happy combination under the guiding influence of science, in an earlier 'dark age' a certain moral outlook was permitted to sustain itself, unrelieved by the penetration of scientific truths. On this view of things the scientific elaboration of a mental illness such as schizophrenia proceeded in relative independence from a social history, and we are led to think in terms, for example, of the scientific *discovery* of schizophrenia. The relation of scientific ideas (of what comes to count as authoritative forms of knowledge) to forms of moral-political discourse (the authoritative conceptions of social life) is left unclarified: social history appears sometimes as background and sometimes as hindrance, but the 'insides' of the scientific discourse are left untouched by it.

There are good reasons why we should want to affirm the promise that is available to use in our contemporary schemes of understanding and treating the mentally ill, but promise is, as we shall see, a delicate and sometimes ambiguous plant. More particularly, by detaching scientific ideas from the historical conditions of their emergence, the rhetoricians of progress have in a number of respects obscured the origins of psychiatry and its attendant practices as moral projects, and impeded recognition of the continuing entanglement of those same projects in an active moral inheritance that does not find much to value in those who suffer from a mental illness.

In recent years, however, a number of historians have provided a different cast on these matters and helped us to see that, as Georges Canguilhem has put it, 'every science more or less gives itself its given and thereby appropriates what is called its domain.' The 'object' of a science thus takes on a new kind of meaning: it is 'no longer simply the specific field in which problems are to be resolved and obstacles removed, it is also the intentions and ambitions of the subject of the science, the specific project that informs a theoretical consciousness.'[1] On this line of argument 'modern psychiatry is not a pure scientific discourse but is necessarily situated in institutions and practices which make both its phenomena and its discourse on them possible.' It does not therefore 'encounter a natural phenomenon "insanity" '; rather it 'deals with a population constituted in specific institutional conditions.'[2]

In this chapter we shall illustrate some of the senses in which the 'disease entity' of schizophrenia can be said to be implicated in a social history, and explore various aspects of the social circumstances that prepared for the emergence of the schizophrenic as an object of scientific discourse and for the identification of the chronic schizophrenic as a definite social type. We shall come to see that the scientific elaboration of schizophrenia played a very considerable role in promoting a form of organized neglect, and in cementing images of pessimism and hopelessness, and that the origins of the project of schizophrenia are inseparably woven into a structure of feeling that is best characterized as the legitimation of contempt. Scientific ideas were more subtly — and deviously — interlinked with social beliefs and commitments than we have generally been led to suppose, the one in various ways feeding into, providing support for, and interacting upon the other.

The context of emergence of the chronic schizophrenic

A debate of the 1870s

A convenient and instructive point of entry is a controversy that appeared in the *Journal of Mental Science* — the precursor of what is now the *British Journal of Psychiatry* — in 1871 and 1872. The choice of date is apt in at least two ways. The 1860s and 1870s marked a point of critical reappraisal in the dominant currents of late Victorian thought that declared itself not in a disillusion with progress as such but in a recasting of the grammar of progress, of the terms in which it was conceived and expressed. The dimensions of the 'social question' presented themselves ever more sharply and extensively so as to make earlier doctrines of moral reform seem lamentably inadequate; and in the organization of responses to the poor, the unemployed and the 'dangerous classes' more generally the naive optimism of earlier reformers gave way to a stance of enlightened pessimism. The appearance of biological and determinist interpretations of history, and of doctrines of progressive social selection, lent justification to beliefs that the unfettered competition of the marketplace operated for the common good and that the artificial preservation of those least able to take care of themselves was a form of interference in the 'natural' expression of market forces. Francis Galton had published his *Hereditary Genius* in 1869 and the influence of Herbert Spencer was approaching its height.

In the case of the insane the previous 30 years had witnessed a massive increase in the population of asylums and in the population officially designated as insane taken as a whole; and in the same period the percentage of asylum inmates judged to be curable had dropped sharply. In question, therefore, were both the amenability of the insane to cure *and* the status of the asylum as an instrument of their welfare. How was insanity now to be conceived? Were new kinds of approaches to the problem of insanity necessary? Was the asylum to be displaced or should it be given a new kind of role? As we shall see, different kinds of evidence were adduced and different styles of argument put forward, and the period is interesting because at this stage things had not settled: we can note the conflicting choices of direction, and the pressures and enticements that urged this way rather than that.

Second, the debates of this period preceded by a number of years the systematic elaboration of scientific ideas about schizophrenia. In 1851 Morel had identified a process of severe intellectual deterioration starting in adolescence that he termed 'demence precoce', and Kahlbaum was shortly to publish his account of catatonic states; but Wundt had not yet established his experimental psychology laboratory in Leipzig where Emil Kraepelin was to be an early pupil. It was only in 1893, in the fourth edition of his textbook, that Kraepelin brought together the syndromes of demence precoce, hebephrenia, catatonia and dementia paranoides under the heading of 'psychological degeneration processes', and in 1899 that he endowed these processes with the name 'dementia praecox' as comprising a single disease entity.

The occasion is Henry Maudsley's presidential address to the Royal Medico-Psychological Association. Maudsley addresses himself boldly and provocatively to a number of themes that taxed the late Victorian psychiatric imagination, and he embarks first on a polemic on the pretensions of some sections of the psychiatric profession in endeavouring to limit the propagation of insanity.[3] 'It must', he writes, 'be admitted that a regular increase of 1000 a year in the insane population for the last twenty years, to whatever cause the increase be due, is a startling fact.' Should we then, he asks, institute measures to limit the propagation of insane or potentially insane persons? Whilst we can assume, he argues, that there exists an 'inherited liability' to insanity, none the less that liability may be 'strong or weak; it may be so weak as hardly to peril the individual's sanity under the most adverse circumstances of life, or so strong as to issue in an outbreak of madness under the most favourable circumstances. Here, then, our practical difficulties begin.' So, for example, 'if all persons in whose families there was a history of nervous disease were placed under the ban of a compulsory continence, or at any rate were debarred from marriage, it is clear that there would be some danger of unpeopling the world.' Moreover there 'are individuals marking every step in the gradation between the mildest form of the insane temperament and downright idiocy.' And it has therefore to be asked whether it is legitimate to 'fix upon a certain point in this gradation and to declare with the authority of science that hitherto and no further it shall be lawful and right to procreate children.' His answer is clear: 'No doubt there are persons who could consider themselves competent to do so; but we may, without further ado, take the opinion to be testimony of their incompetence.'

Not content with this, he then proceeds to some remarks on the role of insanity in the context of human and social development, taking as he does so a sharp jibe at associationist doctrines:

I have long had a suspicion, which experience is strengthening into a conviction, that mankind is indebted for much of its individuality and for certain special forms of genius to individuals who themselves, or whose parents, have sprung from families in which there has been some indisposition to insanity. They have often taken up the bye-paths of thought, which have been overlooked by more stable intellects, and, following them persistently, discover new relations among things; or they display special talents or energies which they discharge in originalities or perhaps even eccentricities of action. . . . And the world is notably the gainer by their existence. Indeed, I wish someone would undertake the task of examining and setting forth how many of the great reforms of thought and action have been initiated by persons sprung from insane families, or some of whom might themselves have been thought insane. . . . There is sufficient truth in the saying 'men think in packs, as jackals hunt' to make welcome in any age, and especially in an age that seems rather to lack the originating impulse, the man who can break through the usual routine of thought and action, and think some new routine or do some new thing.

Then, in a characteristic move, he devises a compromise between the conflicting claims of two traditions, of determinism on the one hand and of the 'capability of self-formation' on the other. It is proper to speak of the 'evil inheritance of a talent of insanity', yet none the less 'a person who is so unfortunate as to have inherited a predisposition to insanity is not necessarily a helpless victim of fate or destiny; he has, or might have, a certain power over himself to prevent insanity; human will counting for something not only in the modification of physical nature, but in the modification of a man's own nature.' It is, so Maudsley believes, 'in the capability of self-formation which a man has, if it be only rightly developed', that there lies 'a great power over himself to prevent insanity. Perhaps not many persons need go mad — at any rate from moral causes — if they only knew the resources of their nature and resolved systematically to develop them.' Thus those who 'have practical experience of the insane know well what a power of self-control they sometimes evince when they have sufficient motive to exercise it. . . . It is, indeed, in consequence of this power of self-control, and of the way in which those who have the care of them elicit it, that asylums have become quiet and orderly institutions, instead of being, as formerly, dens of disorder and violence.'

Asylums may be 'quiet and orderly' institutions, but we should

not for this assume that they are the appropriate instruments
in the cure of insanity; indeed, the conditions of institutional life
may militate against just those improvements of which the insane
are in principle capable:

> The confinement, the monotony, the lack of interest and
> occupation, the absence of family relations, which are in-
> evitable in any asylum, especially in men of the better classes,
> do, after a certain time in some cases, more than counter-
> balance the benefit of seclusion. The patient has no proper
> outlet for his energies, and outlet is made for them in mania-
> cal excitement and perverse conduct; he goes through re-
> current attacks of that kind and finally sinks into a state of
> chronic insanity — becomes an asylum-made lunatic.

'Asylum-made lunatic': the phrase is hedged about with reservation
in Maudsley's usage, but it is no less striking for that. Nor is it to
be viewed as an ill-tempered polemic assault, displaced from any
firm body of reasoned argument. Other versions of it had surfaced
before - Arlidge in 1859 characterized the 'gigantic asylum' as a
'manufactory of chronic insanity'[4] — and, as Andrew Scull has
ably documented, the strictures of Maudsley and others like him,
all of them authoritative and experienced spokesmen, were testimony of long years of observation and reflection on the effects
and consequences of asylum regimes. So, for example, it was clear
to Bucknill writing later in the decade that:

> The curative influences of asylums have been vastly over-
> rated and those of isolated treatment in domestic care have
> been greatly undervalued. . . . It has long been the accepted
> dogma among psychiatrists that insanity can only be treated
> curatively in asylums. . . . A wide knowledge of insanity would
> have taught them that a very considerable number of cases
> of insanity run a short course and recover in domestic life
> with no great amount of treatment, and that perhaps not of
> a very scientific kind.[5]

Here, as elsewhere in his writings, Maudsley insists on the malign
influences of asylums. Those who 'advocate and defend the present
asylum system', he argues, 'should not forget that there is one
point of view from which they who organize, superintend and act,
regard the system, and that there is another point of view from
which those who are organized, superintended and suffer, view
it.'[6] Thus to 'the medical officer these are not so many *individuals*,

having particular characteristics and bodily dispositions, with which he is thoroughly acquainted, but they are apt to become so many lunatics, whom he has to inspect as he goes on his round of the establishment, as he inspects the baths and the beds.' [7] Moreover, whilst we cannot ignore the 'fact that there are some chronic lunatics who have been in asylums for so many years that it would be no kindness to remove them — who have, indeed, so grown to the habit of their lives that it would be cruel to make any change', we should not take this as 'argument for subjecting anyone else to the same treatment in order to bring about the same result'. [8]

All this comprises a forceful body of utterances that are borne upon us with something of a shock, not least because they speak to us across a divide that is filled by long years of confinement and institutional neglect. In a number of respects they prefigure (and, as Scull has rightly remarked, at points upstage) the newly discovered critiques of the asylum of our own period. And what they also offer is an intimation of a view, and a body of evidence in support of it, of the chronic mental patient (and thus chronicity) not as a natural category or process but as a historical event, as a product in part at least of social conditions and circumstances. From the writings of the critics of the asylum system we can extract a perspective on the phenomenon of insanity which suggests that whatever the discriminations to be made between this or that case, or this or that supposed category of disorder, there were in general terms no grounds for adopting a pessimistic attitude towards the insane, nothing about insanity as such that rendered reform (leaving aside, for the moment, the question of just what this might mean) unfeasible, even indeed that the weight of the evidence seemed positively to demand it.

But this perspective was to be sharply jettisoned by subsequent events; even in the writings of the critics themselves it vies with other tendencies and there are, in this connection, other things to be said about Maudsley's address of 1871. Maudsley presents us with the spectacle of a man at the pinnacle of his career taunting his colleagues and subordinates, but there is about his utterances a measure of romanticism and irresponsibility. He offers the seeds of an alternative perspective on the insane but no practical address to late Victorian dilemmas, nothing in the way of a firm proposal for policy that could be taken hold of and implemented; he introduces only complications — moral, intellectual and practical. In what is an honourable but none the less limiting tradition he extrapolates from the individual case to a general social vision; but it is here

that the limitations of his perspective are apparent. Thus there is
an ambiguity about the cast of his thought: when he speaks of the
'bye-paths' of thought and the discovery of 'new relations among
things' we may suppose that it is a certain class of persons that he
has in mind; applied to pauper lunatics who comprised the vast
majority of the asylum population, or to their own kin, this sort
of thing would have seemed ridiculous, not to say dangerous. And
when we learn that a man 'has, or might have, a certain power over
himself to prevent insanity' we may suppose that the balance between determination and the 'capability of self-formation' is differently weighted for different classes.

And critical rejoinder was not long in coming. Writing in the
Journal of Mental Science early in the following year, Edgar
Sheppard, Professor of Psychological Medicine at King's College,
London, complains about 'comparisons instituted injurious to
systems and establishments which have been rightly regarded as
among the best evidence of humanitarian progress'.[9] And he
delivers a sharp rebuke to Maudsley:

> There is nothing elsewhere approaching the elaborate care
> which our asylum inmates receive from the hour of their
> admission to that of their discharge, and yet because they
> have not the one thing which they know not how to use —
> liberty in its largest sense — men are now beginning to en-
> courage the reactionary idea that the mad world is unneces-
> sarily confined; and those from whom we should have ex-
> pected better things, are found to talk to their professional
> brethren about 'asylum-made lunatics'.

He gives us a taste of how those who 'organize, superintend and
act regard the system':

> I will venture to say that there is no class of persons in the
> United Kingdom so well cared for as the insane. The best
> sites in the country are selected for their palaces, within
> which a cubic space per lung is measured for them. . . . The
> fat kine of our fields are laid under contribution for them;
> the corn and wine is stored for them; clothing of the warmest
> and supervision of the best are provided for them. Every sort
> of indulgence within reasonable bounds is theirs. Though a
> large number of them are of the most degraded type, and
> have made themselves what they are by their own vice and
> wickedness, they are equally (if not altogether wisely) sus-

tained and sheltered. They are rained upon by sympathy and sunshined by kindness. They are fenced about with every sort of protection which the legislature can devise. Magistrates, guardians, commissioners, friends inspect them, visit them, record their grievances, register their scratches, encourage their complaints, tabulate their ailments.

The 'capability of self-formation' is not, as in Maudsley's account, to be set against the forces of insanity. Quite the reverse — it is in the very activity of self-formation among the insane that their degradation and wickedness is most in evidence: 'with few exceptions, those who are most desirous of liberty are those who are least capable of properly using it — malcontents, letter writers, men and women who are continually thrusting their individualities upon you, clamouring about incarceration, and finding no warmth (as our Thackeray phrases it) either in the kitchen fire or in the sun.' And in the discovery of 'new relations among things', and the breaking of the 'usual routine of thought and action', Sheppard detects more invidious couplings and consequences. Alluding to Nathaniel Hawthorne's notion that the 'world owes all its onward impulses to men ill at ease', he remarks caustically that 'it is equally true that "men ill at ease" are they who are ripe for antagonistic bearing towards the laws which society sets up for her protection; so that intellectuality would seem to have two strange bedfellows in insanity and crime. The alliance between the latter is much more capable of demonstration than that between insanity and "great wit".'

And we can now see where this is going to lead. 'Sufficient thought', Sheppard alleges, 'is not given to what is due to society itself' and to the 'baneful influence' of the insane 'upon the sound members of the community'. Thus 'those who support private (home) as against asylum treatment are, it seems to me, not sufficiently mindful of what is due to that larger and saner institution called society, of which they themselves are a part.' The looks of the insane person,

his ways, his grimaces, his recognized unstrung condition, excite a curiosity or interest, or fear, which cannot fail to be prejudicial to young and sensitive persons of both sexes. Although the most elaborate and costly machinery has been set in motion to bring under proper care and surveillance those who had formerly no screens behind which to hide themselves when they were no longer fitted for public observation, and who were exposed to the jeers of the thoughtless and unfeeling, the latest phases of philanthropy clamours for their periodical release. For some of the incurable as well as the curable cases nothing will now do but immoderate freedom. Our mad folk are to be seen at public amusement, theatres, concerts, churches, seaside resorts, where they attract the notice of everybody and disturb the equanimity of many. Surely the sound members of the state have some claim to protection from the unsound members, a large proportion of whom have conditioned their own craziness by the vices and follies from which others have been preserved by self-discipline.

Pauper lunatics

Maudsley's strictures and Sheppard's riposte must be set against the background of the massive increase over the previous 20 years not only in the actual numbers of lunatics confined in asylums, and in the proportion of these relative to the rapidly increasing population, but more particularly also in the numbers of *pauper* lunatics so confined. From between 1844 and 1870 the numbers of private lunatics rose from 4072 to 6280 and of pauper lunatics from 16,821 to 48,433. Moreover, in this same period the proportion of pauper lunatics judged to be curable by asylum superintendents declined sharply. In 1844 asylum superintendents estimated that 15.4 per cent of the pauper lunatics in their charge in county asylums were curable; by 1860 the estimated number of curable lunatics in asylums in England and Wales had dropped to 11.2 per cent and by 1870 to 7.7 per cent.[10]

Within the space of a remarkably compressed history the 'loose and scattered madness of the country' had been brought under observation in vast aggregations of seemingly chronic lunatics. But who exactly were these people, and what were they like? Was all of this evidence of a real increase in chronic insanity, of the operations of a natural disease process? Or did it instead serve as testimony of a new and more exacting set of standards and requirements in the management of social life, in the terms on which lives were to be lived and judged, whereby certain kinds of troubled, vulnerable and socially incompetent people for whom the market had no use came to receive authoritative confirmation of their ineptitude? Maudsley and others did, as we have seen, put questions against the rhetoric of 'incurability' and contrive to outline a more benign view of the nature and capacities of the sorts of people confined in asylums. Yet in the closing decades of the century these liberal lines of argument became less and less admissible and, together with the refurbishment of the asylum as a custodial as distinct from a curative institution, the image of an inexorable decline into chronicity was reinforced ever more strongly. In order to understand this process we must identify some of the determining features of the social matrix in which Victorian responses to the problem of mental disorder were formulated and worked out.

The insane and wage labour

As Scull has described, the origins of the institutional solution to the problem of insanity are 'tied to the growth of the capitalist market system and to its impact on economic and social relationships'.[11] With the development and refinement of the capitalist system, economic relationships came to be more fully assimilated into the terms of the market, and the market thus attained a form of purity as the exclusive condition in which lives were lived and defined, unsullied by paternalistic dependencies or by traditional forms of obligation towards the poor. The expansion of the labour market — what has been termed the 'proletarianization' of labour — resulted in the erosion of non-wage sources of income through, for example, the revocation or restriction of those 'customary and common rights, such as access to land, game or fuel, which saved some people from having to seek any or all of their income as cash from wage labour'.[12] Labourers thus found themselves, in consequence, more and more at the mercy of market conditions, and of the fluctuations in those conditions, and for lack of alternative means of support became increasingly dependent on poor relief.

The organization of institutional responses to the indigent seemed, in this context, to promise a means both to maintain control over those claiming relief and to make the administration of relief more economical and efficient. Of crucial significance in this developing system of controls was the distinction, enshrined in the Poor Law Amendment Act of 1834, between the able-bodied and the non-able-bodied, the undeserving and the deserving, poor. The efficient functioning of the capitalist system presupposed the 'existence of a large mass of wage labourers who were not simply "free" to dispose of their labour power on the open market, but who were actually forced to do so', and just for this reason the availability of aid 'to the able-bodied threatened to undermine, in a radical fashion, the whole notion of a labour market'.[13] Under the terms of the 1834 Act the able-bodied poor — those whom it could be assumed were either temporarily unemployed or had put themselves out of work by their own idleness or mismanagement — were thus to be set to work in harsh and exacting workhouse regimes, and the non-able-bodied were, some of them, to be given outdoor relief and others their own distinctive, but less punitive, institutional regimes. The specialization of responses to different problem groups, and the expansion of the asylum in particular, have to be seen against this background of segregation — the pressure to elaborate a system of controls that permitted a rigorous demarcation between the deserving and the undeserving, and thus the application of the principles of 'less eligibility' in all their severity, undistracted by the presence of less amenable elements.

Yet if the objective of this whole operation was control, what was intended was a form of control that included — in the earlier phases in particular — the differentiated aims of training and rehabilitation. Scull has distinguished between the *extensive* structures of domination characteristic of societies where 'the rationalizing impact of the marketplace is still weak' and in which 'the quality and character of the workforce are taken as a given rather than as plastic and amenable to improvement through appropriate management and training', and the *intensive* structures of domination that arise under conditions of strong 'rationalization forced by competition'. Under the latter conditions the population comes to be perceived as 'modifiable and manipulable human material whose yield could steadily be enlarged through careful management and through improvements in use and organization designed to qualitatively transform its value as an economic resource'.[14] So, for example, the legislation of the 1830s brought with it a range of measures geared to the reform of 'character' on the part of the individual workman and to the inculcation of habits and attitudes that would further the sort of ambition expressed by Josiah Wedgwood to 'make such machines of men as cannot err'. As the historian H.L. Beales has put it, what Poor Law reformers such as Chadwick and Nassau Senior desired to achieve 'beside economy, was a system of social police which would open up the labour market and render the labour factor of production mobile and docile, that is, disciplined and as nearly rational and predictable as may be'.[15]

Rehabilitation of the insane

In the early decades of the nineteenth century the insane were eagerly assimilated into this rehabilitative endeavour. For, as Scull describes, the secular rationalities of the period brought about 'a transformation of the paradigm of insanity away from an emphasis on its demonological, nonhuman, animalistic qualities towards a naturalistic position which viewed the madman as exhibiting a defective *human* mechanism, and which therefore saw this condition as at least potentially remediable'.[16] Thus pioneers of moral treatment such as William Tuke were no longer content to limit their efforts to the 'outward control of those who were no longer quite human' but instead 'actively sought to transform the lunatic, to remodel him into something approximating the bourgeois ideal of the rational individual':

> Just as the peasantry who formed the new industrial work-force were to be taught the 'rational' self-interest essential if market system were to work, the lunatics, too, were to be made over in the image of bourgeois rationality: defective human mechanisms were to be repaired so that they could once more compete in the marketplace. And . . . just as hard work and self-discipline were the keys to the success of the urban bourgeoisie, from whose ranks Tuke came, so his moral treatment propounded these same qualities as the means of reclaiming the insane.[17]

In the proclamation of its ideals, however, we can acquire a measure not only of the vaunted ambitions of a remedial programme like moral treatment but also of the obstacles that stood in the way of their realization. For the reason that the very concept of rehabilitation – and thus the judgement of what could count as rehabilitative potential or success – was so ineluctably tied to the interests of the market and to the demand for a predictable, regulated and rationally self-interested workforce, it rendered itself also acutely vulnerable. Either the lunatic was restored to the disciplined army of labour in flawless conformity with the standards that bourgeois rationality required of him, eager and able to compete in the market, or the rehabilitative exercise was deemed a failure, and the lunatic lamentably lacking in remedial potential. 'Mature industrial societies of all varieties', E.P. Thompson has noted, 'are marked by time thrift and by a clear demarcation between "work" and "life".'[18] The valuation of time in the nineteenth century was, with developing urgency, the valuation of a commodity. Pauper lunatics, in common with other denizens of the 'landscape of disciplined industrial capitalism, with the time-sheet, the time keeper, the informer, and the fines',[19] were identified, described and judged in terms not of the time of a life but of the time valuations of the workplace and by the standard of the 'useful worker'. Once apprehended in this way, the individual who showed himself unable to satisfy these standards could only be negatively marked: there was no scope for negotiation, no space left for mitigating accounts, for the invocation of another time perspective through which he might be shown still to possess value. In failing to comply with the time valuations of production he was cast outside time altogether, outside the real labours of history, an encapsulation of badness in the closed system of the self.

In making appeal to the lunatic's desire for esteem, moral treatment endowed him with a degree of credibility and dignity as a moral agent, but in beckoning to him across the gap that separated him from the norms of right thinking and right living that he had eschewed, the terms on which respect was to be merited for the future were made unassailably plain. The 'elective affinity of a market system and the restorative ideal (the former emphasizing the notion of a free, rational self-determining individual; the latter the repair of a damaged human mechanism so that it once more fulfilled these preconditions for competing in the market)'[20] placed a peculiarly onerous and constricting burden on any form of re-habilitative endeavour. No matter how benign the intentions of certain asylum practices, they could escape neither the clutches of the ideological pressures to define the rehabilitative enterprise in the most exacting terms — and from the record there is no evidence that they attempted to do so — nor the institutional pressures to accommodate more and more people within the precincts of the asylum for whom the market could find no use and who in addition had proven themselves a positive social hindrance. Across the years of the century the protagonists of moral treatment brought about, by dint of their effort and dedication, some remarkable individual therapeutic achievements, but when evaluated in this wider and embracing critical context there lurked always the suspicion that the restored individual was not quite the predictable mechanism that was sought after — that, as one psychiatrist was later to put it, he was not 'as useful a social unit as he was before'.[21]

Notions of 'incurability' partook of a much deeper set of valuations than the strictly medical — above all, of the belief that late Victorian society was encumbered with a burgeoning army of inadequates who could perform no useful function and (much worse) who would, if left to their own devices, conscript others into their aberrant ways. In the invective of a psychiatrist like Sheppard, suggestions that the insane were capable of improvement, and that long-term confinement in an asylum was not in their best interests, received the short shrift that they did, not because they could not be substantiated in this or that individual case, but because the very plea for further *individuation* of treatment could do nothing to relieve — and could only seem to exacerbate — the weight of what was perceived to be a *collective* problem.

The insane and outdoor relief

But even if the claims for the rehabilitation of lunatics could not be made good, why in addition was it considered essential to retain the 'loose and scattered madness of the country' under conditions of observation and confinement? In 1871, for example, Dr S.W.D. Williams, superintendent of the Sussex Lunatic Asylum at Haywards Heath, worries that asylums are losing their 'proper characteristics as curable hospitals' and 'degenerating into vast poor houses for incurables', and proposes that 'a more extended trial' might therefore 'be made of discharging chronic and harmless lunatics' to live with their relatives.[22] His experience has strongly impressed him 'with the fact that, as a rule, the poor are more willing and anxious to have the personal care of their insane relatives than those in a higher station of life'. So far as a scheme of this sort can be furthered, 'the minds of the poor will be eased of one of their great superstitions, viz. that their relatives, when once sent to an asylum, have little if any chance of leaving it alive, the belief of many being that it is to the interest both of the justices and doctors not to discharge the patient.' But we have, he contends, to reckon with the fact of strong prejudices 'in the minds of many, especially of the middle and higher classes, against the discharge of lunatics'. To Williams:

> It appears the grossest injustice that because a father, or husband, or wife, is poor, therefore he is not, if he desires it, to be allowed the charge of his relatives afflicted with the most distressing of all maladies, always provided he be fitted for such a charge and will not abuse it.

At the present time:

> It is an unpleasant fact, but nevertheless a true one, that the
> Lunacy Laws utterly ignore the possibility of the relatives
> of pauper lunatics having any affection for their afflicted
> kin. The relations of a pauper lunatic have no voice in the
> question of sending him to an asylum and still less in his
> discharge therefrom.

But special pleading of this sort was, in the prevailing climate of
suspicion around the demands for outdoor relief and the management of the boundaries between the deserving and the undeserving
poor, thoroughly unrealistic. The 1834 Act had assumed that
most unemployment was voluntary, but the events of subsequent
years were to make this a difficult notion to maintain, even among
those most earnestly wedded to it. The category of the 'deserving'
was from the outset a reluctant creation, but it was to show itself
also to be vulnerable and poorly fortified and thus accessible to
expansion and appropriation. It became apparent that the Poor
Law commissioners of 1834 had seriously underestimated the
numbers of those eligible for outdoor relief; the workhouses were,
moreover, able to accommodate only a small percentage of able-
bodied beneficiaries, and over the years 1834–1870 there was
thus a massive increase in the numbers of those claiming outdoor
relief.

In 1870 the central Poor Law Authority (renamed the Local
Government Board) determined to make amends for the relaxation of the principles of 1834 in the intervening years, and in particular to give firm expression in action to what Scull has termed
'the abhorrence of payments to individuals in the community' as
a means of 'dealing with the problem of extreme incapacity of one
sort or another'.[23] From about 1871 through into the 1880s the
Poor Law inspectors exerted strong pressures to reduce outdoor
relief and above all to make the category of the deserving much
more difficult of penetration. So, for example, as Pat Thane has
described, single women were 'now treated exactly as men – as
potentially recalcitrant members of the labour force'. To qualify
for outdoor relief, cleanliness and good character were essential
requirements, and relief was denied to 'applicants "residing with
relatives of immoral, intemperate or improvident character or of
incleanly habits", living in a cottage "kept in a dirty or slovenly
condition", or "in premises in which it is undesirable on account
of its sanitation condition or locality that they should reside",

or simply living "amid insanitary or immoral surroundings" '. And given these sorts of constraints it is not difficult to see that not many of the poor were deemed eligible.[24]

Not only would the dispersal of harmless lunatics into the community have added to the disproportionate numbers of paupers already receiving outdoor relief, but more especially it would have rendered them also 'beneficiaries of something approximating a modern social welfare system while their sane brethren were being subjected to the rigours of a Poor Law based on the principle of less eligibility'.[25] Furthermore, the notion of a 'harmless' incurable lunatic was not, for most of Williams's contemporaries, easily assimilable; there were, as others were quick to point out, other forms of danger and contagion than those that resulted from direct acts of violence. As Sheppard's criticisms make very plain there was that about the insane that was ambiguous, that rendered their entitlement to the designation of 'deserving' doubtful if not downright suspect. In Sheppard's account the lunatic is in his various guises an affront; and Sheppard is in this more nearly representative of what was — and was to become increasingly so — a dominant tendency.

The insane and their associates

There was, of course, a wider context of affront to which Victorian pauper lunatics, through the instabilities of their actions and above all of their speech, seemed to supply their own particular contribution. Alongside the demands of the 'malcontents. . .clamouring about incarceration' and the individuated intensities of those who, instead of occupying themselves silently in purposeful activity and finding in their capacity to speak only a means to express their docility and compliance, made themselves a nuisance through the insistent — and, on a conventional register, scarcely articulate — vocalization of their grievances and desires, we can detect a proliferation of other voices and stances, other rebellious claims on the privileged attention.

In the language of Sheppard's recoil in 1872 from all those lunatics 'continually thrusting their individualities upon you', and putting themselves about in an irregularity of speech and action, we can sense the recoil from more extensive contemporary expressions of individuality, from the consolidation of individual lives into organized movements intent upon asserting the right to assemble freely and to make themselves heard. Behind Sheppard's reactions to the importuning lunatics we can hear Matthew Arnold's rebuke to the sort of 'rough' who took part in the Hyde Park Riots of 1866, 'going where he likes, assembling where he likes, bawling where he likes, hustling as he likes', who has not 'yet quite found his groove and settled down to his work'.[26] And against the force of these judgements, writers of a more liberal political persuasion like Mrs Gaskell found themselves constrained to undertake an awkward brokerage between the realities of an individual working-class existence and consciousness and the habituated responses of a middle-class readership: 'he is, I say, bewildered and (to use his own word) "aggravated" to see that all goes on just as usual with the mill owners.' And they were constrained also to offer apology for the intensity and complication of feeling in the individual working-class life: 'the thoughts of his heart were touched by sin, by bitter hatred of the happy, whom he, for the time, confounded with the selfish.'[27]

The middle classes had their reasons for linking the movement of an individual life with the movements of a class and with the potential or actual upheavals of a period, and for being fearful of the collective humanity that was emergent in the individuations of working-class lives. As John Dunn has described, since shortly after the fall of Robespierre in Thermidor of the Year II there had always been men in western societies who 'saw their life in strictly secular terms and devoted the whole of it to the project of transforming the political and social order of their country by an attempt to seize power within it', men who lived 'in closed or open conspiracy or in the solitude of their own fantasies, in the hope and with the purpose of changing the political and social world by their acts'.[28] There was, of course, nothing to link directly the mass of Victorian pauper lunatics with an incipient revolutionary consciousness, but belief in the contagious powers of forms of mental unrest and excitement was reason enough to look askance upon suggestions (even from such moderate advocates as Maudsley) that insane people merited differentiated attention not as 'so many lunatics' but as 'so many individuals' with whom to become more 'thoroughly acquainted', and that the individuation of such people be entered upon more deeply as a matter of policy.

From the standpoint of those who held power in late Victorian England there were already enough pressures to yield, in sharp opposition to the forms of relation of industrial capitalism, to newly emerging voices and patterns of individuation, and to reach

beyond the settled habits and circles of privileged discourse into
quite new forms of proximity and language. All those lunatic
letter writers, 'most desirous of liberty' but 'least capable of properly using it', were only a worse case of what was already an un-
wholesome general condition. This was a form of acquaintance
that could be done without, and Granville gave as sharp a summary
of the dominant view as any when he asserted in 1877 that:

> No insane person is *harmless* in the only true sense of the
> term; he is ever doing mischief in mind and body and may
> at any moment add physical violence to the sinister mental
> influence he is perpetually exerting on himself and those
> with whom he is associated.[29]

But with whom did he associate? In describing his doctrine of the
association of ideas, John Locke had instanced a particular form
of connection in which an idea 'no sooner at any time comes into
the Understanding but its Associate appears with it; and if they
are more than two which are thus united, the whole gang always
inseparable show themselves together.' [30] In Locke's usage the
image of the gang is primarily literary, but the late Victorians
perceived a more definite and sinister connection between peculiar
forms of association in the sphere of ideas and undesirable forms
of association and influence among men, between cognitive and
social forms of disorder. 'Intellectuality', so Sheppard alleged, had
'two strange bedfellows in insanity and crime.' In place of 'gang'
we find a harsher set of collective images to represent the developing sense of the reproduction of repugnant human forms within
the urban process. So, for example, the lower end of London's
working class in the second half of the nineteenth century were
termed the 'residuum' and perceived as 'almost a separate race of
urban degenerates'. And the diatribes of Herbert Spencer proved
so attractive just because they appeared to legitimate the view
that all manner of evil would result from any relaxation of vigil-
ance against the further propagation of such people. The ethics
of the state, Spencer argued in *Man versus the State*, must be
predicated on the principle of justice rather than generosity and
involve the 'rigorous maintenance of those normal relations
among citizens under which each gets in return for his labour,
skilled or unskilled, bodily or mental, as much as is proved to be
its value by the demand for it: such return, therefore, as will enable him to thrive and rear offspring in proportion to the superiori-
ties which make him valuable to himself and others'. The indivi-

dual must only receive 'benefit in proportion to merit' and 'reward in proportion to desert', merit and desert 'in each case being understood as ability to fulfil all the requirements of life — to get food, to secure shelter, to escape enemies'. Were the state to pursue an opposite course such that 'the benefits received by each individual were proportionate to its inferiority — if, as a consequence, multiplication of the inferior was furthered and multiplication of the superior hindered, progressive degradation would result.'[31]

Useless human types

From within the field of social forces set in motion by the celebration and invigoration of the market economy as the essential condition of life, and by the concomitant expansion of wage labour as the dominant social relationship, we can identify the emergence of quite a new set of responses in the second half of the nineteenth century. There is the sharpened sense of a range of human types as essentially and irrevocably incompatible with the onward march of social and industrial progress, of a growing body of people as comprising a form of human effluent whose only discernible aptitude lay in a proclivity to corrupt others, and hence a much keener effort at marking off the wasteful from the valuable, the useless from the useful. Schemes for the rehabilitation of the socially incompetent or recalcitrant merited approval only so far as at the close of remedial business there was a human product on display that fulfilled the requirements for an enhanced *quality* of labour power; human material that showed itself to be less pliable in this respect was destined only for rejection. In the case of those sorts of people who appeared to suffer from mental tribulation in one form or another, these exacting conditions rendered them peculiarly vulnerable to being picked out for allocation to the category of the socially unwanted or useless: not only were more and more such people dispatched to asylums but they arrived there fettered by a final and unshakeable judgement as to their social worth.

The creation and designation of this new population of the unwanted and the useless is vividly brought out in a description by John Bucknill. Among the 'inmates who filled the new madhouses which existed before the alleviating action of the lunacy laws', he writes, 'outrageous madness was the rule, and detention of patients after they had become tranquil and harmless was against the rule.' In his own period, by contrast:

Our numerous asylums swarm with a motley crowd of persons of weak minds or low spirits; with tranquil and reasonable persons said to have suicidal tendencies if they are not always under supervision;. . . . no doubt all of them, with very rare exceptions, persons of unsound mind, but not madmen or lunatics, or even insane persons, as our fathers understood these terms . . . Since 1845, medical science has discovered whole realms of lunacy, and the nicer touch of a finikin civilization has shrunk away from contact of imperfect fellow creatures, and thus the manifold receptacles of lunacy are filled to overflow with a population more nearly resembling that which is still at large.[32]

All the significant determinations came, as we have described, from a wider field of forces but the pressures to define these people as unwanted were most palpably felt at the level of their own families. Except among 'the opulent classes', the Lunacy Commissioners reported in 1855, 'any protracted attack of insanity, from the heavy expenses which its treatment entails, and the fatal interruption it causes to everything like active industry, seldom fails to reduce its immediate victims, and generally also their families with them, to poverty and ultimately to pauperism.'[33] An asylum superintendent like Williams certainly had his own special reasons for wanting to rid the asylum of harmless incurables, and thus to permit psychiatry to apply itself to the more prestigious business of effecting cures, and on this account he doubtless underestimates the reluctance among many of the poorer classes to take on the burden of care for their insane relatives. Yet at the very least his claims provide an indication of a resistance in thought and feeling to what in the prevailing circumstances had to be done that is at odds with unanalysed attributions of public intolerance towards the insane.

What Williams holds for one of the 'great superstitions' among the poor, namely the belief that 'their relatives, when once sent to an asylum, have little if any chance of leaving it alive', was of course anything but that. In the second half of the nineteenth century, with a much sharper emphasis from the 1870s onwards, the asylum came to be affirmed as a definitively custodial institution, and the insane person as utterly lacking in any kind of potential. Attempts to moderate the severity of these strictures, together with proposals for the support of 'harmless' lunatics in settings in the community, were as we have seen greeted with consternation. Furthermore, quite apart from doubts about their efficacy, the intense individuation of effort of rehabilitative practices did not help to commend them to those who were already concerned about the cost of asylums. With a vengeance, therefore, forms of tribulation that did not of themselves entail incapacity were made over to custodial institutions and to the category of chronicity, and converted into total and lifelong incapacity. The social type of what in our own period we have come to term the chronic mental patient was, then, created against this background of a perceived population of useless people; in the last decades of the century the incurable character of insanity came to be divested of its controversial or contestible aspect and to be taken very much for granted and, as Scull describes, 'the asylum doctors gradually maneouvred to redefine success in terms of comfort, cleanliness and freedom from the more obvious forms of physical maltreatment, rather than the elusive and often unattainable goal of cure.'[34]

There is perhaps no better way to describe the formation of the distinctively modern type of the chronic mental patient than through the shifts in meaning of certain keywords in which the determining changes in social relations — the development of wage labour as the predominant social relationship — were both expressed and reinforced, in particular the words *idle* and *unemployed*.[35] 'Idle' had developed from an original sense of empty and useless to take on a harsh ambiguity between 'employed but not working', 'unemployed because unwilling to work' and 'doing nothing'; and with the word 'employment' we find a shift of emphasis (and also a parallel specialization in the meaning of *work*) from the productive effort itself to a condition of paid employment by another. The mental patient was thus unemployed in the descriptive sense of being outside paid employment but with the additional suggestion that he was therefore also outside any recognizable condition of useful work; and when we add to this the judgement that he was also idle, and therefore responsible for his predicament, we can see how he came to be taken as *unemployable* and (within the definition of the term) incapable of any form of useful activity. But to make matters worse, if in the senses that counted he was unproductive and did nothing, he was at the same time guilty of another form of productivity, a form of doing that was socially valueless but none the less threatening and contagious, to which psychoanalysis was later to pay special attention, and which was nicely characterized by a turn-of-the-century psychiatrist as 'the contemporaneous existence in one brain of morbid apathy and active, though misguided, cerebration'.[36]

The medical legitimation of the useless

The figure of the chronic mental patient was not produced by the asylum as such but by an act of exclusion generated from within a wider field of social forces. Nevertheless, by virtue of its transformation into a custodial institution, the asylum came to play a crucial role not only in making the mental patient more nearly resemble what others in any case took him to be but also – and crucially – in providing the conditions of observation in which the social judgements made about these unfortunate people could be given authoritative scientific ratification. Within the prevailing social conditions, asylums may very well have provided the least punitive sites for such people, but psychiatrists of the period had other interests at heart beyond offering them accommodation. As Karl Figlio has shown, medicine generally in the late nineteenth century played a powerful role in, for example, promoting ideologies of 'constitutional weakness' to deal with failures of individual self-regulation and depletions of vitality among the workforce, and it fell to psychiatry to forge an authoritative account of the chronic tendencies inherent in cases of mental disorder.[37]

Thus neurologists like Hughlings Jackson and Charles Mercier came to insist on the crucial and overriding role played by deficiency or defect in the production of insanity. As Michael Clark has described, mental symptoms were seen as 'indicative of a general diseased condition affecting the entire physical organism, of a regression to lower evolutionary levels, manifesting itself principally in a failure of inhibitory control of the lower by the higher functional levels of the central nervous system'.[38] Not only did all mental symptoms

> share in this negative quality of defect or deficiency, but, arising as they did from what Mercier described as 'an inability to appreciate the true circumstances in which the individual is, and his true relation to these circumstances', they could hardly be expected to become any more intelligible in the light of the patient's life experiences either. Such positive symptoms were, in Jackson's phrase, only 'indirectly caused, or rather permitted', and could not, therefore, immediately be interpreted within any causal system of explanation. They were mere epiphenomena, which bore

no direct or immediately intelligible functional relations to the underlying somato-pathological realities to which, indirectly and unsystematically, they testified.[39]

Furthermore, medical psychology held to 'the conviction that all cases of mental disorder, if not rapidly arrested, would sooner or later evolve inexorably into cases of chronic dementia'. In the textbooks of the period much emphasis was given

> to the characteristic mental and behavioural symptoms believed to presage the imminent onset of general conditions of progressive dissolution — to the telltale improprieties of the early stages of general paralysis, the 'morbid introspection', 'solitary habits', and emotionally self-indulgent religiosity of the 'insanity of adolescence', and to the recrudescence of sexual desire in incipient senile dementia. But none of these characteristic patterns of symptomatic behaviour was regarded as possessing any particular interest or significance, since they all partook of the same fundamental character of defect, and dementia, 'the common form of all insanity' as Mercier described it.[40]

On this view of progressive deterioration:

> Dementia was, so to speak, the 'explanation' of the symptoms, which thus only acquired significance when interpreted retrospectively, in the light of the subsequent development of the diseased state toward dementia. But dementia was, by definition, a state in which the very possibility of meaning, let alone of particular meanings, had been lost — in which the mental manifestations signified only the chaotic disintegration or even extinction of mind itself. Therefore, with its onset the phenomena of mind and behaviour passed once and for all beyond the reach of rational interpretation, regardless of whatever intelligible meanings they might once have possessed in previous life-historical contexts.[41]

The arrival of the chronic schizophrenic

The receptivity to the type of the 'chronic schizophrenic' had thus been prepared for, and we only await the announcement that he has arrived. To further our grasp of the process that we have described we cannot do better than to look at the reception accorded him when he did arrive, and for this purpose we may turn to the account of a debate between members of the Royal Medico-Psychological Association that was held in 1909 to discuss Emil Kraepelin's recently published theory of dementia praecox. And the account is, as we shall see, all the more vivid and revealing for being the record of a live discussion.[42]

Objection to the term 'dementia praecox' has been voiced by a certain Dr Robert Jones of Claybury Hospital. 'Dementia', claims Jones, means 'mental enfeeblement' and thus excludes by definitional fiat any possibility of recovery. In Jones's view the symptoms of dementia praecox are much better subsumed under Thomas Clouston's description of adolescent insanity, and here from Clouston's own account we find a 60 to 70 per cent recovery rate. But Jones, several of the interlocutors claim — and it is a claim that is to carry the day — has misperceived the true nature of the course of the illness. Thus a Dr Stoddart invokes the standard of 'the useful worker' to justify Kraepelin's usage and asserts that among dementia praecox patients 'mentation is so enfeebled' that they are 'totally incapacitated from ever doing any useful work'. And Dr Devine urges similarly that, in 90 per cent of the cases where the symptoms of dementia praecox are observed, 'such mental deterioration will follow as will lead to a permanent incapacity to lead a useful life', and thus 'one knows one is dealing with a disorder which is the commencement of a downward career leading to mental deterioration.'

A number of speakers allow that a few cases temporarily recover, but, retorts Stoddart, 'we know that the same may occur in dementia paralytica.' Dr Bevan-Lewis argues that all cases of dementia praecox 'in the long run inevitably betray notable mental enfeeblement of a grade which fully entitles them to the term "dementia praecox" '. Devine acknowledges that one sometimes comes across what at first meeting appear to be recoveries, 'but this does not destroy the value of the conception'. 'It is', he asserts, 'necessary to carefully watch the future of the patient and to see if he is really as useful a social unit as he was before and if this is merely a remission, a temporary arrest as it were.'

Thomas Clouston brings out the excitement that Kraepelin's theory has aroused when he says that Kraepelin had been 'oppressed with the idea — as they had all been — could he find out something, some series of symptoms, by which he could prognose the existence of an incurable mental state at the earliest stages?' The merit of Kraepelin's scheme, claims Devine, is that it enables the psychiatrist to predict 'by observation of symptoms what will probably eventually happen to a patient'. And seen in this light Kraepelin's descriptions have, he announces, 'given a meaning to the incoherent mutterings, the gait, attitude, conduct of even a terminal dement, all these features having acquired a significance which previously they had entirely lacked'. And in consequence 'one finds it hard to look on dementia praecox, to which one owes so much, as an "undesirable alien".' Dr Hayes-Newington acknowledges that 'it is difficult from the book point of view to contemplate the contemporaneous existence in one brain of morbid apathy and active, though misguided cerebration', but none the less he takes the term 'dementia praecox' to 'admirably denote the quiet collapse of jerry-built brains under the strain of their own weight or on the first contact with the responsibilities of adult life'.

But there are others who are more sceptical. The relationship between adolescent insanity and dementia praecox in particular is a subject of considerable dispute, and that the ground is clearly set for confusion and acrimony is evident when we read that 'in dealing with adolescent insanity Dr Clouston says that the inmates of public asylums consist of about 50 per cent of such cases, and Professor Kraepelin puts the figure even higher for dementia praecox.' 'The adolescent insanity of Clouston with its 66 per cent recovery rate', Dr Dixon asserts, 'cannot be the dementia praecox of Kraepelin' − but he has little to add to this. Dr Lewis Bruce, among others, concurs, but Dr Percy Smith takes the view that Clouston's description of adolescent insanity covers 'practically the whole of the ground' which is now covered by Kraepelin. He had, we learn,

> listened very intently during Dr Stoddart's speech for a statement as to the symptoms of dementia praecox. He asked Dr. Stoddart whether there was any common symptom in all the group of what was called dementia praecox except dementia, which might not itself occur, or might not be persistent. And Dr Stoddart said there was no symptom which was pathognomonic of dementia praecox. So they were in a difficulty. If there was no specific symptom, what was dementia praecox? They recognized the clinical groups described by Kraepelin. If there was no pathognomonic symptom it was rather difficult to accept the term 'dementia praecox'. He (Dr Stoddart) said the one characteristic was a dissociation of the receptive and executive sides of the mind. . . . He (Dr Smith) would ask whether that was the only form of mental disease in

which there was dissociation between the receptive and executive sides of the mind, because he could not grasp that that
was so.

Dr Savage is more sceptical still. 'Definition', he says, 'is like the
outposts in a new country, it is an approach to the unknown and
indefinite which will lead to more complete knowledge. A definition should be something which gathers but does not fix our
experience, its use should be to enable us to advance. If we are to
be satisfied with a *name*, then a definition is a danger.' And he
continues: 'That there is a definite entity, a real disease deserving
the name "dementia praecox" I cannot believe. . . . I am never tired
of quoting myself in saying there is no such *thing* as insanity.' But
Savage's colleagues tire of him more easily than he does of himself;
to have taken his admonitions seriously would have rendered their
hold over the 'new country' precarious indeed. Devine brings the
discussion back to the real instrument of colonization, the concept
of 'mental deterioration', and tries to resolve the dispute between
the standpoint of Clouston and that of Kraepelin with the suggestion that

the two eminent observers in question are not describing the
same thing. They are adopting an entirely different point of
view, both illuminating and valuable, but not comparable in
any way. The lesson I learn from Dr Clouston's masterly description of the insanities of puberty and adolescence, a
description which is now classical, is the influence which a
developmental period has in the production and content of
disordered mental states which occur at that period. He shows
how such states, whether mania, melancholia, or confusion
are coloured by the state of mind, which is normal at such a
period. His point of view is, therefore, chiefly a biological
one. Kraepelin, on the other hand, is *not* describing the
insanities of adolescence. What he is describing is a group of
cases, the essential feature of which is a tendency to mental
deterioration. It is true that such a group is more common
in adolescence, but it frequently finds expression later in
life, and if one limits his conception to a particular biological
epoch its value is quite lost. The utility of Kraepelin's work
consists in the fact that, given, let us say, a case of adolescent
insanity, which may be one of several varieties of mental
disorder, he has furnished us with something tangible by

which one may judge if it is likely to lead to a permanent mental enfeeblement or not.

The individual who stood to lose most from the adoption of the Kraepelinian view was Clouston himself. As he puts it, Kraepelin's dementia praecox was 'manifestly ousting his "adolescent insanity"... the one bowed out at the window, while the other came in at the door.' His account of his own equivocations and uncertainties over Kraepelin's theory, and the resolution he has reached, are thus of particular interest. From what he says we derive a fine sense of the excitement with which Kraepelin's formulations were received, of the temptations that they offered to a profession eager to secure a firm scientific status for itself, mixed with not a little suspicion – perhaps the more so in Clouston's case – of the credentials of these foreign importations with their idiosyncrasies of style and emphasis, together with an evident anxiety lest the decision to back the wrong horse should leave British psychiatrists lagging behind their colleagues overseas. Clouston has had, so we learn, the

> peculiar advantage of lately being associated with a pupil and friend of Kraepelin, a man who had been for something like twelve months in an American asylum where Kraepelinism was dominant. ... That gentleman, Dr MacFie Campbell, was on his staff, and he was in daily intercourse with him. He, Dr Clouston, was, like everybody, exceedingly impressed with the fact that the term 'dementia praecox', as well as some of the other members of the Kraepelin classification, seemed to dominate the psychiatric world of America but not that of France or of Italy, and that it was rapidly taking possession of the minds and imaginations of the younger men in this country.

He determined to take advantage of this Scottish representative of the German master, and

> He said to Dr MacFie Campbell day by day, 'I place myself, as it were, at Kraepelin's feet, through you, in order to do him full justice: will you tell me whether this case is one of dementia praecox or not? And if so, will you kindly tell me wherein you make it out to be dementia praecox ...

As a result of – or perhaps despite, we cannot be sure – his periods of intercourse with Dr MacFie Campbell, Kraepelin's 'enthusiastic pupil', Clouston decides, with a good deal of equivocation, to back Kraepelin. This is how he argues his change of view:

> He need not say he agreed with Dr Jones that it was a most evil thing that they should use the term 'dementia' for anything except an incurable mental condition. It led to nothing but confusion and it could not lead to anything else. . . . The use of the term 'dementia' to describe a disease which was to a large extent curable was necessarily and of itself an objectionable thing.

None the less,

> with all that, and with all objections to Kraepelin's terminology and his clinical studies, there was no doubt that modern psychiatry owed an enormous deal to him. And there could be no doubt that, imitative as the Americans were, and fond as they were of following in the fashion of things, it yet could not be that all the young Americans were such psychiatric fools as to follow Kraepelin strongly if there were nothing in him. That had been impressed upon his mind strongly and had made him endeavour to take a judicial-minded view of Kraepelin and his terminology. What if his terminology was wrong, if his facts were right? Therefore they must not be too critical with regard to the mere terminology of the words 'dementia praecox'. He thought that in a short time they would evolve and have clinico-pathological groups which were unassailable. Meantime they should be thankful for having got a little way on through the agency of Kraepelin's studies and, if they pleased, through his wrong terminology.

This is truly a sad muddle. Clouston contrives to suggest that in distinguishing 'facts' from 'terminology' he can dispense with the terminology and acquiesce in the 'facts'. But this is confused thinking; for the meaning that Clouston dislikes in the term 'dementia praecox' is intimately bound up with Kraepelin's conception of the facts. It is, as Devine remarked earlier, the notion of a naturally deteriorating disease process that lends significance to features of a patient's behaviour — 'the incoherent mutterings, gait, attitude, conduct' — which 'previously they had entirely lacked'. Where Clouston sees individuals who are to 'a large extent curable', the majority of his colleagues see lunatics 'totally incapacitated from ever doing any useful work', all of whom 'in the long run inevitably betray notable mental enfeeblement of a grade which fully entitles them to the term "dementia praecox" '. From his colleagues' point of view, Clouston has failed to perceive properly: if he would only 'carefully watch the future of the patient' he would then detect that the patient was not 'really as useful a social unit as he was before'. Clouston's colleagues knew very well that it was the conception of a deteriorating disease that gave the 'facts' point, lent them their interest and enticement, and held them together; that is why they were at such pains to labour — above all else, as though the life of the 'facts' turned on it — the case for the conception. And we must, I think, assume that Clouston knew it also; for he was, after all, himself no 'psychiatric fool'.

Against the power of Kraepelin's theoretical edifice the misgivings of Clouston and others could carry little weight.[43] For in the image of the type of the chronic dementia praecox patient elaborated by Kraepelin we can see encapsulated in a single life history all the late Victorian fears that we have described. For all that the dementia praecox patient was morbidly apathetic and depleted in vitality he was also obstinate, truculent and unpredictable; his was not the individuality of the well-regulated worker and the private citizen but a wayward, uncontained form of individuality that ran with (and gave encouragement to) the crowd. Perhaps most serious of all were the 'extensive and varied morbid manifestations in the domain of work and conduct which specially give the clinical picture its peculiar stamp':

> The patients have lost every independent inclination for work and action; they will sit about idle, trouble themselves about nothing, do not go to work. . . . They experience no tediousness, have no need to pass the time, 'no more joy in work', but can lie in bed unoccupied for days and weeks, stand about in corners, 'stare into a hole', watch the toes of their boots or wander aimlessly about. . . . For work they have 'no inclination'; 'their nerves can't stand it.' A patient did no work for two years 'in order not to deprive people of gain'; another had in view, after having used his last sovereign, to go into the Lake of Constance; a third asked 'for an easy job, perhaps as a clergyman'.[44]

Images of the chronic schizophrenic in the early twentieth century

The horrendous and unprecedented conditions of the First World War gave rise to a category of reactions among soldiers at the battlefront that came to be known as 'shell-shock'. Such were the dimensions of the problem of traumatic reactions that the traditional disciplinary systems for dealing with malingerers could not adequately cope with the numbers foisted upon it. Medicine seemed to promise an alternative option, but the official doctrines could offer only a crude materialist gloss on the conventional moral invective. In the dominant Kraepelinian view, shell-shock was for the most part attributed either to an organic state brought about by punctate haemorrhages in the brain or to an innate biological and psychological inferiority, a psychopathic constitution. As the War Office *Committee of Enquiry on Shell-Shock* reported in 1922, patients found themselves as a consequence shuffled about indiscriminately, 'lines of treatment were interrupted and replaced by others, different explanations were given, different prognoses, different promises . . . *until the patient lost all faith in any doctor, became hospitalized and settled down in a chronic depression with incapacity*'.[45]

That the War Office committee of 1922 could have reported with such acuity on what had befallen these unhappy people in the ravages of war was in large part due to the efforts of a small group of psychiatrists who demonstrated to good effect that the traumas of battle could both be understood and treated by setting them in the context of the psychological history of the subject. But the schizophrenic was to be brought no such relief from his chronic and degenerative predicament. In the decade that followed the 1909 debate Clouston found himself vindicated in this, that Kraepelin's term 'dementia praecox' was to a large extent replaced by Eugen Bleuler's coinage 'schizophrenia' — though even 30 years later we still find some psychiatrists persisting in the earlier usage. But this was a strictly terminological shift that, whilst serving to specify the characteristic symptomatological picture more accurately, did nothing to detract from a belief in the Kraepelinian conception of a deteriorating disease process. If the 'shell-shocked' were represented as the ineffectual 'fall-out' from the system of modern warfare, the schizophrenic was cast in a similar role in the sphere of social and industrial progress. Writing some 50 years later of the attitudes towards schizophrenics in this period, Manfred Bleuler has described how the schizophrenic was conceived as suffering from a 'final and irrevocable loss of his mental existence':

> So it happened that the clinician became increasingly accus-
> tomed to seeing in his schizophrenic dementia cases an autis-
> tic attitude on the part of the patient. The patient and those
> who were healthy had ceased to understand one another.
> *The patient gives up, in abject resignation or total embitter-*
> *ment, any effort to make himself understood.* He either no
> longer says anything or says nothing intelligible. In so do-
> ing the naive observer declares, out of hand, that the patient
> has lost his reasoning powers.[46]

'Insanity', Brower and Bannister had asserted in 1902, 'is a more
or less permanent disease or derangement of the brain producing
disordered actions of the mind.' The 'general course of all adolescent insanity is towards more or less complete mental breakdown.
... It is essentially, in all its forms, a degenerative type of insanity.'[47]
Cole could say in 1913 that 'insanity is now generally recognized
by the laity as a disease of the brain',[48] and in 1914 Knowles-
Stansfield described how 'patients in asylums may be roughly
divided into two distinct groups, namely those who have a pros-
pect of recovery, forming about 10 per cent, and the hopeless
chronic cases who make up the remaining 90 per cent.'[49] In 1926,
in their textbook of psychological medicine, Craig and Beaton
could see in the dementia praecox patient only the remorseless
decline into autism to which Manfred Bleuler referred. The disorders of dementia praecox, they wrote, 'have no other cause than
the patient's failure to master life'. Involved in one such group of
disorders ('schizoid reactions') is a 'gross failure of development in
the central nervous system' which 'causes a failure of adaptation
from birth', and in a condition such as hebephrenic dementia we
find 'an ever-increasing gap between the subjective capacity for
development and its practical application to life'. At a certain
point, perhaps after some critical life event, the loss of a job or
girlfriend,

> The patient whose behaviour had hitherto been regarded as
> 'neurotic' or 'idiosyncratic' and treated accordingly begins
> to show conduct which is definitely psychotic. He becomes
> irritable and liable to emotional outbursts on no apparent
> provocation: he is negligent, dreamy, and self-absorbed. His
> habits become individualistic and asocial; he masturbates fre-
> quently, avoids other people, shuts himself away or wanders
> from home.[50]

The connection of doctrines of degeneracy and deterioration with concerns about social and industrial progress is well brought out in the writings of W.H.R. Rivers, psychiatrist, psychologist and anthropologist. In common with other authorities on mental life, Rivers was in search of an explanation for the seeming inability of certain sections of the population to stand up to the rigours and requirements of modern life, both in the workplace and on the battlefront. How, the questions were asked, could the robust personality be procured and early indications of constitutional weakness be detected? Rivers described his enterprise as 'the examination of the mental constitution of different peoples and by an extension of the term of the differences which characterize the members of different races'. He was impressed by what he variously termed the role of 'the morbid in sociology' and the malign operations of 'degeneration' in social life. 'With the incoming of the idea of evolution', he announced in a lecture to students of anthropology in Cambridge in 1919, this last factor 'was thrown wholly on one side' and in consequence there has been 'a complete failure to appreciate the vast part which degeneration is continually playing in the history of human institutions'.[51] In one aspect his aim was to tease out the constitutional factors that led to loss of energy and vitality. Before the turn of the century he studied under Kraepelin at Heidelberg for a period and collaborated with him on an investigation of mental fatigue, and after the First World War he was a member of the Industrial Fatigue Research Board, a body established to enhance the efficiency of the workplace and to weed out the constitutionally unsuitable. In a second aspect his concern was to strengthen the understanding of the biological basis of mental disorders. He borrowed from Hughlings Jackson's account of the release of lower-level activities from higher-level controls, but went further in seeing in these lower-level activities the expression of racial activities which the later stages of evolution had either controlled or suppressed. And he was thus 'naturally led, wherever possible, to interpret abnormal mental conditions in terms of regression to more primitive, hitherto suppressed, activities'.[52]

The fatigued worker and the 'primitive': these are distinct cultural images, the one a jeopardy to the workplace and the other to the race, but we can see how in the representations of schizophrenic lassitude and schizophrenic thought disorder they could be made to combine into a composite image of constitutional weakness and degeneracy that offended against all the standards of

efficiency and 'right thinking' which civilization was alleged to require. 'One finds it hard', Devine remarked in 1909, 'to look on
dementia praecox, to which one owes so much, as an "undesirable
alien".' But the rapture accorded the scientific conception is not
to be confused with the dominant perception of its objects, for
Kraepelin's theory of dementia praecox did indeed appear to lend
a particular legitimation to a view, established as we have described
over the last decades of the nineteenth century, of those who
languished in asylums as 'undesirable aliens'. 'One now finds it
hard', as we might say, 'to look upon the dementia praecox patient
as anything other then an "undesirable alien".' From this process
of scientific construction and rationalization, the rationalization
of what in an important aspect is the bitter history of struggle
between classes in the social process of our period, a body of
human actions is pitched beyond the realm of ordinary understanding. 'What is a strike?' Mrs Gaskell makes one of her characters
ask, peering across the divide that separates her suburban residence
from the crowd that has gathered around the factory gates in
another part of the town;[53] 'What is a schizophrenic?' we have
come to ask, with the same measure of puzzlement, in our own
time.

The specific renderings of the dementia praecox patient must,
in an obvious respect, be seen as partaking of a wider, and more
generalized, set of perceptions of 'the Other'. Thus George Orwell,
writing about very much the same period that included our debate
on dementia praecox, has described how at school he had 'no
notion that the working class were human beings. At a distance I
could agonize over their sufferings, but I still hated them and des-
pised them when I came anywhere near them. . . . To the shock
absorbers of the bourgeoisie such as myself, "common people"
still appeared brutal and repulsive.'[54] The difference in the case
of the dementia praecox patient, however, is that with him things
could only get worse, to him were attached all the ideas associated
with the word 'deterioration': He was deemed to be: on the wane;
on the decline; out of repair; out of tune; depraved; decrepit;
done for; worn out; used up; broken down; fit for the dust-hole;
fit for the waste-paper basket; past work; past cure; behind the
times; washed out; beyond hope.

2

Schizophrenia and history

The destinies of schizophrenics

Scientific progress and the schizophrenic

Perhaps, writes Oliver Sacks,

> *Every* story is surprising, for no two are the same, and none is
> a mere continuation of what went before: for we are not
> speaking of cases and uniform process, but physiology as it is
> embedded in people, and people as they are embedded and
> living in history. One may have *intended* the replicabilities
> and uniformities of science, but one *encountered* the vicissi-
> tudes of history or romance.[1]

Psychiatrists of the late Victorian and early twentieth century eras
did, of course, speak of cases and a uniform disease process that
ran a course of constant deterioration over the years. In doing so
they certainly *intended* a scientific undertaking with a powerful
predictive capacity that was consonant both with a particular
set of scientific aspirations and with a particular form of social
experience, with a view of schizophrenic 'uselessness' and all
that we have seen conveyed by the term 'deterioration'.

Over the decades of this century, however, those investigators
and practitioners who have ventured outside the Kraepelinian
stockade have *encountered* not a process of progressive deterioration, the ravages of a disease-in-itself, but the struggles, misfortunes,
hopes, griefs, satisfactions and, above all, the indeterminateness of
people who, whatever the constraints and liabilities under which
their inherited natures have placed them, and even when confined
to psychiatric institutions, are indeed embedded and living in
history. These encounters have called not only for a new under-

standing of what is at issue in schizophrenic lives but necessarily
also for a highly developed and testing form of self-understanding
on the part of those scientists who have engaged in them and made
it their business to tell others about them. The rigours of historical
dialogue have, on occasions, proved too demanding. Where some
have beaten a hasty retreat to the stockade, others have been
tempted to tell stories about what they have seen that, whilst they
may have satisfied certain cultural urges, have done little to
enhance our grasp of how we might begin to foster conditions of
community that are less detrimental to the well-being and viability
of schizophrenic people.

On any serious reading of how things now stand it can justifiably
be claimed that the scientific understanding of schizophrenia has
made remarkable progress in the last decade or so. But the form
of progress I have in mind is not, I fear, the form of progress that
many (though certainly not all) scientists will identify as such or
that, on a particular view of what scientific achievement ought to
look like, they aspire to. We have, I believe, to conceive it as a
form of progress that has emerged from (and is thus inextricably
dependent upon) the recognition and understanding of the historical embedding both of schizophrenic lives *and* of the lives and
practices of scientists. Progress has, that is to say, come from
those painstaking efforts that have tried to find new terms (terms,
that is, that are new to science though not to common language)
in which to articulate the enterprise of schizophrenic lives and
thus to extend the bounds of community so as to help us grasp
schizophrenia as one of the forms of tribulation with which in any
actual human community schizophrenics and non-schizophrenics
alike have to contend. All this is perhaps to say that the kind of
progress which matters most is that which is available to the social
sciences conceived as a form of moral science, as distinct from
the kind of progress that is available to the natural sciences.
However, for this reason and also because welfare has come to
find itself — and perhaps has always been — such a beleaguered
presence in our type of society, it is necessarily a vulnerable
achievement; in recent years the bad old ideas about deterioration
have been reconscripted to perform another tour of duty.

One group of scientists who have extended our social vision
in this way are the Swiss psychiatrists Luc Ciompi and Christian
Müller and their collaborators, who in an investigation known as
the *Enquète de Lausanne* have given us a revealing historical
retrospect on the destinies of a number of schizophrenic patients

born between 1873 and 1897.[2] In studies such as this the stories of schizophrenic lives have shown themselves to be very surprising indeed, not only for our own period but, more astonishingly, for schizophrenics first admitted to hospital during the decades we looked at in the last chapter. In the Lausanne study the lives of 228 schizophrenics were charted over a period of at least 37 years from first admission to hospital to re-examination, in many instances for much longer. As Ciompi describes, these are probably the longest follow-ups of such a large group of schizophrenics in the world literature. What did the investigation disclose? In the first place Ciompi and Müller discovered remarkable variations in the clinical course of schizophrenia, which they reduced to eight types. But not only was the clinical course much more varied than the traditional view of a uniform process would have led them to suppose, but they discovered also that the outcome was much more favourable. Thus almost half of the patients in the inquiry achieved a favourable outcome (27 per cent complete remissions and 22 per cent 'minor residuals'), 24 per cent an intermediate outcome and 22 per cent a severe outcome. (The remaining 9 per cent fell into an unstable or uncertain category.) Only 6 per cent of the subjects were judged to be suffering from the so-called 'catastrophic schizophrenia', an acute form of onset leading directly to a severe and unremitting chronic psychosis. Furthermore a comparison of the clinical condition at follow-up with that at first admission revealed that 'mental health was completely or partially improved in about two-thirds of the cases'.

The picture is further amplified when we turn from the depiction of the fluctuations and variations in the clinical course to the account of the social circumstances of these patients over the period of observation. Over these decades about one-quarter of the group spent more than 20 years in hospital but as many as 47 per cent less than one year. At the time of study the mean age of the subjects was 74, yet more than half were still working, about two-thirds of these in part-time and the remaining third in full-time occupations.

Viewed in one light, the Lausanne study is a tale about the relatively more benign hospitalization practices of Switzerland in the early decades of this century, as compared with those of, say, Britain and the United States. In the latter countries the hold of the asylum, and of the pessimistic outlook that went with it, was much stronger, and as late as the 1930s, about 60 per cent of all patients hospitalized for schizophrenia were likely to remain there indefinitely.[3] But the story of these schizophrenic lives has, of course, a wider import than this, for what it effectively does is to puncture the traditional representations of schizophrenia as entailing a remorseless clinical decline and inevitable hospitalization due to incapacity. Moreover, a number of other accounts have helped us to see that the stories of those severely disturbed individuals who have been maintained in psychiatric institutions over long periods are equally productive of surprise, and that these people are not as moribund or deteriorated as had been believed and as some, indeed, would still claim. The circumstances that obtained in Britain and the United States make it impossible for us to extract a countervailing social history from the historical record for the early decades of this century to set against the traditional doctrines about what a schizophrenic life amounted to. However, as for example, J.K. Wing has argued on the basis of his own investigations, it is not to be believed that all these long-term schizophrenic patients were seriously clinically ill, and we should not therefore read the hospital statistics as providing confirmation of those doctrines.[4]

Scientific story-tellers

The *Enquête de Lausanne* is one of a number of studies that have done much to deepen our understanding of the enterprise of schizophrenic lives. But whilst the schizophrenic lives out the story of his life, it is a story that is recovered and told by the scientist. Moreover, to speak of schizophrenic lives as embedded and lived in history presupposes a recognition and understanding on the part of the scientist of the historical embedding of his own life. In one aspect this concerns the moral character of his undertaking for, as Alasdair MacIntyre has remarked, 'it is only in the context of human relationship that acknowledging the pains and griefs and hopes and expectations of others makes sense. Hence our knowledge of others — or our lack of it — depends on what the form of our moral relationships are.'[5] However, quite properly the scientist wants not only to characterize, and hence acknowledge, what is at stake in a human relationship or set of relationships — though surely this has proved difficult enough — but also to provide an explanation, whether this is to take the form of the clearing up of a puzzle or, more ambitiously, a developed causal account. Hence there arises the question of the kinds of claims that within any such context of relationship can legitimately be made by any one person or set of persons about another person or set of persons.

The scientist who has produced the most illuminating and — in terms of its implications — the most far-reaching study of the long-term course of schizophrenic disorders is Manfred Bleuler. To Bleuler's particular contributions in this respect we shall turn later. Not only did he set out to tell the stories of schizophrenic lives; he has also given us the most incisive and critical account that we have to date of the history of schizophrenia — the history, that is, of the diverse tales that scientists have mustered over the decades of this century and of the claims that have been made for them.[6] Bleuler wants to show that if there has been a problem about how to characterize what is happening with a schizophrenic patient, there has also been a closely connected problem around the kind of self-understanding possessed by scientists.

A characteristic tale was, as we have seen, that there was no narrative of a human life to be grasped, and that what we were witness to was the process of a disease-in-itself that set the sufferer irrevocably outside human community. Thus Bleuler describes how

All suspicions and assertions to the effect that schizophrenias are the manifestations of organic idiocy, a brain atrophy, a progressive process, or of an event that continues to propagate its own development, that defies understanding or perception by the emotions, have created unfavourable presuppositions for the scientific exploitation of clinical experience with chronic schizophrenics. The clinician who discovered after years of observation that there was an improvement, and who found an abundance of inner life, of emotional perception, of human rationale in his chronic schizophrenic patient — rather than the expected inexorable progression of the disease — during certain periods in history almost had to be ashamed of his discoveries. On the other hand he felt secure and in concert with the accepted hypotheses if he was able to record an increasingly severe state of idiocy and dehumanization of the patient.[7]

Generally speaking, Bleuler tells us,

The physician is accustomed to assume the presence of physical diseases when physical symptoms are in evidence. When they are absent, one is most reluctant to make authoritative statements that some physical illness lies concealed behind any sorts of complaints or behavioural disturbances. At the utmost a hidden physical illness might then be suspected, but one would never dare to represent it as a certainty in such a case.

However:

> Amazingly, up to now, these fundamentals were barely valid for the field of schizophrenia. Through to the present day, many clinicians and researchers are fully convinced that primary physical disorders (functional or structural) consitute the most essential onset conditions for schizophrenia, although they are unable to identify any clear symptoms indicating such supposed physical disorders. At certain times, researchers were even in danger of being reproached for having an unscientific, uncritical mentality, of being insulted and ostracized, if they did not conform by 'admitting' that there were physical explanations for schizophrenia. In a peculiar reversal of otherwise valid norms, assumptions used to be declared 'scientific' that resulted from pure speculation or emotional needs, and any attempt to consider only information that could be proved was rejected as 'unscientific'.[8]

Bleuler describes the dogma of 'incurability in principle' that governed psychiatric thinking in the years after Kraepelin introduced the concept of dementia praecox, and remarks on the bitterness of psychiatrists of this epoch at their inability to discover a brain disease as explanation for schizophrenia. So firmly entrenched was 'faith in the incurability of the disease' that what looked to be a recovery was made subject to reinterpretation. Thus 'if a patient was released after a schizophrenic psychosis, and if he remained socially well integrated for many years, and finally died, it was suspected that he would eventually have become schizophrenically demented again, if he had only lived long enough.' Representative of the type of attitude that prevailed was H. Luxenburger's assertion in the 1930s that the existence of a 'schizophrenic somatosis' was to be assumed 'with a priori certainty'. And Bleuler comments against this background on the levity with which serious physiological researchers 'conclude that they have discovered physical causes for schizophrenia on the basis of insignificant information and a minimal number of schizophrenics'.[9]
At the time of its introduction the concept of dementia praecox brought to mind a type of dementia 'similar to what is known as

"dementia senilis". One thought of it as a perpetual state of being "out of one's mind" — a final, irrevocable loss of one's mental existence.' Though he introduced the term, Kraepelin did of course recognize that the primary thinking capacity remained intact in dementia praecox patients. But later generations of research workers have proved themselves less discriminating, and even in contemporary studies on heredity the so-called schizophrenic dementia

> is still being interpreted as if it reflected the 'actual process of the disease' in its purest form, and as if it were the most direct expression of a hereditary pathological predisposition. In this context scientists write of the 'demented' forms of schizophrenia as being the 'core syndrome' of the disease, to which related psychoses that do not end in dementia are appended.[10]

If, on this view, the only story to be told about schizophrenic lives was a story of natural causality, others have extended the same compliment to the families of schizophrenics. Thus in the early part of the century if it was discovered 'that a patient's parents were divorced, that his father had abandoned the family, that his mother had callously turned over his child to foster care, such circumstances served as definite indications of a psychopathic constitution of the progenitors and of an inherited background favourable to schizophrenia in the patient.'[11] In the post-war decades, however, some have eschewed tales of natural causality in favour of accounts that implicated the origin of the schizophrenic's suffering in a social order of causality. Here was a genre that sought to draw the development of a schizophrenic psychosis into the narrative of a family history, whether the interactions of the family as a whole or the development of the child in relation to its mother. But if in this genre it appeared that there was now a story of human relationship to be told about how human beings living in close proximity affect each other, 'environmentalists' have shown themselves to be no less assertive than those of contrary persuasions in offering their accounts as a foundation for decisive causal claims. Thus for example some investigators came to hold 'the dogmatic conviction that the long sought-after etiology of schizophrenia could be found in the severe chaotic childhood experiences. Bias and prejudice led even serious investigators astray in past decades in supplying "proof" that cannot be sustained by honest criticism.' It was discouraging to

find, Bleuler remarks, that the 'very same circumstances — the
frequency of the broken home — (in some cases not even proved)
should indicate to one investigator proof of hereditary factors at
work and to another proof of the psychogenesis of schizophrenia'.[12]

Narratives and vocabularies

Where Ciompi and Müller helped us to recognize that schizophrenic
lives are embedded and lived in history, Bleuler helps us to see
that there has been something very peculiar about the sorts of
self-understandings possessed by scientists as to the form and
character of their own embeddedness in history. On Ciompi's
view, what has traditionally been 'called "the course of schizophrenia" more closely resembles a life process open to a great
variety of influences of all kinds than an illness with a given
course'. From other quarters similar questions have been raised
against the applicability of concepts of 'natural history' to schizophrenic disorders. So, for example, Rue Cromwell has argued that
the schizophrenic's 'destiny is determined much the same as the
destinies of all people are determined' and that schizophrenia is
not therefore 'an all-encompassing illness which sets the patient
apart from his fellow man'.[13] These writers do not of course mean
to propose a concept of schizophrenia that abolishes illness,
neither do they mean to imply that schizophrenia is not infrequently a chronic illness; what they offer, rather, is a way of
thinking about the schizophrenic and his condition that emancipates
him from the determinateness of the type of the chronic schizophrenic that we have inherited from the nineteenth century.

But what does it mean to speak of a 'life process' and of the
embedding of lives in history? How are we to grasp the connection
between the historical embedding of human lives and the historical
embedding of the enterprise of human understanding? The most
promising route into these questions is, I believe, to take seriously
Richard Rorty's recommendation that we adopt an approach to
social science and morality which 'emphasizes the utility of
narratives and vocabularies rather than the objectivity of laws and
theories'.[14] Already in this discussion I have introduced notions of
story-telling and narrative, and I shall now go on to explore these
more fully and to highlight their significance for our understanding
both of schizophrenic people and of the difficulties which the
science of schizophrenia has encountered. To proceed in this way
will be to opt for a style of analysis that is less concerned with

questions of causality than with sequences of action and reaction. Human lives are certainly not devoid of causal properties, but the extraction of these from the historical texture within which lives are lived has shown itself to be a more hazardous affair than has sometimes been supposed. So, for example, whilst there is now incontrovertible genetic evidence of an inherited predisposition to schizophrenic illness in a large number of cases (though it must be said also that the evidence is equally incontrovertible of just such a predisposition in a wide body of people who do not become schizophrenic), we reach well beyond the terms of that evidence if we then try to use it to refurbish a conception of a 'natural history' and to claim that we have identified the significant determinations in the unfolding of an individual life.[15]

The sort of approach that Rorty recommends cannot exhaust all that a science of human beings is able to achieve; least of all can it tell us all that we should like to know about schizophrenia. What, perhaps, an exploration of the concept of narrative can do is to help give us our bearings, to further our understanding of the terrain within which human lives are lived and efforts at human comprehension are carried out, and to grasp the connection between the form of human action and the appropriate form for the understanding of human action. But to propose this line of thought is, of course, to propose something that is alien to the conceptions of scientific inquiry that we are most familiar with. We shall need first, therefore, to look briefly at why this is so, and to do so may perhaps give us a further clue as to why, if what the writers quoted above have to say about the life of a schizophrenic is true, it has taken so long to find this out.

Scientific reason and historical reason

The individual, the scientist and the project of the Enlightenment

From Descartes onwards in what has been, and in many respects is still, the most influential tradition of Western thought, thinkers have abjured history as a means to truth. Indeed one way to characterize the Enlightenment project of understanding of the late seventeenth and eighteenth centuries is as a series of claims to have done away with all those mundane historical impediments to clear vision and thought that had clouded classical views of the world. Enlightenment thinkers were united in the belief that 'whereas the scholastics had allowed themselves to be deceived about the character of the facts of the natural and social worlds by interposing an Aristotelian interpretation between themselves and experienced reality',they, by contrast, 'had stripped away interpretation and theory and confronted fact and experience just as they are'.[16] The spectacle of human nature stripped of its metaphysical pretension that displayed itself to such a discerning observer as Thomas Hobbes may not have been particularly pleasant, but it did at least possess the singular merit of a claim to scientific veracity.

From Descartes, Locke and their successors we have inherited the notion of 'scientific method' as the search for 'an absolute conception of reality'. As Richard Rorty has elegantly described, we have in this

> The Cartesian form of the archetypal philosophical fantasy — first spun by Plato — of cutting through all descriptions, all representations, to a state of consciousness which, *per impossibile*, combines the best features of inarticulate confrontation with the best features of linguistic formulation. This fantasy of discovering, and somehow *knowing* that one has discovered, Nature's Own Vocabulary seemed to become more concrete when Galileo and Newton formulated a comprehensive set of predictively useful universal generalizations, written in suitably 'cold', 'inhuman', mathematical terms. From their time to the present, the notions of 'rationality', 'method', and 'science' have been bound up with the search for such generalizations.[17]

'Method' came to be conceived as a transaction between the competent 'knowing subject' and reality, a transaction that involves 'not simply ordering one's thoughts but *filtering* them in order to eliminate "subjective" and "non-cognitive" or "confused elements", leaving only the thoughts which are Nature's Own'.[18]

In the philosophy of Descartes, and the epistemological tradition that succeeds him, mind comes to be conceived as a principle of science, as somehow peculiarly equipped to perceive things as they truly are and to codify reality in Nature's Own Vocabulary. To achieve the direct access to Nature which mind permitted was to be able to distinguish between 'the parts of one's mind which do and don't correspond to reality', a distinction which thus comes to be equated with that between 'rational and irrational ways of doing science', or between doing science and doing something else. On Locke's account knowledge consisted of 'rightly ordered inner representations' that derived from mental processes, and for both Descartes and Locke the elucidation of the workings of the mind provided access to a 'method of discovering truth, and not just truth about the mind'. On the view of mind as a closed space, sufficient unto itself, and doing combat with other influences, 'the difference between the man whose beliefs were true and the man whose beliefs were false' thus came to be understood as 'a matter of "how their minds worked"'.[19]

Doctrines about the source of knowledge as residing in the individual — thus on the empiricist account the notion that knowledge arises from sensations received within the closed realm of the individual mind — were developed and pursued in close connection with doctrines about the origin and nature of the individual himself. If the origin of knowledge is to be accounted for solely on the basis of individual experience, then it must also be possible to account for the individual himself without reference to social causality. Thus from the late seventeenth and eighteenth centuries we have inherited a conception of the individual as *given* in his most essential aspects, a picture of the encapsulated, self-possessed and self-centred individual comprising a distinct and separate reality from what is called 'society', and also a conception of society as made up of citizens who are 'independent centres of consciousness'.[20]

The Cartesian epistemological tradition thus furbished a conception of objective scientific inquiry that could serve as a model for individual self-possession, for what it was to be in touch with reality and to see clearly. And to see human beings clearly, to render them perceptually fit for scientific understanding, was certainly not to resort to vocabularies that retained terms referring to intentions, purposes and reasons for acting; rather it was to favour mechanistic sorts of explanation that sought to uncover the physiological and physical mechanisms that underlay action. In the image of the scientist carefully filtering his thoughts, and distinguishing between the parts of his mind which do and don't correspond to reality, is to be found the most consummate expression of the properly functioning mind, of an acutely self-possessed consciousness that endeavours to establish a solid foundation for perceptions and to preserve thought from contamination by social, religious and metaphysical elements.

Thus post-revolutionary French philosophers such as Antoine Destutt de Tracy and Pierre Cabanis saw in the work of writers

such as Locke and Condillac a means to put social life on to a
scientific footing. As de Tracy explained in outlining the programme of the Idéologues, the basis of certainty is to be found in
individual sensation; by examining how our ideas are combined
and deduced we shall be able 'to discover the character and causes
of truth and error'.[21] Truth was thus directly available from basic
perceptual processes, and error and falsehood, by contrast, resulted
when the individual permitted the purity of his sensations to be
contaminated by social influences and processes. In this connection,
language, whilst it could not be disregarded as an expedient
instrument for conducting the business of social life, none the less
fell under suspicion as dissipating the clarity of the perceiver's
access to truth. 'Another thing that is of great use for the clear
perception of truth', Locke had written, 'is if we can bring ourselves to think things abstracted and separate from words.' When a
man 'thinks, reasons and discourses within himself' it is better to
lay words 'aside and have an immiedate converse with the Ideas
of things'. And de Tracy reached the conclusion that the ambiguity
and variety of meaning by which words in the language were
enveloped was 'the source of all our errors and all our disputes'.[22]

It is, of course, not difficult to identify numerous successors
to the programme initiated by the Idéologues at the turn of the
nineteenth century, both in the work of what came to be known
as the logical positivists or logical empiricists and, more widely, in
the main currents of twentieth century scientific psychology. One
of the most formidable opponents of notions of 'pure observation'
and 'ultimate sources of knowledge' has been Karl Popper. What
we should do, Popper suggests, is to 'give up the idea of ultimate
sources of knowledge, and admit that all knowledge is human;
that it is mixed with our errors, our prejudices, our dreams, and
our hopes; that all we can do is to grope for truth even though it is
beyond our reach.'[23] Scientific theories, he argues, are not as
adherents of sense-observation theory believed 'digests of observations' nor moreover are they 'just the results of observation'.
We need, instead, to think of what we call 'science' as a form of
myth that is

> differentiated from the older myths not by being something
> distinct from a myth, but by being accompanied by a second-
> order tradition — that of critically discussing the myth.
> Before, there was only the first-order tradition. A definite
> story was handed on. Now there was still, of course, a story

to be handed on, but with it went something like a salient accompanying text of a second-order character: 'I hand it on to you but tell me what you think of it. Think it over. Perhaps you can give us a different story.' This second-order tradition was the critical or argumentative attitude. It was, I believe, a new thing, and it is still the fundamentally important thing about scientific tradition. If we understand that, then we shall have an altogether different attitude towards quite a number of problems of scientific method. We shall understand that, in a certain sense, science is myth-making just as religion is.[24]

In this way Popper brought the historically sundered vocabularies of scientific method and story-telling into closer connection with each other. Similarly, in sharp contrast to the empiricist conceptions of the scientist engaged in a solitary transaction with reality, he insisted on the importance of tradition in science and thus on the communal basis of scientific achievement. Nevertheless in introducing the connection Popper did not, of course, mean to blur the line between the 'scientific' and the 'non-scientific', or to suggest that it could not be definitively drawn. Above all, he has always held out for the idea that the form of critical discussion characteristic of science is of a privileged kind to be distinguished from other such forms, for a view of science as hedged about in a context-free transaction with reality sharply marked off from historical contexts of justification. Other philosophers, however, have argued that the history of science licenses no such sharp distinction between one form of critical discussion and another, and that scientific story-telling is no less historically embedded than other forms of story-telling. Put very summarily, the argument in the case of the natural sciences is that critical debate between scientists is more like an ordinary conversation than the Enlightenment view of it had led us to suppose, and in the case of the social sciences that notions of story-telling and narrative serve to identify crucial features not only of what social scientists do but also of the form of human action itself, of how human life is lived and sustained. On both these fronts, therefore, the conception that we have inherited from the late seventeenth century of scientific discourse as *normal discourse*, as providing the standard which all other forms of discourse must emulate, becomes distinctly questionable.

The debates about the relations between historical and scientific rationality, and about the project of social scientific understanding, are to say the least treacherous. Happily, we have in a number of discussions by Alasdair MacIntyre an exploration of notions of story-telling and narrative that is peculiarly germane to our purposes, in that it illuminates in a very graphic way a number of the connections between the historical embedding of human lives and the historical embedding of the enterprise of human understanding.

Science and narrative

We shall look first at that part of MacIntyre's argument in which he tries to show that an understanding of the dramatic and historical character of human action can help us grasp a connection between the resolution of a personal crisis of understanding, a crisis of understanding in an individual human life, and the resolution of a crisis of understanding in a scientific tradition. To instance such a personal crisis he gives an account of the turmoil into which Hamlet is thrown upon returning to Elsinore from Wittenberg. To share a culture, MacIntyre argues, is to share schemata by means of which members are able to act intelligibly both to themselves and to others and to understand and interpret the action of others. But suppose a condition in which the agent discovers not only that the schemata on which he has so far relied have led him into error and deception and are thus put into question, but also that the circumstances in which he finds himself are open to radically different possibilities of interpretation. Whom is he now to believe and how is he to repair his means of understanding?

Just these problems arise for Hamlet when he is confronted by the events at Elsinore. How is he to make sense of them? Which schema is he to choose? 'There is the revenge schema of the Norse sagas; there is the Renaissance courtier's schema; there is a Machiavellian schema about competition for power.' Not only does he have the problem of which schema to apply, he also has the problem: 'Whom now to believe? His mother? Rosencrantz and Guildenstern? His father's ghost? Until he has adopted some schema he does not know what to treat as evidence; until he knows what to treat as evidence he cannot tell which schema to adopt.'[25]

Hamlet is, as MacIntyre describes, a classic study of an epistemological crisis, a crisis that is at one and the same time a crisis in beliefs and in human relationships. How is such a crisis to be resolved? Hamlet's problems can be put in the form of questions like: 'What is going on here?' 'How am I to understand the human drama here of which I am part?' 'How ought the narrative or story of these events to be constructed?' His 'problems arise because the dramatic narrative of his family and of the kingdom of Denmark through which he identified his own place in society and his relationships to others has been disrupted by radical interpretative doubts.'[26] The way through is thus for him to 'reconstitute, to rewrite that narrative, reversing his understanding of past events in the light of present responses to his probing'. And an epistemological crisis is thus resolved

> by the construction of a new narrative which enables the agent to understand both how he or she could intelligibly have held his or her original beliefs *and* how he or she could have been so drastically misled by them. The narrative in terms of which he or she at first understood and ordered experiences is itself made the subject of an enlarged narrative.[27]

MacIntyre means us to understand human action as a source of narration for which narrative provides the essential form of understanding. As he writes elsewhere: 'It is because we all live out narratives in our lives and because we understand our own lives in terms of the narratives that we live out, that the form of narrative is appropriate for understanding the actions of others.' 'Man', so MacIntyre argues, 'is in his actions and practices, as well as in his fictions, essentially a story-telling animal.' Moreover, 'he is not essentially, but becomes through his history, a teller of stories that aspire to truth.'[28] Thus in aspiring to truth the agent does not cease to be a teller of stories and, as in the case of Hamlet, he can only deal with the errors and inadequacies of a particular story or set of stories by reconstituting them in a new and better account. It is just this form of self-consciousness in respect of the story-telling character of science that distinguishes, for example, the 'new science' of the eighteenth century Italian philosopher Giambattista Vico. But in reconstituting the narrative or narratives in terms of which he first understood and ordered experiences into a new narrative, the agent may be led to revise his conceptions of truth and rationality and thus to ponder the claims that he can make for the 'better account' that he has now assembled:

He has had to become epistemologically self-conscious and

at a certain point he may have come to acknowledge two
conclusions: the first is that his new forms of understanding
may themselves in turn come to be put in question at any
time; the second is that, because in such [epistemological]
crises the criteria of truth, intelligibility and rationality may
themselves always be put in question — as they are in *Hamlet*
— we are never in a position to claim that now we possess the
truth or now we are fully rational. The most we can claim is
that this is the best account which anyone has been able to
give so far and that our beliefs about what the marks of a
'best account so far' are will themselves change in what are
at present unpredictable ways.[29]

It will be obvious enough that this is a very unLockean view to
adopt and implies (among other things) a radically divergent
understanding of the nature of selfhood and of truth and rationality. I shall enlarge on the problem of selfhood in the next
chapter, but for the moment we may grasp MacIntyre's meaning
more fully by looking at what happens to the sort of thinker who
comes to deny the historical character of human understanding
and, unlike Vico, to feel that 'all narratives are misleading fables
when compared with what he now takes to be the solid truth
of physics.'[30]

One such individual is René Descartes. Descartes claimed to
entertain doubts not about one set of beliefs among several
but about the whole background of inherited beliefs. As MacIntyre
remarks, 'Descartes' doubt is intended to lack any such background. It is to be contextless doubt'. Descartes thus 'starts from
the assumption that he knows nothing whatsoever until he can
discover a presuppositionless first principle on which all else can
be founded.' But Descartes misdescribes his epistemological crisis
and fails to recognize those features of his inherited beliefs which
he does not put in doubt at all. So, for example, he is able to use
the French and Latin languages and 'as a consequence he does not
put in doubt what he has inherited with these languages, namely,
a way of ordering both thought and the world expressed in a set of
meanings.' Furthermore, he does not recognize that his thought
is formulated against the background of the conflicts and uncertainties of a tradition of inquiry from which he inherits the
epistemological ideal of knowledge as akin to vision and that he is
therefore 'responding not only to the timeless demands of scepticism but to a highly specific crisis in one particular social and
intellectual tradition'.[31]

It will be apparent that there is a striking difference between Shakespeare's account of epistemological crisis in *Hamlet* and Descartes's, which MacIntyre puts as follows:

> Shakespeare invites us to reflect on the crisis of the self as a crisis in the tradition which has formed the self; Descartes by his attitude to history and to fable has cut himself off from the possibility of recognizing himself; he has invented an unhistorical, self-endorsed, self-consciousness and tries to describe his epistemological crisis in terms of it.[32]

MacIntyre wants to show, in contrast to Descartes, that scientific reason is dependent on historical reason, and that for lack of the historical continuity provided by the context of a tradition human understanding lapses into incoherence.

How can this be so? The argument turns on a demonstration of the conceptual connections between narrative, tradition and conflict and thus between the means for the resolution of a crisis in an individual life on the one hand and a crisis in a scientific tradition on the other. A scientific tradition is constituted by a narrative that tells the story of that tradition and the theories it embodies, and thus reconstructs in a coherent account the incoherencies or anomalies of a previous tradition or of an earlier phase of the same tradition. Furthermore, to be kept alive a tradition must be continuously reconstructed through, in MacIntyre's phrase, argumentative retellings of the narrative that constitutes the tradition, some of which may be in conflict with other argumentative retellings. In this respect a tradition is in part constituted by conflicts of interpretation of that tradition and thus by a history of arguments as to the nature of the tradition. A tradition is thus always in danger of lapsing into incoherence, and coherence can only be maintained or restored by the construction of a narrative that renders intelligible in a new way the errors and incoherencies of previous narrative histories. From this point of view, therefore, a scientific revolution is to be understood as the successful resolution by the scientist of a crisis in the tradition in which he was formed through the construction of a new and more adequte narrative. Where 'we are apt to suppose that because Galileo was a peculiarly great scientist, therefore he has his own peculiar place in the history of science' we ought perhaps, MacIntyre nicely suggests, to incline to the view that 'it is because of his peculiarly important place in the history of science that he is accounted a particularly great scientist.'[33]

Progress thus comes from an argumentative retelling that preserves the historical continuity between different episodes of a tradition and thus presupposes the context of a tradition. On MacIntyre's argument not only is dramatic narrative 'the crucial form for the understanding of human action' but furthermore:

> Natural science can be a rational form of enquiry if and only if the writing of a true dramatic narrative — that is, of history understood in a particular way — can be a rational activity. Scientific reason turns out to be subordinate to, and intelligible only in terms of, historical reason.[34]

But supposing we *were* dispossessed of the historical continutiy that derives from a context of tradition and everything *was* put in doubt simultaneously. What would happen then? We might then find ourselves in the position of radical scepticism that David Hume describes in which 'the understanding, when it acts alone, and according to its most general principles, entirely subverts itself', and the subject declares himself

> ready to reject all belief and reasoning, and can look upon no opinion even as more probable or likely than another. Where am I, or what? From what causes do I derive my existence, and to what condition shall I return? Whose favour shall I court, and whose anger must I dread? What beings surround me and on whom have I any influence? I am confronted with all these questions and begin to fancy myself in the most deplorable condition imaginable.[35]

And as MacIntyre rightly describes, an epistemological crisis of this kind taken to a certain limit, whether in an ordinary human life or in the life of a scientist, must issue in a form of madness. To trust unrelentingly only in what can be based upon sense-experience would be to risk incurring Hume's Disease, a peculiarly painful illness which, so MacIntyre informs us on the basis of his own investigations into the long-term course of the disorder, is 'incurable and ultimately fatal'. But much as the epistemological ideals that we have inherited in the tradition from Descartes through Locke to Kant claim that they do so, scientists have not in fact trusted only in sense experience. Thomas Kuhn's criticisms in *The Structure of Scientific Revolutions* were after all not of what scientists actually do, but of the gap that has been contrived between such epistemological ideals and identifiable scientific practices. As Rorty puts it:

Since the Enlightenment, and in particular since Kant, the physical sciences had been viewed as a paradigm of knowledge to which the rest of culture had to measure up. Kuhn's lessons from the history of science suggested that controversy within the physical sciences was rather more like ordinary conversation (on the blameworthiness of an action, the qualifications of an officeseeker, the value of a poem, the desirability of legislation) than the Enlightenment had suggested.[36]

On MacIntyre's account Kuhn's mistake, however, was not to have noticed the historical continuity that is given by the context of a tradition, and thus makes possible the construction of a narrative that renders intelligible the errors and incoherencies of earlier phases of that tradition. In Kuhn's description 'scientific revolutions are epistemological crises understood in a Cartesian way' where everything is put in question at once, and hence Kuhn has been taken by some of his critics to mean to say that such intellectual upheavals are irrational events.

Once, however, we grasp the role of dramatic narrative in the resolution of crises of understanding, we can be brought to recognize that 'the best account that can be given of why some scientific theories are superior to others presupposes the possibility of constructing an intelligible dramatic narrative which can claim historical truth and in which such theories are the subject of successive episodes.'[37]

Popper, as we discussed earlier, saw the importance of notions of tradition and story-telling, but supposed nevertheless that it was possible to elevate the stories of science to a privileged argumentative footing and to demonstrate the rationality of science for all time by assembling a set of rules to describe how science must proceed. But attempts to formulate context-free rules are always having to contend with counter-examples from the history of science, and it is thus 'only when theories are located in history, when we view the demands for justification in highly particular contexts of a historical kind, that we are freed from either dogmatism or capitulation to scepticism.'[38]

Understanding human action

If on MacIntyre's account dramatic narrative plays such a powerful role in the construction and justification of theories in the natural sciences, and if therefore the scientist in his laboratory, far from severing his connection with the ordinary social world of sense-making, is dependent on the resources that if offers him as a condition for his success, what then holds for those sciences for which the action of human lives constitutes the very stuff of their subject matter? In a justly influential paper MacIntyre has tried to expose the contrasting predicaments within social life of two individual types, Mr Ordinary Agent (with no special qualifications) and Dr Social Scientist.[39] In essence he sets out to answer two questions: what sorts of difficulties do ordinary agents encounter in trying to negotiate and understand social life? And how, if at all, can social scientists manage to improve on the sorts of understandings that are available to ordinary agents?

Social life, MacIntyre argues, is inevitably a precarious affair in which the 'socially established demands of action outrun the possibilities of rationality' and agents find themselves continually subject to confusion, incoherence and distortion. Both in his efforts to grasp the actions of others, and to comprehend his own life situation from within as it is lived, the agent is drawn into a convoluted field of difficulty. How, for example, is he to characterize an action? To the question 'what is so-and-so doing?':

> The answer might be 'digging', 'planting lettuce seedlings', 'making sure that they will have an adequate source of vitamin C', 'doing as his wife told him', 'taking his prescribed twenty minutes exercise', 'filling in time till the bars open', 'earning money', 'overstraining his heart', 'using the wrong tools for the job'.[40]

For want of an understanding of the intentions that underlie the performance of the action the observer has no basis on which to select from a range of possible descriptions. Moreover such an understanding itself presupposes a knowledge and understanding of the individual's beliefs, and of the settings from which those beliefs derive. Thus 'the action of taking a sheep to market presupposes a whole web of beliefs about the economy and about husbandry; the action of assassinating a tyrant, a whole web of political beliefs.' Furthermore, the characterization of any particular action is inherently unstable just for the reason that contrasting descriptions of that action may assume primary significance for the agent involved in it under different conditions.

In his transactions with other agents, and in response to the demands made upon him, therefore, the agent has of necessity continually to refashion the dramatic and narrative forms in which he orders his life (and, as an aspect of that ordering, his understanding of others) and tries to make it intelligible to himself and to others. In his search for comprehension we can think of the agent as an amateur social theorist and of social life as 'a series of historically idiosyncratic, interrelated narratives in which the attempt at comprehension by every agent is an indispensable feature'. In the programme of the Enlightenment there was confidence in the radical separateness and self-sufficiency of the sphere of individual life, and in the potential for epistemological access to an observational stance in which the world could be seen as it truly is, undistracted by the partialities of social influence and process. By contrast, the agent of MacIntyre's description finds himself constrained in his activities as a theorist to work up such comprehension as he can from within an intricate interdependence of individual and social life, action and setting, in which neither 'the individual' nor 'the action', no more than the agent's own vantage point, can be isolated from the historical texture in which they subsist, and made determinate. What the agent has to contend with is never just 'an individual' but an episode or siting within a history of intersecting actions, and thus intersecting beliefs and concepts. Of necessity he must impute intentions, motives, states of mind etc. to others, construct generalizations and attempt to predict future outcomes. However, by virtue of the pervasive instabilities in the field of social action, of the strategic and tactical tasks in which agents are engaged, their capacity for deceit, irony and pretence and for the rational self-monitoring of the concepts and generalizations under which others try to bring their behaviour, the agent will always be forced into imputations and ascriptions which can never be rationally warranted by the available evidence and into predictions and generalizations that constantly break down.

If Mr Ordinary Agent is left in the social and epistemological lurch in this way, how then do matters stand with Dr Social Scientist?:

We all know that those professionally concerned with the human sciences are as liable to astonishment or to mishap as anyone else. Psychiatrists sometimes have broken marriages and breakdowns; anthropologists occasionally expect research grants much as Melanesians expect cargo; and sociologists may exhibit deviance and anomie. But in their professional and professionalized lives, have social scientists acquired a method of understanding social life that, by reason of its scientific objectivity, rescues them from the epistemological limitations imposed upon ordinary agents? Could they have?[41]

And the answer, MacIntyre returns, is that neither have they acquired such a method nor could they do so. Neither in respect of the characterization of human behaviour nor in respect of the formulation of causal generalizations can social scientists render themselves 'invulnerable to the upsets to which ordinary agents are liable.' On this view of the matter the natural scientist, even if he is dependent on historical reason and cannot therefore claim privileged access to nature's way of doing things, is at least able to get on with the job; the social scientist, in contrast, is always at risk of being surprised and disrupted, not to say subverted, by his objects of study. But if the social scientist cannot escape the epistemological limitations to which the ordinary agent is subject, what can he do? He can at least avoid falling or remaining a victim to such limitations by becoming conscious of them and by seeking to carry through forms of inquiry that involve the posing of self-conscious questions of the following kind:

> What categories and concepts am I using in interpreting the actions of others and in forming my own intentions? What characterization can I give of the situation, which I am rendering determinate and intelligible to myself and perhaps to others through these categories and concepts, in terms other than and, if possible, logically prior to, my categorizations? What criteria am I employing in finding these categories and concepts more appropriate to use than any others? What sort of rationality, if any, is involved in the use of these criteria? What in the answers to all these previous questions is bound up with the particularities of my own personal and social situation? What characterizes my situation as that of an agent *as such*, and what characterizes it as that of an agent *of a particular kind*, so providing me with an understanding of others as well as of myself?[42]

To reach such a conclusion is not to cast the social sciences as a forlorn and unwarranted collection of enterprises. It is rather to argue, as for example has John Dunn, that just because of the 'intrinsic epistemic fluidity' of those sciences, and the concomitant difficulty even in 'characterizing adequately what is humanly the case at a particular time', we must conceive them 'as irretrievably moral sciences, cognitive enterprises committed to the *humble* assessment of social and individual potentiality under extraordinarily refractory conditions'.[43] One of the questions that writers like MacIntyre and Dunn ask is: what is it to consider the social and historical embedding of human lives? The other is: how is our understanding of social life can we be preserved from what MacIntyre terms 'epistemological self-righteousness'? These questions are not unconnected, for to see human sociality not, as methodological individualists who would have us do, as an 'external and contingent attribute of human beings', but as informing what we are and the forms of understanding that are available to us, is to see also that our self-understanding, and thus also the understanding we proclaim of others, is to say the least a corrigible affair.

To treat the self-understanding of human beings as a problem is to allow that it is 'deeply interwoven with their understandings of the social settings of their lives, with, that is to say, their amateur social theories' and that they are thus burdened by an 'opacity in self-understanding' that is a function among other things (again in sharp distinction from the sorts of assumptions that we have inherited from the Enlightenment as to what it is to see clearly what is going on around us) of the 'limits of their social vision'.[44] But if methodological individualists cannot recognize the constraints on their social vision then no more can methodological wholists, those theorists for whom the sum of individual life is firmly cast within the machinations of an ineluctable social causality. For individualists and wholists alike, knowledge is reducible either to 'facts about individuals' or to 'facts about society'; they are both epistemologically strident, intent upon furbishing an 'absolute conception of reality', and both therefore suffer from the maladies which it has been MacIntyre's purpose to diagnose.

Science and schizophrenia

The power of MacIntyre's discussion is not only, as I shall try to demonstrate in more depth in subsequent chapters, that it initiates a number of concepts that are of help to us in studying the action of schizophrenic lives, but also that it provides us with a perspective within which both to locate the vicissitudes of the scientific project of schizophrenia and, equally important, to grasp the force of the social history that we described in the last chapter in its connection with an intellectual history.

As we have seen, the project of the Enlightenment licensed a conception of the scientific thinker as standing in direct confrontation with the 'facts' of the natural and social worlds, relieved of the hindrance of earlier forms of tradition and affiliation. Under the sponsorship of secular rationality the framework of social existence was increasingly stripped of those teleological impedimenta by which human beings had previously been burdened; the stage of human activity was, as it were, cleared of the clutter that had got in the way of direct perception: human beings now became fully visible to each other, and what they recognized in each other was the individual. On the one side we can acknowledge in this the great promise of the secular project, the promise of extending rationality across different dimensions of social existence, of drawing different domains of human thought and activity out of the darkness of superstition; yet on the other we can recognize also the risks and temptations by which it was attended. For what it also introduced into social life were not only new forms of power but in addition, as a concomitant, quite new forms of vulnerability, new possibilities for the exposure of the lives of some men to the wills and interests of other men. Above all, perhaps, it introduced a dissipation of the grammar of community such that individuals found themselves easily put beyond the terms of a recognized human order and liable both to be addressed and maintained in this solitary condition — a social order in which individuals came to be judged not as ends in themselves but as means to institutionally defined ends, and thus where the action of a life, so far as it resisted assimilation into institutionally defined purposes, came to possess only negative value and even perhaps to become inexplicable.

This is the social and intellectual space in which the type of the chronic schizophrenic was formed. The chronic schizophrenic is not, of course, the product of an intellectual history alone, but if we cast the tendencies and aspirations we have described into the pressures and circumstances of the period that we discussed in the last chapter we can begin to grasp the conditions under which people became available for diagnosis as chronic types and scientific operators stood prepared to receive them as such. Once we edge our way inside these ways of feeling and thinking, the delineations of the schizophrenic as a chronic type lose their peculiarity, as though it were a wholly natural consequence that he should have been picked out and recognized as such. And if in one aspect the schizophrenic is the negative opposite of the disciplined and regulated worker we can now see that in a second, and complementary, aspect he is the negative opposite of that traditional image of the scientist, trusting only in sense experience and guarding against contamination by untoward influences, which has furnished us with a model not only of how scientific activity and the accumulation of knowledge is taken to work but also of what rational participation in the world consists in.

Yet if we have here an incipient account of why the project of schizophrenia should have come about, and why it should have taken the form that it did, we are now perhaps in a position also to understand why in its subsequent history it should repeatedly have encountered the sorts of difficulties that Manfred Bleuler described. For, following the line of argument proposed by MacIntyre, we can say that precisely those very same characteristics that enabled the creation of the project, and the demarcation of a new scientific terrain, have made an unwitting but powerful contribution to its inability not only to secure a firm hold on its conquest but to its inability also to understand the reasons for its difficulties. So far as social life, and the terms of human agents' participation within it, is not the sort of enterprise that the Cartesian tradition has taken it for, then the loss of the connections between the vocabularies of scientific method and storytelling, and between narrative and the form of human action, are likely to have crippling consequences both for what any particular scientific inquiry into some aspect of human life is able to achieve and for the self-understanding of the scientists involved in such an undertaking. From this point of view it is then not surprising that the sort of definition of the relationship between schizophrenia and history enforced by (at its strongest) a conception of schizophrenic lives as possessed by a *natural* history has historically so often been caught unawares.

Of particular note here have been the embarrassments produced by the 'imperfections' of language, as though language were not the medium within which as human beings we must perforce live as best we can but as something which, useful though it may be in our day-to-day dealings, we can nevertheless for scientific purposes get beyond to a purer set of representations. Here for example is a not uncharacteristic attempt by a group of behavioural psychologists to liberate the patient's speech from all those messy constraints of context and circumstance and place it in a state of virginal readiness for the approaches of the scientific worker. The methodological amenability of speech to scientific scrutiny, the writers tell us, is that 'because people talk much of the time, they are used to being asked to talk or are used to being engaged in conversation':

> This is very important in circumventing the problem of cooperativeness which plagues any psychological techniques requiring patients to do something specific, such as lifting a finger as soon as a stimulus appears, recalling a word, defining a word, tapping as fast as possible, or saying what they see on some peculiar-looking but symmetrical picture.[45]

The fact of the patient's familiarity with speech thus becomes a contrivance through which to dupe him into supplying a supposedly context-free sample of his behaviour. We learn that:

> The situation was presented to the patients as a routine mental hospital procedure, not as an experiment. The patient was brought into the experimental room and seated behind a screen which consisted of a 42 X 50 inch wooden frame covered with a cloth and placed on the top of a table in such a way that the experimenter was able to observe the outline of the patient, while the patient was unable to see the experimenter. A 7.5 watt red light bulb was placed directly in front of the patient. The tape recording apparatus was placed on the experimenter's side of the screen; the patients were told that their speech was being tape recorded and that the purpose of the screen was to obtain clearer recordings.

The patient then had read to him the following instructions:

> When I tell you to start I would like you to begin talking until I ask you to stop. You've probably noticed the light in front of you. Whenever you are saying something of importance the light will flash on and off. By importance I mean information which will help us get a better picture of what's wrong and put us in a better position to help you. You will find that speaking of these important things will make you feel better. Now, I'd like you to talk about your family, your schooling, your work, how you spend your free time, about any problems you have, and anything else about yourself that is related to your being here in hospital. So why don't you start by telling me why you came here to the hospital and then go on talking until I tell you to stop.

As many as 40 per cent of the subjects talked for 30 minutes without questions, and on this basis the writers make a claim for the experiment as

> a situation which provides the researcher as well as the clinician with a sample of speech which could be analysed for any number of characteristics. One could, for example, examine the grammatical nature of the speech sample; one could use it for a content analysis; one could examine the frequency of occurrence of particular words or patterns of repetition; one could do a temporal analysis of the speech; one could measure the comprehensibility of the speech; one could perform a linguistic analysis of it; and so on. This material has the further advantage of containing no such interfering stimuli as questions or other reactions on the part of the interviewer, other than the few standard prods. In fact, for periods of time as short as the 30 minutes used in this experiment, no reinforcement at all need be delivered (provided some has been promised) in order to keep patients speaking.

In another account of problems of language and thought in schizophrenia the authors introduce what they call some 'raw discourse', but then (a few pages into the book) dispatch it on the grounds that it is too fluid and 'may be described or explained in many different ways depending on the bias of the observer'. The way through to Nature's Own Language, they suggest, is rather to collect the sort of data that can be made to 'fit the orientation of the scientist who, starting with the assumption that all phenomena of nature are orderly, is concerned primarily with finding principles that describe the nature of the order'.[46]

The deep muddle into which the whole effort to write out, and pin down, the distinctions between the speech of normals and the speech of schizophrenics in Nature's Own Language has got us is brought out in the following. 'Important questions', D. R. Rutter recently proclaimed, 'remain unanswered.' Thus we do not know how schizophrenic patients behave in free conversation, how they behave in encounters with each other, and whether they behave consistently across different types of encounter. Rutter set out to remedy these omissions, and in a remarkable experiment he compared the conversational behaviour of 12 schizophrenics with that of patients from three control groups: depressives; patients suffering from neurotic or personality disorders; and psychiatrically normal chest patients. The experiment consisted of a kind of conversational musical chairs:

> Each subject was asked to hold two five-minute conversations, one with a partner who was a patient from his own diagnostic category, and one with a psychiatrically normal partner, who was generally a nurse. Thus . . . each schizophrenic subject talked once with a schizophrenic partner and once with a normal; each depressive subject talked once with a depressive partner and once with a normal; and so on.

Rutter was nothing if not scrupulous in his codification of various features of conversational behaviour. For each of the two 'conditions' – 'patient partner condition' and 'normal partner condition' – he carefully measured: the percentage time spent speaking; the total number of words; the number of utterances; the mean word length of utterances; the speech rate (words/sec); the percentage time spent in simultaneous speech (SS); the number of occurrences of SS; the percentages occurrences of SS initiated by subject; the percentage time spent in mutual silence; the number of floor wins; the number of floor changes; the percentage of utterances ending as a question; the number of accompaniment and acknowledgment signals; the filled pause ratio (percentage of words); the speech disturbance ratio (percentage of words); and still more besides.

What did all this effort disclose? The study revealed, Rutter tells us, 'relatively few overall group differences and suggested that, for the most part, schizophrenic subjects behaved similarly to control subjects', and, furthermore, 'the abnormalities of behaviour suggested by previous research into schizophrenic patients did not emerge.' A likely interpretation of the conflicting evidence, Rutter suggests, is that 'some feature of the setting is the important variable. The most widely used setting has been a form of highly structured, doctor–patient, clinical interview, while the present investigation was based on informal conversations with a patient or nurse.' And then finally, in what is a truly remarkable statement:

> *It may well be that schizophrenic patients, like the general population, respond quite differently to different situations.*[47]

Structures of power and structures of culture

To follow in these lines of inquiry is to lend credence to the

tradition of philosophy that runs from Descartes through Locke
to Kant, and to suppose as Locke did that 'we can free ourselves
from the problems of the day and pursue "a plain, historical
method" in examining the emergence of complex experiences
out of simple ones.' Once we grasp, however, that the starting
point for inquiry 'is bound to be the dialectical situation in
which one finds oneself caught in one's own historical period —
the problem of the men of one's time', and that traditional notions
of 'objectivity' and 'scientific method' must be abandoned, there
are, as Rorty describes, two roads to go. One is to emphasize
'structures of power', to bring out 'the way in which the social
sciences have served as instruments of "the disciplinary society",
the connection between knowledge and power rather than that
between knowledge and human solidarity'. The second is to
emphasize 'structures of culture' and to demonstrate 'the moral
importance of the social sciences — their role in widening and
deepening our sense of community and the possibilities open to
this community'.[48]

To take this first road is to follow Michel Foucault and others
in disclosing the dark side of the human sciences: the preferred
style of analysis here is one that shows how people can be helped
to escape from what others have tried to do to them. Here, for
example, is the voice of psychiatric orthodoxy:

> Any adult must be able to define his terms to a reasonable
> degree upon demand. That is, he must be able to become
> more exact by limiting the reference of a term or a phrase he
> uses; and to accomplish this end he must be able to discard
> whatever is unimportant or only partially relevant.[49]

And here, taken from a discussion by Jacques Derrida, is the
voice of the patient:

> They demanded: Tell us 'exactly' how things happened. An
> account? I began: I am neither learned nor ignorant. I have
> known some joy. This is saying too little. I related the story
> in its entirety, to which they listened, it seems, with great
> interest — at least initially. But the end was a surprise for
> them all. 'After that beginning', they said, 'you should
> proceed to the facts.' How so? The account was over. . . .
> I should have realized that I was incapable of composing an
> account of these events. I had lost the sense of the story;
> this happens in a good many illnesses. But this explanation

only made them more demanding. . . . An account? No, no account, nevermore.[50]

Derrida uses this example as a taunt to those who, like the psychiatrist quoted above, strike up commitments to the drawing of firm lines between fact and fiction, science and non-science, 'responsible' and 'irresponsible' discourse, and so on. Yet in doing so he confirms the fears of those who worry that to abandon the citadels of old-style objectivity will be to give up everything.[51] Foucault, Derrida and others have looked at the ways in which people like schizophrenics have been measured against conceptions of community that service the forces of domination in a given society and found wanting: measured, as we discussed earlier, against the time of work rather than the time of life.

This is, as we have seen, a wholly necessary direction to pursue, yet to concern ourselves as these writers do exclusively with the problem of community in its repressive aspect, as an instrument in a cycle of domination or discipline, is to leave a cluster of important questions unaddressed. The problem of community runs deeper than this. In one aspect it focuses the question of how rationality might be reconceived in the terms, as Rorty puts it, of culture as a 'conversation' rather than as a 'structure erected upon foundations'.[52] In a second, and closely related, aspect it is the problem of human action and understanding, of how agents are able to act in a manner intelligible both to themselves and to others, and to understand and interpret the actions of others. Another way to say this is that, whereas writers who emphasize 'structures of power' help us to identify and understand a history of abuse, they fail to locate their criticisms against an adequate countervailing conception of the undertakings of human lives. Ironically, at the end of the day they succeed only in pointing up an opposing strand in the Enlightenment inheritance — that of the individual released from the shackles of tradition, free to make his own way as he pleases and accountable to no-one.

To take the other road that Rorty instances, the road that leads to 'structures of culture', is to follow MacIntyre in seeing that scientific understanding (and in particular the scientific understanding of human beings) is more closely connected with ordinary human understanding than has generally been supposed, and that both these activities are conducted within an inextricable interdependence of individual and history. We can put the matter like this: philosophers like MacIntyre show us life under one kind of description, life not as a matter of observing someone, separating figure from ground, from a fixed vantage point of contemplation, but life in the sense of 'getting to know someone' across a range of circumstances and settings, or of the 'coming-to-grasp' of a situation from within as it is lived, where it is states of affairs that are at issue rather than a tidy separation of individual from environment and where, as we have seen, we are likely to find ourselves very often surprised.

The separation of figure from ground (and the explanatory style that goes with it) is a wholly necessary one for pragmatic purposes, but so far as we privilege this stance as permitting an 'unhistorical, self-endorsed, self-consciousness', and accord a special status to the knowledge that we derive from it, then we will be led to jeopardize not only our capacity for self-understanding but also our capacity for understanding others. Much as we need (and could not envisage doing without) words like 'truth', 'rationality' and 'progress', we cannot ground these in the way in which the major traditions in philosophy have suggested that we could. Far from seeing our 'story-telling' urges as dispensable for scientific purposes, therefore, we need rather to view them as expressions of the medium in which we necessarily (however much any particular story may be improved upon) live and must get along in as best we can. To view people in their 'story-telling' and 'story-comprehending' aspects in relation to the stories of which they find themselves a part is, in this respect, an essential condition for understanding them.

Reconceiving the enterprise of a schizophrenic life

We can perhaps now begin to see that there may be something to be gained from approaching the enterprise of schizophrenic lives more directly within the sorts of conceptions that MacIntyre proposes. On MacIntyre's line of argument we have tended to approach the problem of schizophrenia in a Cartesian way on the model of an encapsulated form of selfhood. Once, however, we grasp the historical embedding of human lives in the terms discussed, then we can recognize the need for a different set of conceptions. And it is, of course, against this background that the discovery of all those surprises in the unfolding of schizophrenic lives assumes such a salience.

As we have seen, the sorts of concepts that we need in the discussion of the enterprise of schizophrenic lives are dramaturgical ones. As Oliver Sacks describes:

The concepts of mechanics, and the concepts of theatre, are radically different, yet need to be joined: they are joined legitimately in the notions of *actors* and *acting*, and illegitimately in the notions of *puppets* and *passive reactions*. The first of these is a living, biological notion: the second a mystical, Golemical notion — a degraded and degrading travesty of life.[53]

Dramaturgical metaphors are biologically apt in a way that mechanical metaphors are not: in their journeyings his patients show themselves to be 'living disproofs of mechanical thinking as they are living exemplars of biological thinking' and 'remind us that we are overdeveloped in mechanical competence, but lacking in biological intelligence'. Diseases, and our reactions to them, 'cannot be considered *in vitro*, in themselves; they can only be understood with reference to *us*, as expressions of our nature, our living, our being-here (*da-sein*) in the world.' Thus:

Diseases have a character of their own, but they also partake of our character; we have a character of our own, but we also partake of the world's character: character is monadic or microcosmic, worlds within worlds within worlds, worlds which express worlds. The disease — the man — the world go together.[54]

We need to find a vocabulary that can begin to indicate what is happening with a patient: 'we are concerned not simply with a handful of "symptoms", but with a *person*, and his changing relation to the world', and thus with disease in its aspect as *strategy* as well as in its structural aspect.[55]

A particular merit of pursuing inquiry along these lines is that in taking the schizophrenic person seriously (within the terms of the sorts of conceptions that MacIntyre proposes) as an active participant in social life, we may be in a position to identify more adequately wherein (at points) he also fails as a social agent. To speak, as we have done, of 'structures of culture' is in one aspect to highlight the 'conventional' character of human practices, but in another it is to ask that we explore the dimensions of the conventional against the reach of our conceptions of human agency, conceptions that could logically be different but that are deeply, and perhaps inextricably, rooted in our capacity to sustain community. The paradox I shall enter is that it is only by rendering the schizophrenic fully social — that is, by extending our sense of community so as to grasp him as a historical agent — that we are able to understand both how he fails and why we are right to judge this failing to be a form of suffering, an illness.

Perhaps the most damaging criticism to be made of traditional approaches to the problem of schizophrenia is not so much that scientists have run to all sorts of peculiar explanations of schizophrenic conditions, but that they have not succeeded in characterizing adequately in the first place just what — in John Dunn's phrase — is humanly the case in schizophrenic predicaments. Psychiatry, as Goffman and others have argued, has always found it difficult to say what is wrong with the schizophrenic, to identify the fatal 'delict': it has only been able to characterize him in terms of 'difference'.[56] Such a poor account have psychiatrists tended to give of what it is that they are trying to explain that it has even been mooted in some circles that, quite aside from the known irregularities of psychiatric diagnosis, there is nothing much wrong with schizophrenic people. In seeking to dispel notions of this sort (if that is still necessary) we shall not be able to pin down distinctions between schizophrenic and non-schizophrenic forms of life in a way that would begin to satisfy orthodox tastes, but because we cannot pin down it does not follow that we cannot distinguish and provide a form of justification for such distinctions as we make.

These questions I shall take up in more depth in the next part of the book. However, in preparing the ground it may be useful to look, finally, at some of the clarifications and insights that Manfred Bleuler has brought to our thinking about the enterprise of schizophrenic lives, because more than any other worker in this field he has endeavoured to find the words in which to grapple with the sorts of problems of human understanding that MacIntyre describes. What Bleuler gives us in his major work are three parallel and interconnected narrative histories: a history, as we have seen, of the scientific project of schizophrenia, a history of the lives of a large group of schizophrenic people, and the history of his own relationship to and within each of these. We may now illustrate some aspects that bear upon our previous discussion.

Thus on the whole difficulty of providing an authoritative characterization of what is at issue in a given situation, Bleuler says:

Naturally a person in my position finds it easy to emulate

what many other investigators have done, namely, at the end, to render a decision after a lengthy interview with a patient or a member of his family, to the effect that his mother was 'domineering' or that his father remained apart from the life of the family. But in the end I am not convinced that I have captured the entire truth of the situation in stating a summary judgment of that sort. And if I carefully allow the patient to continue to speak freely in a relaxed atmosphere, I find time and again that he himself begins, quietly or vehemently, to shake the carefully erected structure of every summary judgment, even though I had earlier skilfully obtained his complete agreement.[57]

And on the notion of the abstraction of individual from environment, Bleuler offers:

In keeping with scientific tradition, we should like to evaluate the milieu itself independently of the child. In line with older methods of thinking we should like to know just how a particular set of conditions — and especially how the parents — influenced a certain child. We should like to assume that a child exists, that this child is placed in a particular environment, and that the child and the environment could exist independently of one another. But this very assumption is incorrect. The child has a part in creating the environment. The child is never merely placed into an environment that is totally independent of that child.[58]

In Bleuler's study we have, as Edward Hare has put it, 'a historical record, perhaps unique in its thoroughness and probably now unrepeatable, of what schizophrenia was like in a particular place and time'.[59] As Bleuler describes in his preface, his intention was 'to depict the life vicissitudes of 208 schizophrenics and their families' as he has 'personally experienced these, together with them, over a period of more than 20 years'. Previous studies had exhibited a number of shortcomings, not least that they had described (and that inadequately) the long-term courses only of hospitalized patients. In consequence 'nothing was really known about the fates of the great numbers of patients with whom, after their release, the doctor lost contact', and it was the life histories of these people in particular that Bleuler wanted to draw into his account.[60]

He was able to show that, contrary to old notions of a 'progressive worsening' of the disease, after an average duration of five years the condition does not deteriorate any further but may improve. Of the 208 subjects in the study about 25 per cent achieved full recoveries and about 10 per cent remained permanently hospitalized as severe chronic psychotics. Between these two extremes there was a large group of people who never achieved a stable outcome but of whom many experienced intermittent recoveries. Bleuler was able to identify a number of types of course which, roughly speaking, could be divided into two categories, the 'benign' and the 'malignant'. Between two-thirds and three-quarters of the subjects could be classified as having undergone a 'benign' course and between one-quarter and one-third a 'malignant' or a virulent one.

The interest of Bleuler's study lies not merely in the facts about oucome, important though they undoubtedly are (though as he remarks himself they will hold 'little meaning for anyone who is not familiar with the history of the theory of schizophrenia'), but more particularly in what he is able to show about the nature of the interaction between the schizophrenic person and the world in which he lives. On Bleuler's view of it schizophrenia does not cease to be in quite a large proportion of instances a chronic condition. However, contrary to notions of 'a continuous regressive process towards a state of idiocy' or, more moderately, of a uniform process leading to inevitable deterioration, he proposes a concept of chronic schizophrenia which recognizes that even patients who have suffered decades of illness 'remain mentally alive' and are 'still involved in a continuous altercation with their own being and their environment':[61]

The closer we live together with patients, even the most chronic ones, the more astonished we are at fluctuations in their condition. The great majority of the alterations in the course of many years after the onset of the psychosis are clearly in the direction of improvement. The improvements are manifold in nature. Some of the patients who have hardly ever uttered coherent sentences start to speak or behave as if they were healthy on certain occasions, for instance, when on leave, at hospital festivities, or on the occasion of a catastrophe such as exploding bombs in wartime. I have seen improvements after 40 years' duration of a severe chronic psychosis. And, what is even more amazing, a schizophrenic may recover after having been psychotic and hospitalized for decades. Such a late, complete recovery is rare, but it occurs.[62]

The following is an example of the sort of improvement Bleuler has in mind. Edouard S. was born in 1912 and hospitalized as a schizophrenic at the age of 30. From 1943 to 1963 he lived at home, but in all this period:

> was able to perform only the simplest tasks, and continued to show peculiar behaviour stereotypes. For instance, every day he scrubbed three steps of the staircase. He voiced numerous delusional associations. If, for instance, an object was broken, he declared stereotypically that it could only be repaired if this or that person would live in a specified location or would die.

However:

> Beginning in 1963, that is, 21 years after onset of illness, a period of improvement set in. It seemed related to the death of his mother, although he had enjoyed a good relationship to her. The proband began to take an interest in many things; he began to read the newspaper again, which he had not done for many years, and especially, he speaks again with his relatives and has become their accepted and beloved family member again. His family no longer regards him as mentally ill, but simply as somewhat odd. After many years he again attends church with his family. To be sure, his case cannot be considered a complete recovery. He still voices delusional associations, as described, and leads a retired life limited to the confines of his family. This marked state of improvement has held for the past 2 years, to the conclusion of the observation period.[63]

Examples such as these are a crucial part of Bleuler's argument but is is important that they be put in a wider perspective. In certain obvious respects Bleuler gives us a much more optimistic account of the outcome of a schizophrenic illness than the traditional view had allowed for, but what perhaps taken overall he does is to *complicate* our understanding of the life histories of schizophrenics and of the enterprise of schizophrenic lives. The lives of schizophrenics show themselves to be unassimilable to the sort of predictive apparatus which psychiatrists of the late nineteenth century had constructed; they are instead replete with surprises, some of which may be for the better but others again for the worse.

The sense of complication in our thinking about the enterprise of a schizophrenic life is perhaps brought out most forcibly in Bleuler's discussion of the concept of 'recovery'. How are we to understand the recovery from an illness like schizophrenia? What is to be the desired stance for an individual to take on his schizophrenic past? How is the fact of having suffered a schizophrenic illness to be assimilated into an individual's biography, into the way in which he accounts for himself to others and organizes the narrative of his life? As Bleuler describes, 'a schizophrenic may be non-aberrant in his own environment but then becomes confused during re-examination when he is questioned about his former illness. Has he recovered or has not not recovered?' We thus have to contend with the question

> as to what is to constitute the healthy processing of a psychosis. Is the patient's complete insight into his illness always an indication of complete recovery? Or is it, on the contrary, an indication of an internal pathological distancing by the patient from his own fate, in understanding something as unprecedented as an experienced psychosis, as if it were something to be shrugged off and forgotten? . . . Is it necessarily pathological, when a schizophrenic who, judging by outward appearances, has recovered, makes confusing statements when he is asked to discuss his psychosis of recent experience?

Perhaps, Bleuler goes on to say,

> It is an indication of recovery when the psychotic events of the past can be discussed only irrationally and autistically, while it does not necessarily indicate well-being when such shocking events are cast in clear, flowing language that could never correspond to subjective reality.[64]

But to ask these questions is implicitly also to ask the question 'What is the individual reacting to?' An illness that has 'befallen' him? But then, asks Bleuler,

> Do we really know whether schizophrenia 'befalls' an individual? Perhaps it is more of a phase or the result of a personal inner development. . . . A radius fracture with all its implications can largely be investigated independently of the rest of the patient's life. We may ask what the 'general' course of a radius fracture is, without becoming involved in extraneous problems. In case of schizophrenia this may be different. This particular schizophrenia may correspond to the patient's

struggle for harmony with his own ego, his inner existence, in the process of dealing with his environment. In such cases, schizophrenia does not endanger the personal fate of the patient from the outside, but it comes into being from the personal lifestyle of that individual.

From this point of view:

> The concept 'recovery from schizophrenia' is something quite different from that of recovery from other illnesses or injuries. When a schizophrenic recovers, it does not always mean that he is rid of a malady that attacked him from without, in the way that the injured patient is relieved of the incorrect position or mobility of one of his bones. The recovery from a schizophrenia denotes instead that his inner development had led him back into society as a unified person.

In the case of the schizophrenic who fails to recover:

> Possibly his schizophrenic life is an inner necessity for him. The deeper we learn to feel our way into the schizophrenic, the less certain becomes our judgement as to what his recovery might mean, and whether a social readaptation would truly be the patient's own well-being — his own greatest personal achievement.[65]

The sorts of considerations that Bleuler introduces have also been developed by others, for example in Britain by J. K. Wing in the exploration of how the personal reactions of schizophrenic people to their conditions (in conjunction with the reactions they receive from others) affect the course and outcome of a schizophrenic illness.[66] Some of Bleuler's terms are, however, perhaps not wholly satisfactory — thus the stress on 'inner development' seems to conjure a somewhat mystical process that cannot be observed but only intuited and emphathized with. To improve on these, to widen and deepen our conception of the 'observable' to include the recognition of what someone else is doing that comes from our mastery of our language, and more generally to take this discussion about the enterprise of schizophrenic lives further, we must look more closely at the enterprise of human lives in general and at the conceptions we need for thinking about selfhood.[67] It would in any case be peculiar if in a book that treats of schizophrenic people as social beings they were not to be allowed to speak for themselves, and for a more detailed encounter with the action of schizophrenic lives we must now prepare.

Part II

The Action of Schizophrenic Lives

3

Selfhood, identity and narrative

From this the poem springs: that we live in a place
That is not our own and, much more, not ourselves
And hard it is in spite of blazoned days.
　　　　　Wallace Stevens, Notes Toward a Supreme Fiction

Selfhood and narrative

A good many of the difficulties that the project of schizophrenia
has encountered, we have suggested, have arisen out of captivating
but mistaken assumptions both about the nature of human action
and about how the enterprise of understanding human action is
to be conceived. A key to the difficulty was to be found in the
concept of narrative, both for what it clarified about the project
of social scientific understanding and for what it indicated about
the form and character of human selfhood. I shall now explore in
more depth what a narrative conception of selfhood amounts to.

It emerged from our earlier discussion that we cannot set about
the characterization of an agent's actions independently of the
characterization of the beliefs and intentions that underpin those
actions. And similarly we cannot adequately characterize beliefs
and intentions independently of the settings — social milieus,
institutions etc., and what MacIntyre terms practices — that give
such beliefs and intentions shape and significance. Another way
to say this is that in attempting to characterize an action we have
to contend with the histories both of the agent and of the setting.
'In successfully identifying what someone else is doing we always
move towards placing a particular episode in the context of a set
of narrative histories, histories both of the individuals concerned
and of the settings in which they act and suffer.'[1] So, for example,
the history of a particular individual within a particular marriage
is set within the history of development of the institution of
marriage. An action, or set of actions, is thus an episode in an
individual history that must be viewed in the context of the history

of a setting, 'a history within which the histories of individual agents not only are, but have to be, situated, just because without the setting and its changes through time the history of the individual agent and his changes through time would be unintelligible.'[2]

The characterization of action thus requires of us that we grapple with the interconnections between the intentional, the social and the historical:

> We identify a particular action only by invoking two kinds of context, implicitly if not explicitly. We place the agent's intentions . . . in causal and temporal order with reference to their role in his or her history; and we also place them with reference to their role in the history of the setting or settings to which they belong. In doing this, in determining what causal efficacy the agent's intentions had in one or more directions, and how his short-term intentions succeeded or failed to be constitutive of long-term intentions, we ourselves write a further part of these histories.[3]

Narrative thus provides the appropriate form for understanding the actions of others or, as the case may be, for not understanding such actions. For when we declare a particular action or set of actions to be unintelligible we mean that we either lack the narrative context in which to place it or, more drastically, that we cannot conceive a narrative context that *could* account for such an action (i.e. render it intelligible as an action which we could in principle ask the agent to account for himself). But both in coming to understand, and in failing to understand, it is through an apprehension of the narrative form of human action that we approach the matter.

Narrative holds the importance it does because human action has a basically historical character and the narrative conception of selfhood gives us the necessary terms with which to discuss the historical continuity of a human life. In Western societies each human life is characteristically partitioned into segments and so, for example, 'both childhood and old age have been wrenched away from the rest of human life and made over into distinct realms. And all these separations have been achieved so that it is the distinctiveness of each and not the unity of life of the individual who passes through those parts in terms of which we are taught to think and feel.' We therefore need a concept of the self that can help us restore the continuity of a human life, 'a concept of a self whose unity resides in the unity of a narrative which links birth to life to death as narrative beginning to middle to end'.[4]

But to say that the individual agent lives out narratives in his life, and that he is not only actor but also author, is not, of course, to imply that he lives whatever story he pleases. Each individual finds himself drafted into a story — the dramatic history of a setting and its intersection with other settings — that precedes him and is not of his making, and the narrative of his life is thus composed within the constraints and resources of this wider action. Thus:

> What the agent is able to do and say intelligibly as an actor is deeply affected by the fact that we are never more (and sometimes less) than the co-authors of our own narratives. Only in fantasy do we live what story we please. . . . We enter upon a stage which we did not design and we find ourselves part of an action that was not of our making. Each of us being a main character in his own drama plays subordinate parts in the dramas of others, and each drama constrains the others. In my drama, perhaps, I am Hamlet or Iago or at least the swineherd who may yet become a prince, but to you I am only A Gentleman or at best Second Murderer, while you are my Polonius or my Gravedigger, but your own hero. Each of our dramas exerts constraints on each other's, making the whole different from the parts, but still dramatic.[5]

For the same reason that the agent can never be more than co-author of the narratives he lives out, so also the narrative enterprise of a life can never be fully predictable. The agent lives out his life in relation to a conception of a future, a conception which to be intelligibly held must partake of culturally shared images of the future, but in virtue of the dramatic character of social life, of the intermeshing of individual life projects and of the reflexive possibilities of which agents can avail themselves, the agent can never be certain how the plot is going to develop. Furthermore, to live out a narrative in interconnection with the narratives that others live out is to be the subject of an individual history that not only can, but must, be narratable as an essential prerequisite for making one's actions, and the continuity of one's life, intelligible to others. And just as the individual agent is always potentially accountable to other agents in this respect, so also they are accountable to him:

> I am not only accountable, I am one who can always ask others for an account, who can put others to the question. I am part of their story, as they are part of mine. The narrative

of any one life is part of an interlocking set of narratives. Moreover this asking for and giving of accounts itself plays an important part in constituting narratives. Asking you what you did and why, saying what I did and why, pondering the difference between your account of what I did and my account of what I did, and vice versa, these are essential constituents of all but the very simplest and barest of narratives.[6]

We can now begin to see how interwoven is what we term the course of a life (from the Latin *currere*, to run), the onward progress of a life through successive stages, with another uniquely human form of running, the running to and fro (from the Latin *discurrere*) of dis-course. Similarly the world (from the Anglo-Saxon *weorold*, meaning the course of a man's life) in which the course of a life is run is both the world that is external to us, and into which we can try to intervene but which preserves an obdurate independence from whatever interpretations that we may choose to give of it, and a world that has been historically made up, into which any one of us finds himself or herself thrown as on to a corner of a stage that we did not design but which is none the less a cultural product and a culturally sustained and modified enterprise. As Hannah Pitkin describes, 'the world is necessarily both objective and subjective, both independent of language and structured by language.'[7] And thus there is an important sense in which we need to envisage the process of finding one's way in the world, or learning how to negotiate and maintain a course through life, on the analogy of learning to find one's way into (and thus to discover, or fail to discover, a part in) a conversation that has already been long in progress before one entered the room. The 'key question for men', MacIntyre argues, 'is not about their own authorship; I can only answer the question "What am I to do?" if I can answer the prior question "Of what story or stories do I find myself a part?"'[8]

Human socialization is in a crucial aspect the process of learning to make sense of the world through hearing and coming to understand the stories that others tell — stories of 'good' and 'evil', of what it is to be a child, mother, father etc. — and which the dramatic resources of a particular culture make available. The sense that the agent makes of the stories that he has heard, and the stories that he comes to tell in his own way, will not necessarily accord with the understandings that those around him would wish him to have or possess themselves, or with the part they would like him to play. He may, for example, come to decide that the stories in which the history of a setting is articulated are untrue: but as we discussed earlier he can only come to grips with a recognition of *this* sort through reconstituting the original story into a different story.

The narrative enterprise of childhood

But what are the narratives from which we all set out on our course through life? How are we to understand what MacIntyre terms 'the narrative enterprise of childhood'? The psychoanalyst Bruno Bettelheim provides us with some useful insight into these questions when he tells us that 'myths and fairy stories both answer the eternal questions: What is the world really like? How am I to live my life in it? How can I truly be myself?' At a certain age the child comes to ask himself questions like: 'Who am I? Where did I come from? How did the world come into being? Who created man and all the animals? What is the purpose of life? What must I become?' He wonders 'who or what projects him into adversity, and what can prevent this happening to him. Are there benevolent powers in addition to his parents? *Are* his parents benevolent powers? How should he form himself, and why? Is there hope for him, though he may have done wrong? Why has all this happened to him? What will it mean for his future? Fairy stories provide answers to these pressing questions, many of which the child becomes aware of only as he follows the stories.'[9]

Bettelheim wants to make a point about the importance of fairy-tales in the development of the child: it is, he argues, through listening to fairy-tales (alongside, of course, other cultural experiences) that the child comes to acquire ideas about how to interpret social reality and to give some sense and definition to his experience of himself as a developing actor and author within a story that both precedes him and calls him into being; to bring some order to what we may think of as an active entanglement that for lack of such clarification must remain chaotic. So, for example, 'when the hero of a fairy-tale is the youngest child, or is specifically called "the dummy" or "simpleton" at the start of the story, this is the fairy-tale's rendering of the original debilitated state of the ego as it begins its struggle to cope with the inner world of drives, and with the difficult problems which the outer world presents.'[10]

But Bettelheim's argument has, of course, a much wider bearing in that fairy-tales are able to possess the importance they do just because of the hold of the symbolic on the formation of human subjectivity. The idea of the child identifying and defining himself through listening to, and taking part in, narrative enactments draws attention to the need for a theory of human socialization — an interpretation of how the human subject comes about — that neither views the individual as a *tabula rasa* moulded by a process called 'society', nor takes the 'reflexivity of the cogito' for granted as an 'inherent property of human beings'. As Anthony Giddens has put it, we need a formulation that can help us look upon consciousness not as 'a unitary or indivisible substance, but as a fractured or fragile set of processes'.[11]

The British psychoanalyst D. W. Winnicott has given us a vivid and relatively straightforward account of what is meant by consciousness as a 'fractured and fragile set of processes', of what at a very basic level is involved for the child in beginning to establish himself as a narrative participant. 'At first', Winnicott writes, 'the individual is not the unit. As perceived from the outside the unit is an environment–individual set-up. The outsider knows that the individual psyche can only start in a certain setting. In this setting the individual can gradually come to create a personal environment.'[12] The 'process of development through which the individual passes from dependence to independence is an extremely tricky developmental era', but if 'all goes well the environment created by the individual becomes something that is like enough to the environment that can be generally perceived', or, as we might say, the individual discovers that the narrative that he begins to create for himself can interact fruitfully with the larger narrative in which his development unfolds. Thus 'the personality does not start off as a completed whole thing if we think of the infant's point of view. By various means the unity of the individual psyche becomes a fact, at first at moments and later over long and variable periods of time.'[13]

The individual moves, that is to say, from a state of being merged in with the object into a phase where he comes to form a conception of external reality, of a repudiated world of the *not-me*, a world which 'the individual has decided to recognize (with whatever difficulty and even pain) as truly external' and as outside magical control.[14] We can think of the transition from a world of *me-extensions* as a transition into a shared condition of being-in-the-world in which it is relevant to speak of the world both as given, as truly external, and as co-operatively made up in various ways. If this condition has proven to be philosophically perplexing, then it is no surprise that it should also involve personal pain and that Winnicott should describe the individual as 'engaged in the perpetual human task of keeping inner and outer reality separate yet interrelated'.[15]

A key conception in Winnicott's formulation is the *potential space* which is located between me-extensions and the not-me, 'at the interplay between there being nothing but me and there being objects and phenomena outside omnipotent control'.[16] This is the 'intermediate area of living' in which most of the time we live when we are experiencing life, a 'place for living that is not properly described by either of the terms "inner" and "outer"'.[17] In terms of the early development of the child we can think of the potential space as 'the hypothetical area that exists (but cannot exist) between the baby and the object (mother or part of mother) during the phase of the repudiation of the object as not-me, that is, at the end of being merged in with the object'.[18] The potential space can only be made use of so far as the child has sufficient confidence in the mother, and in the environmental conditions, and can thus risk making the separation between the me and the not-me. But if the potential space is the space of separateness it is also the space of union and, most significantly, of these in their interrelation.

The means by which this interrelation is effected (and thus in which separation, as distinct from separateness, is avoided) is most powerfully brought out in Winnicott's discussion of that particular use of objects, together with certain kinds of activities, which he designates transitional phenomena. Transitional phenomena include, for example, objects such as the rag, teddies, dolls etc. to which all young children form attachments, together with 'an infant's babbling and the way in which an older child goes over a repertory of songs and tunes while preparing for sleep'.[19] When 'we witness an infant's employment of a transitional object, the first not-me possession', Winnicott suggests, 'we are witnessing the child's first use of a symbol and the first experience of play.' An essential feature of such phenomena is that 'we agree never to make the challenge to the baby: did you create this object or did you find it conveniently lying around', did you make it up or did you discover it in the external world?[20] We can think of the object as a symbol of the union of the baby and the mother (or part of the mother). This symbol can be located. It is at the place in space and time where and when the mother is in transition from being (in the baby's mind) merged in with the infant and alternatively being experienced as an object to be perceived rather than conceived of. The use of an object symbolizes the union of two now separate things, baby and mother, *at the point in time and space of the initiation of their state of separateness.*[21]

So far as the baby does not suffer a break in the personal continuity of existence that cannot be repaired, the baby 'becomes able to allow and even to benefit from separation'. The potential space is therefore the space of a 'separation that is not a separation but a form of union'.[22]

The growing child thus becomes able to reach out into, and move about in, an area of shared reality beyond me-extensions and to make use of the resources that he finds there — so, for example, the repertory of songs referred to above — to fashion that reality in ways that are decidedly his own, but that none the less mesh with the way in which it is fashioned by others. He comes to learn — and this is Winnicott's main point — about the interrelation between separateness and union ('the balance of separateness and communication' in a phrase of George Eliot's),[23] about the embedding of his own uniqueness in conditions of community, and to find in the co-operative putting together and sustaining of a world the means to ensure personal continuity of being. And Winnicott echoes MacIntyre's discussion of these themes when he remarks that at more developed cultural levels originality is only possible in the context of a tradition, and that 'the interplay between originality and the acceptance of tradition as the basis for inventiveness' seems to him 'to be just one more example, and a very exciting one, of the interplay between separateness and union.'[24]

But the achievement that we have described for the developing child is precarious, and Winnicott instances Humpty Dumpty:

He has just achieved integration into one whole thing and has emerged from the environment–individual set-up so that he is perched on a wall, no longer devotedly held. He is notoriously in a precarious position in his emotional development, especially liable to irreversible disintegration.[25]

Thus the environment may prove to be not a source of encouragement in the process of individuation but a source of impingement, and the newly formed individual may then take up a pattern of reacting to such impingements that disturbs the continuity of his 'going-on-being'. Under these circumstances movements into the area beyond me-extensions provide not the conditions of continuity – an integrated experience of selfhood through space and time – but a perpetual source of threat and disruption. Relationships produce loss of the sense of the self which can only be regained by return to isolation, and the potential space instead of becoming a source of meaningful symbols is felt to be 'cluttered up with persecutory elements' of which the individual 'has no means of ridding himself'.[26] Here the individual never properly achieves 'unit status' and his energies are taken up in mobilizing defensive strategies – modes of omnipotence and magical control, for example – in order to maintain some measure of intactness in his experience of himself and his relationships with others. There may result a repudiation of the conditions of intersubjectivity and, still more alarmingly, sometimes also of the distinction between that which is me and all of that which is not-me.

We shall examine some of these vicissitudes in more detail in subsequent chapters, but it is perhaps as well to be clear at this point that there is no suggestion in my argument that we can extract anything from Winnicott's account of the achievement or loss of selfhood in infancy and early childhood about the *causes* of schizophrenia. What accounts like these can do, however, is to help us situate schizophrenic predicaments within a deeper understanding of the sort of undertaking that human selfhood is, and thus recognize the way in which, to use Winnicott's own words, 'emotional development in its primitive or earliest stages concerns exactly the same phenomena that appear in the study of adult schizophrenia.'[27] Ideas about the 'potential space', and about the 'interplay between separateness and union', take our earlier discussions of the interconnections between the agent and the setting, the agent and the story or stories of which he finds himself a part, to a more intimate level of personal organization. In addition, the ideas forge a link between the capacity for play – it is in the potential space that the child plays – and the dramatic productions of adult lives; between, if you like, the gradations in the narrative enterprise of human life. Above all, Winnicott attempts to get beyond Freud's thoroughly reductive treatment of cultural experience and to 'tackle the question of what life itself is about', 'to describe what life is like apart from illness or absence of illness' — i.e. to get beyond formulations of health or aliveness in terms of the state of the ego defences or some such notion — and to convey something about the *risks* of the life process, of human living in an area beyond me-extensions.[28]

We can take this discussion a little further by turning briefly to Jacques Lacan's account of how the child moves into an area beyond 'me-extensions'. For all its difficulty and obscurity the great merit of Lacan's contribution is that it helps us to see how deeply interwoven is the genesis (and thus the complications of the genesis) of human subjectivity in the action of language. Thus for Lacan the question 'What does becoming a human subject involve?' is intimately bound up with the question 'What does it mean to enter language?' And to enter language is to pass from what he calls the 'imaginary' into the 'symbolic'. The imaginary is akin to that undifferentiated state that Winnicott described in which there is as yet no clear distinction or boundary between subject and object, child and external world, child's body and mother's body. The discovery of the symbolic and the movement into it from an undifferentiated state produces not 'an individual' as a reality distinct from and to be offset against the reality of 'the environment' but a process of individuation within a matrix that is also peopled by the emotional states, intentions, desires etc. of others. Where once there was *direct* access to reality in the form of the mother's body, there are now only substitute objects in the form of the movement of signification. Language presupposes *difference* in the sense that a sign only has meaning by virtue of its difference from other signs, and also *absence* in the sense that the sign comes to 'stand in' for an absent object.

The paradox that Lacan wants to convey to us is that where in moving into the symbolic the child discovers new possibilities for making himself, he discovers also a pre-existing order, a drama in which he has to try to find his way, to locate the doors that can be opened and those that are firmly locked, and in which he bumps against the affirmations that others have already made, whether consciously or in phantasy, of what he is or should be. He has, that is, to find his way into a dramatic narrative where his arrival has already been prepared for, and a 'place' for him to some extent designated, and where answers to questions like 'Who am I?' or 'What should I do?' do indeed turn on an answer to the question 'Of which story do I find myself a part?' It is in this sense that we need to think of the constitution of the 'I' as brought about through the 'discourse of the Other'.

Terry Eagleton gives us as clear a summary of these aspects of Lacan's thought as we could hope for:

> When we enter the symbolic order, we enter into language itself; yet this language, for Lacan as for the structuralists, is never something entirely within our individual control. On the contrary . . . language is what internally *divides* us, rather than an instrument we are confidently able to manipulate. Language always pre-exists us: it is always already 'in place' waiting to assign us *our* places within it. It is ready and waiting for us rather as our parents are: and we shall never wholly dominate it or subdue it to our own ends, just as we shall never be able entirely to shake off the dominant role which our parents play in our constitution.[29]

Perhaps the most illuminating illustration of the theme of absence and loss on which Lacan puts such emphasis is Freud's account of a little boy's game with the reel and string in *Beyond the Pleasure Principle*. As Freud describes, the boy throws the reel out of the pram to the sounds 'o' 'o' 'o', representing the word *fort* (gone) and pulls it back up again with the exclamation *'da!'* (here). In the *fort-da* game the child uses objects within his reach to stage, and thus to bring under symbolic control, the disappearance and return of his mother. Eagleton puts forward the interesting suggestion that we can also read the game as 'the first glimmerings of narrative. *Fort-da* is perhaps the shortest story we can imagine: an object is lost and then recovered.' Its brevity notwithstanding, it carries a deeper significance, for 'even the most complex narrative can be read as variants on this model: the pattern of classical narrative is that an original settlement is disrupted and ultimately restored. . . . Something must be lost or absent in any narrative for it to unfold: if everything stayed in place there would be no story to tell.'[30]

Personal identity

This discussion has perhaps given us some idea of what it means to speak of the 'narrative enterprise of childhood'. The sorts of complications that Winnicott and Lacan describe are in certain respects peculiar to the genesis of subjectivity, but as the connection between narrative and loss brings out we should not therefore suppose that there arises a point at which the complexities of selfhood disappear, at which, as it were, the making of 'the individual' can be said to be 'completed' or 'finished'.

Once we have identified the role of narrative in the constitution and understanding of individual and social life we can be brought to see why the concept of personal identity is inexplicable in the sort of account that the empiricist tradition provides which restricts itself to the description of psychological states and events. As MacIntyre argues, philosophers such as Locke and Hume 'have failed to see that a background has been omitted, the lack of which makes the problems' of personal identity with which they wrestled insoluble:

> That background is provided by the concept of a story and of that kind of unity of character which a story requires. Just as a history is not a sequence of actions, but the concept of an action is that of a moment in an actual or possible history abstracted for some purpose from that history, so the characters in a history are not a collection of persons, but the concept of a person is that of a character abstracted from a history.[31]

Problems of personal identity are thus properly understood as problems in the narrative ordering of human lives, as difficulties that arise for the agent in his efforts to make his life intelligible either to himself or to others. In seeking to make his life intelligible the agent finds himself subject to liabilities that are intrinsic to social life, to all that being a social agent involves and gives rise to. Efforts at comprehension, and at the reworking and renegotiation of narrative histories, are unlikely to achieve full coherence and completion and to rid themselves of areas of incomprehension, tension and conflict. To bring out some of the characteristic difficulties in adult life MacIntyre instances the conflicts in the post-war history of the French Communist Party (PCF) between revolutionary demands and reformist practices as these find expression in the life of a trade union official who is also a PCF militant. We may view the trade union official/PCF militant as engaged

> in trying to locate his actions within a number of quite distinct narrative histories. At one level there was that of his own biography as a Communist militant. . . . At the same

level there is his biography as a trade union official with a career, a record of successes, failures and promotions, a pension, and a retirement. There are also the larger narratives in which the more individual are embedded: the history of French communism, and the post-war history of the French economy. Interwoven with these are the personalia of child-hood, adolescence, marriage, fatherhood or motherhood, and ageing, in addition to encounters with religion. The narrative of romantic love and of conversion or loss of faith may be the most crucial of all.[32]

Some of these narratives may not always knit together and some (or parts thereof) may not do so at all:

> Each act of each militant is made coherent and determinate at the level of one or more of the narratives and perhaps left incoherent at other levels, as a result of a number of different types of interaction. Consequently, his theoretical grasp of his own life, and its social structuring, may receive confirmation at one level and disconfirmation at another at one and the same time. To maintain adequate coherence here, very adroit manoeuvring will often be necessary.[33]

There are, of course, numerous other complexities that arise out of the consideration of the concept of the narrative self and I have, in any case, provided only the barest indication of Alasdair MacIntyre's own discussion of these matters. But we can now perhaps be brought to see what is meant by the paradox of human agency, the idea that 'society must be understood as a process constructed historically by individuals who are constructed historically by society.'[34] Once we recognize the interplay between individual and setting, agent and story, separateness and union, we can no longer rest content with simple-minded conceptions of 'the individual'. The notion of the individual, Philip Abrams declares, is 'an abstraction from the process of individuation', and individuality must therefore be studied as a process of 'becoming' that, for better or worse, involves the 'meshing of life history and social history in a singular fate'.[35]

4

Chronic schizophrenics: Joseph and fellows

It's so difficult to find things to talk about in here. I mean all we can talk about is the hospital. The only life we're practising is in this hospital, aren't we? I mean, some of us don't even go out of the ward to be interested in anything.
Arthur, chronic schizophrenic

To the singular fates of a group of troubled agents, all of them chronic, working-class schizophrenics and − with the exception of one day patient − inmates of several years service in a psychiatric hospital, I shall now turn. With the help of the sorts of conceptions I have outlined I shall illustrate different facets of these agents' altercations with their environment and explore how, under circumstances that are far from ideal, they grapple with their own life projects and with those − including myself − with whom they most immediately have to do. To highlight some of the most bewildering and painful but none the less characteristic features of these kinds of life predicaments I shall, to a large extent, focus the discussion around one individual whom I shall call Joseph. It is as well to say here that with regard to Joseph in particular the going will be hard. Joseph is already well on the road to becoming one of the 10 per cent of Manfred Bleuler's worst-outcome schizophrenics who remain permanently hospitalized as severe psychotics; to tackle the narrative enterprise of a schizophrenic life under these circumstances is to engage with it at its most problematical. But we may perhaps suppose also that if we can make some headway in relation to these states of affairs our arguments will possess some wider significance. At various points in the pages that follow we shall also meet a supporting cast in the persons of Eric, Arthur, Terence and Henry. Let me first briefly introduce those who will figure most prominently.

Joseph

> If things get worse I won't be able to cope with my
> direction gear. I see myself heading for the life of a
> recluse, being valued at 7 and ½ pounds per calendar
> month.
>
> Joseph

A gaunt-looking man with piercing blue eyes and a doleful and
expressionless face that nevertheless on occasions quite unexpec-
tedly creased into a warm and disarming smile, Joseph was first
admitted to hospital at the age of 26. There followed a period of
intermittent hospitalizations which culminated in what proved
to be a long-term admission, so that by the time I came to know
him he was aged 33 and had been a permanent inpatient for three
years. He was brought up in a working-class family in a small
town in the North of England where his father was a skilled
labourer. The town was once the centre of a thriving mining
industry, but the last surviving pit had closed down when Joseph
was in his teens. The family consisted of Joseph, his parents, and
his two elder sisters, both of whom left home early to marry.
There was no history of mental illness in the family.

Shortly before his final admission he wrote to his GP with the
worry about his 'direction gear' quoted above. The consultant's
report at the time of admission reveals that he had been 'very
difficult at home, aggressive to his mother and sisters and not
looking after himself, playing the gramophone all day, and practising archery to the hazard of the neighbours'. Apparently he was,
for example, given to 'shooting arrows tipped with nails from a
home-made bow into a busy thoroughfare'. On one occasion he
fired at his father from the roof of his parents' house as his father
tried to coax him down (fortunately, he missed). At night, the
report continues, he was up most of the time 'lighting fires, rattling
doors, running water taps and flushing toilets'. He is given to
'talking as if he were lecturing and says that if it were not for the
lecturing he would go mad'. He is grossly deluded and thought
disordered. He says, for example, that 'though people think a sail
drives a ship it doesn't. It's pulled round the world by cables and
capstans and blocks and tackles.' He also claims that there are two
versions of Edward Heath, the Prime Minister at the time, 'one
who's gone to live in Ireland, and one who's come back.' His
premorbid personality is said to have been solitary, shy, pessimistic
and health conscious. The diagnosis is now chronic schizophrenia.

His behaviour after admission was, it would appear, equally difficult — 'surly and rude in his attitudes to the staff and boastful of his accomplishments with female patients on the cricket pitch' — and shortly he was transferred to a locked ward. From the records it is evident that for the first two years after his final admission Joseph regularly petitioned to be given help in finding employment outside the hospital. The following is characteristic: 'He has been agitating to be assisted in finding employment with a view to discharge.' His psychiatrist during this period replied to an enquiry from his mother as follows: 'He has been seen by the Resettlement Officer who will do what he can to find something suitable for Joseph, but as you will be aware employment is very short in this area and it is not possible to pick and choose too much. We have tried to help Joseph accept this situation and not be too demanding in the exact job he will take.' Six months later the psychiatrist reports that Joseph is 'very vague and makes no effort to work regularly, saying that he is too old to work and that more work would kill him. He is unrealistic in his whole attitude to treatment and work, and expresses no ideas at all about getting well or ever coping outside the hospital.' From this point on there is no mention in the records of subsequent requests by Joseph to be found work outside the hospital.

Over the three years from the time of his last admission he has been a permanent resident on a locked ward, for the most part on 'Male 15s', within the patient subculture generally reckoned to be the most 'crazy' ward in the hospital. The staff on the ward have not by and large found him easy to deal with. Here are some characteristic entries from his ward notes:

Has bad habit of writing on mirrors with soap.

Hallucinated and talking complete nonsense.

Gross thought disorder and no insight.

Restless and agitated. Frustrated through lack of cigarettes. Occasionally gets a little frustrated with his lot.

Grossly hallucinated and deluded, believes there is a war going on between the Americans and the Vietnamese. (1976)

Very argumentative and emotional at times, stating that he is sick of work and looking after other people and would like to go home and have a bit of peace and quiet.

Disturbed behaviour a.m., refusing to go out with ward group, given 100 mg intra musc. Largactil as prescribed.

Agreed to be interviewed by Dr X at case conference this week, revealed considerable deterioration of whole personality and gave a confused and vague account of himself. Dr X considers him a classic case of schizophrenia.

On occasions, when his behaviour has been more settled, he has been granted 'parole' and permitted to carry messages for the nursing staff to different parts of the hospital. His work in the hospital has mainly consisted of domestic ward duties. He has sometimes also worked with the 'garden parties' — contingents of patients assigned to sweep the leaves etc. in the hospital grounds — and on 'bottle tops' in the 'industrial training unit'.

It is perhaps appropriate to add here that whilst some of the examples from Joseph's case file that I have quoted certainly resemble the sort of discrediting statements that Goffman highlighted as characteristic of asylum regimes, it is not part of my purpose to single these out for special mention as exemplifications of a form of dominance or as exhibitions of an arbitrary and unwarranted power over the lives of vulnerable subjects. Our discussion will implicitly involve some critique of 'the asylum', but not so much because of the malign things that have been done under its auspices as because of the pressures and exactions of a historical process that has made the asylum carry the burden of its disregard for people like Joseph.

As argued earlier, critiques from within 'structures of power' have been pushed too far, and taken as the exclusive pivot of analysis can only serve to fuel an opposing tendency in the Enlightenment view of the human subject. I would certainly claim that the sort of account I shall provide is better than the representative institutional version in the sense that it attempts to extend our conceptions of 'community' rather than to service a peculiarly narrow and banal understanding of what community might mean. In doing so it will, for example, endeavour to take seriously Goffman's recommendation that in contrast to the traditional psychiatric case record we declare an interest in 'the occasions when the patient showed capacity to cope honourably and effectively with difficult life situations'.[1] But we should not suppose that in probing beyond institutional descriptions there is an autonomous subject to be recovered whose heroic career is to be assimilated under the rubric of a history of resistances to what others have tried to make of him. Schizophrenics like Joseph certainly suffer from 'contingencies', but they also suffer from other things besides, and it is with the unravelling of some of these strands that I shall in considerable part be concerned.[2]

Arthur

Arthur was first admitted to hospital at the age of 18 and there followed six further admissions over the next seven years. He was 26 when I came to know him and he was then a day patient, sleeping at home with his parents and spending the best part of his days at the hospital. A tall, bespectacled, lanky man with a shambling gait, he spoke in a soft and gentle voice that seemed to express an inconsolable sadness. I never saw anything extreme in him: he was never outwardly angry, or exuberant, or badly depressed; always attentive, but slightly bemused and quietly despairing, his voice conveying the sense of the arrested life that he now lived.

His typical day went something like this: up at 7.00; breakfast at 8.00 with perhaps a few words shared with his family about 'food, and what we're doing like'; off to work in the hospital at 8.50; work in the gardens till 11.00 and then to the ward; dinner on the ward at 12.00 and then back to the gardens at 1.00; returns to the ward for tea at 4.00; after tea he sometimes walks over to the hospital tea rooms, but most days he just goes home; supper at home at 7.30; after supper he perhaps goes for a walk on his own, otherwise he watches television; at 10.00 he goes to bed. On an ordinary day he exchanges no more than a few words with anyone. He has no special friends either in the hospital or outside and the ward on which he still spends part of the day he finds depressing: everybody sitting around, no communication – 'I read a book, someone else talks to himself.'

His thoughts during the day are mostly about religion and the things he has read in the Bible: 'I think about whether I'm doing any good and that, doing God's will.' It is, he tells me, difficult to get clear as to what is meant by religion: 'knowing what the words stand for, what they mean, knowing the difference between good and bad. . . . If a person's clean then he'll go to heaven. "Clean inside", that's what's meant by the Holy Ghost in the Bible, not drabness at all. I often worry about me in case I'm going drab, in case I aren't healthy enough.' He often feels frightened of temptation, particularly when faced with bad influences like television. 'I can't get interested in that because there are things I don't like, for example crime, making fun out of that like cartoons.' On a number of occasions he has felt a spirit coming up in his body and has been frightened of losing control. For example, at one time the word 'kill' would come into his mind − 'it used to happen every day, I could think of nothing to stop it' − and a feeling run up his spine, followed by the statement 'I shall not kill.' The only way to deal with this sort of occurrence is to say of himself 'I am strong.'

He is not very happy at home and feels unable to talk to anyone in the family about what concerns him. His father, he says, is a bit of a bully and shouts at him for no reason. For example, he drinks a lot of tea and his father 'plays up about that'. He sometimes thinks that he would have 'more self-reliance' if he found board and lodging for himself: 'only it's my mother, I don't want to upset her.' About once a fortnight he breaks with routine and goes to bed at 7.00, but then gets up again because he can't sleep: 'and then my dad plays hell with me and I go to bed again at the usual time.' He has never had a girlfriend in his life: 'I've fancied a few but I've found nothing to say to them.' 'Before I have a girlfriend I must be able to chat them up and attract them, and then I think, what have I got to attract them? Sometimes I feel frightened to stand very close to a girl anyway.'

Terence

Terence was 28 when I met him and had spent most of the past ten years in hospital. He still received weekly visits from his parents and sometimes he went home for the weekend. He was a puzzling person to make out: what struck one most forcibly was his air of innocence and naïvety; it was as though he had never quite grown up or been encouraged to grow up. Indeed he worried a good deal over what it meant to be 'grown up' and sometimes complained that his parents treated him like a two year old when he went home: 'behave yourself, Terence, lie down on the settee, have a rest, have a sleep.'

One of his favoured devices was to rehearse remarks that his parents had made about him: '"Am I barmy?", I say to my dad. "Yes", he says, "you're barmy, you've been barmy for years and you'll never be any different. Only your mum and dad know you're barmy, no one else knows", he says.' According to Terence his parents tell him that he is cunning and crafty and all he thinks about is cigarettes: 'yet my father piles cigarettes on us. Contradiction isn't it?' For a while now, he tells me, he has fancied one of the female patients in the hospital but his father has discouraged him: 'My dad says if I got married I'd die. He says "don't give money to women, they'll just take it off you. I've got to work for that money", he says, "all I'm concerned about is your health."'

For a period he was in an open ward but was transferred back to a locked ward after he had walked home eight miles without permission. 'The charge nurse said I might have been killed. When I got home I said to me dad: "Aren't you going to give us a cup of tea before you take me back to the hospital?" "Come on Terence, Dr Y has been on the phone. You mustn't upset Dr Y. Keep in with Dr Y and everything will be all right." My dad says the doctor says my nervous system's not functioning properly, it's stopped working.' He tells me that he walked home on this occasion because: 'I thought, well I've had enough of the regular routine, going out every morning after breakfast. I'll go home!' He found himself asking questions like: 'Am I wasting my life here? Is my dad wasting my life here? Is Dr Y helping me? Why does my dad put all the burden on Dr Y? Does my dad want me home or not?' He gives me an analogy: 'If you were sitting there writing and got sick of it, you'd say "OK Terence, you can go now." Well it's the same with me. I had a sudden impulse to down tools and go home.' He often put questions like these to himself, and at the end of the two years in which I knew him he had come no closer to being able to answer them to his satisfaction. And the questions were invariably followed by feelings of guilt that led to remarks such as: 'I feel I'm not co-operating sufficiently with different people. As long as you suit other people, play the game, you're all right.' What, he asked me on this occasion, would happen if 'everyone took it into their heads' to down tools and go home: 'If Dr Y left, he might leave me here!'

Eric

Eric was 29 when I first met him and had been in hospital permanently for the past ten years. His father died when he was an infant and he had been brought up by his 'mother and the National Assistance'. He had one sister, 20 years older than himself, whom he sometimes visited. His mother died three years previously. Of all the inmates described here Eric was the most obviously 'normal', indeed self-consciously so. A boyish, rather effeminate-looking man he endeavoured to present himself as a model of the 'sensible' and the 'proper' that would not have been out of place at a vicarage garden party. The group, he once told me, must be a 'good' group and avoid 'dirty' discussions; we may all be men and have 'dirty' thoughts but it would be wrong to give expression to these. Until his mother's death, he said, he hardly spoke at all: 'I was very dependent on her. I couldn't put things together then. I wasn't dumb, but I wasn't articulate.' For the most part he carried himself in the role of the well-adapted, 'career' mental patient, giving no more than a hint of the disruptive beneath the pleasant and co-operative surface, but as the occasion required he was capable of incisive comments on his institutional predicament. The nurses, he reported, 'make up jokes about people. It's part of the treatment. It isn't very nice for the person they're laughing at if he has any intelligence left at all.' And: 'I'm nearer now to being a paranoid than I was two years ago. If you treat a man like an animal he'll behave like one.'

The group meetings

We now turn to three sequences taken from a series of discussions which I organized between these and other schizophrenic patients. These discussions took place in a hospital setting, usually on a weekly, sometimes on a twice-weekly, basis over a two-year period. Joseph, Arthur and Eric took part in all of the meetings, Terence, Henry and two or three others in some of them. These were not intended to be 'therapy groups' in any formal sense. Whatever else may need to be said about them, the sequences are perhaps best approached as a record of discussions between a group of troubled agents within a historically located social world who met together to discuss various features of their respective situations, their ideas and beliefs about the social world, their hopes, griefs, prospects, discontents and so on.

The participants did, I believe, come to view these meetings as rather special occasions. They did not have to attend and could, if they so wished, have declined the invitation. We should not make too much of this: offers in a mental hospital are hard to refuse and there was undoubtedly an implied suggestion somewhere that it would reflect well on their case if they did attend. Nevertheless it became plain to me that in the participants' minds the meetings were set apart, and provided a welcome relief, from the duties and obligations of the daily round. They would otherwise have been working, either on the garden parties, on 'bottle tops' in the industrial training unit or on domestic duties in the ward, and attendance was seen as something of a privilege. There was the idea, perhaps, that what they had to say was of some interest and value beyond an assessment of their individual cases (so for example on a number of occasions other inmates mentioned to me that they had heard about the meetings from the participants and asked if they too could take part). There was also the added promise of a free cigarette or two (all of us with the exception of Eric were heavy smokers) and endless cups of tea, served with a certain civility (a tray with not inelegant cups and saucers) in more congenial surroundings than they were accustomed to on the wards. The setting was itself important, a pleasant room furnished with a carpet and comfortable, if somewhat decrepit, armchairs on the corner of the hospital admission block, a modern structure separated from the main hospital building — a vast nineteenth century edifice where all the chronic patients were housed — by a wide acreage of lawn.

All of this contrived to lend some credibility to the idea that we were 'somewhere else': mental patient status could not altogether be forgotten, yet we were none the less at a certain distance from the main institution and thus from the expectations and perspectives that it embodied. I made an undertaking with the participants not to report on anything that was said in the meetings to anyone else at the hospital unless they specifically requested me to do so, a commitment that was, I believe, taken in good faith. Participants made their own decisions on the discussion topic for any particular occasion; this arrangement worked quite well, though sometimes it gave rise to difficulties in settling on something that everyone found congenial (so, for example, Joseph proposed to me privately one day that we discuss 'reality and unreality' at the next meeting).[3]

A   Life prospects and other matters

(In this sequence I have run together extracts from two consecutive meetings.)

Joseph:	Worse this last week than ever. I suppose we've been in this hospital too long. Everybody's wanting to go home. Everybody's fed up and we're getting on each other's nerves. We're sick of the place and we just want to go home.
Me:	And yet last week you were saying . . .
Joseph:	I know, I've changed my mind now, I just want to go home. I don't want to be in that place for another week. I've changed my mind. I've been in there too long. I'm going round the bend, I'm getting headaches now. It just confuses you somehow in there. They're marching around that much. The racket, the marching.
Eric:	You just sit about until you can bear it no longer, and then you start walking up and down!
Joseph:	There's nowhere to go you see. You're in the ward, and can never go out. The only exercise you get is walking up and down on the ward.
Me:	Where would you like to be living if you weren't in the hospital?
Joseph:	Well, I like my friends, what I call my friends, like old Billy Jones. I like living in a commune.
Arthur:	Where there's a lot of people living?
Joseph:	If I was living in a house by myself which I would have to do because I have nobody except for two old people, I'd go crackers. I'd have nobody to talk to all day. Well I like to see the two old people, what I call my mother and my father, on a weekend, but the place I've moved into it's impossible.
Henry:	If I had money I'd be able to do things, move around, live in hotels by myself, this is what I'd do.
Joseph:	Well you see it's like this. You were born in a certain place. Wherever you were born you always return to. It's very difficult to leave the country and go to an entirely different country and settle down there. Very difficult indeed. Managing a job, I mean.
Eric:	The hospital's just a backwater. There's nothing to do. A home's much better. It's mixed in with ordinary life.

Line numbers (right margin): 5, 10, 15, 20, 25, 30, 35, 40

Joseph: I found that when I was living at home I was
still working all the weekend typing notes out
for somebody, doing some clerking for some- 45
body. In fact when I got home on a weekend I
did more work than when I came back here.
That's what I found. I was glad to get back on
a Sunday night. Just simply to go to bed and
go to sleep. Because I never got any sleep at all, 50
all the weekend. I was up all night writing
things out for people.

Arthur: You weren't forced to, were you?

Joseph: No, I wasn't forced to. I suppose I decided I
had a job to do and had to do it. 55

(silence)

(Talk of 'moving around' reminds Henry that on the way over to
the meeting from the ward he met another patient who had just
received a letter from his psychiatrist telling him that his compulsory detention order had been renewed. Henry is disturbed
by the news since his own case is shortly due for review.)

Joseph: I'm having trouble with me ears and eyes now.
I can't see properly. I want a pair of glasses. My
hearing's dull, I can't hear properly.

Arthur: I don't understand it, he seemed all right to me
this lad. 60

Joseph: There's no hope for him. He's subnormal. No
amount of drugs can do anything for him.
There's something wrong with his brain. He
lives in the past all the time.

Henry: Someone else takes all the decisions in here, 65
that's the trouble.

Joseph: If you can work out how a two-way switch
(laughing) works you've signed your life away. You put
the light on at one end of the room and go to
the other end of the room and put it off. If 70
you can work that out you've signed your life
away.

Eric: You mean you must be raving mad to work
that out?

Me: The same person turns it off as turns it on? 75

Joseph: Of course not. There's three wires and one
bulb and two switches. If you can work that
out you can work anything out. (laughter)

(The talk turns to 'tablets' as another area of hospital life over which patients have no control.)

Joseph: You get into this routine of taking tablets, relying on tablets for everything. Before I 80 came in here they told us that psychiatry was dependency on tablets. We didn't quite understand this, we thought surely to God we weren't put on earth to live on tablets all the time. Eventually we threw them away, and 85 they locked us up. I mean if you take sleeping pills all your life you get to a point where you can't sleep at all.

Arthur: I mean these tablets, they interfere with human nature don't they, in that they interfere with 90 your own system.

Me: But some people feel that they can't manage without them?

Joseph: You see this is the point like, you see during the world war nobody, people got no sleep at 95 all.

Arthur: Doesn't make them the same you know.

Me: In what way?

Arthur: I couldn't rightly say. I've been taking tablets so long I don't know what it's like to be 100 without them. I feel that the tablets interfere with your reactions to certain emotions. I should have a will of me own to meet the opposite sex. It makes me lose the will power to be sort of interested in the opposite sex. 105 I try and make myself . . . but . . . you can't force it on yourself can you?

Eric: We should be able to make these kinds of decisions for ourselves.

Joseph: I don't know, I just . . . more or less . . . the 110 people who look after us in our ward . . . well like . . . they've been working at their job for so long that they know exactly what they're doing. We rely on the nurses you see. We rely on them all the time to decide what *we* have 115 got to do.

Eric: But we should be able to do it for ourselves. Decide more for ourselves. We should have a will of our own.

Joseph: I tell you what's occurred to me. Somewhere   120
            in the world there's a group of people who tells
            everybody else what to do.
Me: You think that's good?
Joseph: It is in a way like. It is for me like. For some
            people it isn't. Somewhere in the world there's   125
            a genius who knows everything, and he tells
            everybody else what to do. He must be very,
            very, old!

(pause)
(Arthur says that he is fed up with himself and with everybody
else.)
Arthur: I wish that everybody would be a bit brighter.
Joseph: Feel depressed do you?   130
Arthur: The ward is so depressing. Everbody sitting
            around. I read a book, someone else talks to
            himself.
Henry: I don't understand what you're getting at.
(pause)
Arthur: I'm angry with myself for not getting on in the   135
            world.
Joseph: Nothing you can do about it at all.
Arthur: When I'm at home I think about the front
            garden . . . full of weeds . . . and the more I
            think about it the more I put it off . . . full   140
            of weeds and the dahlias need standing up
            with canes. I haven't made much progress.
            I haven't got a job. The only entertainment
            I have is going to a nightclub. I'm by myself
            most of the time.   145
Joseph: The best thing to do is to get some wood and
            make something. Improvement bit by bit.
            Start a project or something. Start off with
            something simple.
(pause)
Arthur: I don't feel that I have anything to say that   150
            would interest anybody.
Joseph: I mean, I suppose the best thing we can do is
            for everybody here like to sort of find some-
            body who's your own type, who thinks
            the same way as yourself. Get together, and   155
            like start a business. Find something to do like.

Me:	Start a business?
Joseph:	Why, start a car factory or something like that. I think we're entirely different, that's what's wrong with us. We can't get on together because we're all in a different mood. I think people should be free to go wherever they want to in the world and see what they want to see, whatever they're interested in. But to do that you need a car, and you need to build good roads, and to build the roads you need tractors.
(pause)	
Arthur:	I think a lot of people are different, but I think you're a lot different than anybody else here myself.
Me:	In what way?
Arthur:	Well, his opinions about things, about what's going to happen. His thinking about dangers happening and that you know. I don't believe some of the things he says.
(silence)	

Line numbers: 160, 165, 170, 175

B   Going outside

(During the opening few minutes of the meeting Joseph has been recounting a story about someone on his ward called Jack Watson.)

Joseph:	He's carried on once or twice at the dances. At least you get some laughs.
Terence:	I see Jack Bodell was knocked out.
Joseph:	I never saw it.
Eric:	I never saw it. I just heard.
Joseph:	Jack Watson is going to be the next heavyweight champion of the world. (laughs) He's getting his boxing gear together. You get some laughs with Jack. My name is Jack. He keeps changing his name like me. We keep changing our names.
Me:	What do you change your name to then?
Joseph:	Well, I just put, I put Jacky Waterhouse one day.
Me:	Why Waterhouse?

Line numbers: 5, 10

| Joseph: | It was pouring down all the time, it was raining all the time. They're using gases on us in here you know. | 15 |

Terence: Nice in here isn't it?

Joseph: They're using gases on us all the time.

Terence: Do you like it in here? Joseph, do you like it in here? 20

Joseph: Not bad, all right. They're using gases in here all the time you know.

Terence: Makes you feel like a cup of tea, doesn't it, to feel at home. 25

Joseph: They keep filling Ward 15s full of gas. (laughs) It's terrible. I've put myself on a weight-reducing diet. Jacky's about 16 stone you know.

Eric: We're all doped in here, with the tablets and that. 30

Joseph: Ay, makes you in a bad temper doesn't it, this place, puts you into a bad temper. (laughs)

Terence: That's why I want to drink tea all the time.

Joseph: Puts you in a bad temper. You're fighting with each other all the time. (laughs) I don't know, you get to a point where you think 'oh, have I hurt his feelings or has he hurt my feelings?' People of the same weight seem to get on best. You're best off on a ward where everybody weighs 16 stone. 35

40

(Arthur arrives at this point. He is now a day patient and I ask him how he finds it living at home.)

Terence: He often talks to me, Arthur.

Arthur: Eh?

Terence: You often speak to me don't you?

Arthur: Ay, living at home? It's better than living here like. 45

Joseph: Have you been to F. lately? (Joseph's home town) Old F., you know, there used to be a fish and chip shop there. It's in a terrible state you know like. You couldn't live there now. The village is in a terrible state. Nobody lives there at all now. It's just a deserted village. 50

Me: Your parents live there don't they?

Joseph: No, no.

Me:	Where do they live now then?	55
Joseph:	Oh ay. I don't know like. I suppose they're living at home. They've *moved*.	
Me:	They've moved?	
Joseph:	Why I think they've gone up north like. Why the old F., there was houses about there, bingo halls and that, all finished now, nobody lives there, the old buildings are still there, but there's nobody.	60
Me:	Why's that?	
Joseph:	It's impossible to live there now. It's just solid rock you know. You couldn't live there. It's just dust you know. You see, you can't live anywhere you know, you've got to have the weather conditions to live in. I mean if you buy a house and find you can never go out of the house. If you buy a house on dry land like, you find that you're never out of the house.	65

70 |
Me:	Why?	
Joseph:	Why, because if you go outside you get dust up your nose and down your throat.	75
Me:	In F.?	
Joseph:	Why anywhere, don't you. (with some irritation)	
Me:	So we're not just talking about F.?	
Joseph:	No, even here. What they do is they get a pressure suit when you take seriously ill and you have to live on tablets. And when you take seriously ill they put you on a crash course in a pressure suit and you go crazy altogether, crackers altogether, for about three weeks. There's one on M15s. That's psychiatry that. You see the whole world is, you see there's so much dust and dirt and things like that, you can't live. Most people live in communities under big domes. Now you don't know the dome is there. They build a whole village, and then they build a dome over the top, and they paint the dome and you see aeroplanes flying about inside.	80

85

90 |
| Me: | Inside the dome? And what is there outside the dome? | 95 |
| Joseph: | Certain death. There's domes under the sea. | |

Me:	Is there a dome over this hospital, or does the dome extend over the whole of England?
Joseph:	No, just over this area, for about five miles around. You see aeroplanes only that big (demonstrates with his hands) they put hypnotic gas in and there's little bits of aeroplanes flying about.
Me:	Inside the dome?
Joseph:	*Inside* the dome. Some of it's possibly in me. It's the only way to exist on a world like this.
Me:	Why?
Joseph:	Because there's so much impurities in the outside atmosphere. You just turn into a caveman if you went outside. If you went out of this environment of the dome, you would die within half an hour. It's like being on another world or another planet.
Me:	But does each village have its dome, or how does it work?
Joseph:	Of course, they're connected with tunnels.
Me:	Between one place and another?
Joseph:	No, between one dome and another.
Me:	Have you been outside the dome?
Joseph:	No, only in a pressure suit, when I went to F. like. At one time people existed outside this world of dome, agriculture and things like that, living outside like cavemen, you know, and they died you see, and were buried you see, and then they learnt to make things. And so the first thing they made was a . . . I suppose they cut this tree and all sorts growing outside you know. They made a big dome like. And to sort of give them a sense of security against the breakage of the dome they build brick houses inside the village, inside the dome. And there's another dome which manufactures gases and things like that, and we are living in what's called an environment which is suitable to ourselves. The dome could collapse at any time, it has to be kept in a constant state of repair. It's impossible to live in the outside world for the simple reason that there is too

Line numbers: 100, 105, 110, 115, 120, 125, 130, 135

much dust. You might get hit by a meteorite coming down from space or something like that.   140

Me: How is it that you seem to be more aware of these dangers than the rest of us?

Joseph: I don't know really. I suppose at time you realize where you're at through living in an   145 artificial, in this environment, you see.

Me: And what's brought this realization to you?

Joseph: I don't know really. You take so many tablets to get you fit you see, and you realize what you're living in. You're seeing aeroplanes and   150 you realize it's only that (he points towards the ceiling) high above your head and it's only that big. Then you realize you're living in this artificial environment.

Me: I don't really understand about the aeroplanes.   155

Joseph: Why, size, you see, size. You realize that the aeroplane going overhead is only just above your head and is that big. (opening his arms) They put hypnotic gas into the dome. The gas affects your eyes in the dome and so you think   160 that there's a big aircraft miles up.

Me: But not so?

Joseph: Not so. In fact there's little aircraft about that big probably just about the height of that light there.   165

Me: You said earlier on that there were bits of aeroplanes.

Joseph: Well, there is at times. At times you see there's one crashed you know. So you maybe just drive down the motorway . . . like that . . . that   170 is a dome about that big, and make probably a full-sized aircraft and just stick it somewhere, you see. We're living in a world which is impossible to live on unless we live in this, some people call it an artificial environment   175 but it isn't. If we lived outside we would die. Some people say 'where did we originally come from? Why are we here?' We're living on a world where you're not sort of accustomed to living. We're stuck on this place like, we   180

have to live in these domes. We have to produce
our own food, inside the domes and that, so
we can't have come from this world.

Me: We don't really belong here then, in your view?
Joseph: I'm not sure. Debatable isn't it? Maybe people   185
                from another planet came here and the space-
                ship crashed. We've had to build this thing, see.

(pause)

Joseph: No, but what I was saying before, they tell you
                an aircraft is a form of transport, but it doesn't
                work you see, nothing can fly. All these birds   190
                you see flying around are flying food parcels
                or clockwork. You see, an animal is part of the
                human body. People talk about breeding cattle.
                A bull is how you feel. There's different kinds
                of bulls. A bull is your mind. People say, why   195
                a bull you know. Breeding cattle and things
                like that you know. Well that is part of your
                mind you see, you see bulls. Now every animal
                that has ever been designed or existed is part
                of your body. You design your own animals.   200
Me: Why is a bird a flying food parcel?
Joseph: Well a bird is something to do with your
                stomach you see, the hands you see, you eat
                with your hands, that's the bird's wings, and
                when it goes down into here.   205
Arthur: You mean that when we eat these things they
                become part of us?
Joseph: Well they do, you see I mean.
Arthur: You have to eat them though to be part of us?
Joseph: Well you see animals are part of the human   210
                body. You X-ray a human body and it's made
                up of parts isn't it — like a car. It's against the
                law to X-ray anybody like, you couldn't do it
                in any case, but this part here that would be
                the head of a snake you see, and that would be   215
                a bird flying. Activity you see. Animals are
                nothing. That's where life would have started.
                I suppose it'll probably have started with a
                bird, some people say that you see, and then
                they would sort of have interbred, and interbred   220
                till you got a caveman like a gorilla you know.

	But that didn't happen, that was impossible.	
Me:	How's that?	
Joseph:	Why, it worked the opposite way you see. It would work the opposite way if you went outside this dome.	225
Me:	What would happen?	
Joseph:	Why there would be animals produced from our bodies.	
Me:	But instead we're produced from animal's bodies?	230
Joseph:	No, no, it's the opposite way round. People think that we're produced from animals but we're not. If we went outside the dome animals would produce themselves from us.	235
Me:	Well, what happens *inside* the dome?	
Joseph:	Why, inside the dome, you more or less, I don't know like, you more or less, why inside the dome the most important thing is your medicines isn't it.	240
Me:	You're saying animals don't exist, they're just part of us?	
Joseph:	They probably do outside the dome like, what's left of somebody who went out.	
Me:	But in fact the animals are, we are the animals, inside.	245
Joseph:	Ay, the animals exist in us you see.	
Terence:	God invented the apple tree, and Adam and Eve.	
Joseph:	Ay, apples are a form of medicine aren't they, you know.	250
Terence:	Where did Adam and Eve come from?	
Joseph:	Well, they reckon at one time the world was a big desert and there was only one man like.	
Terence:	No, it wasn't, it was rocks.	255
Joseph:	Rocks, and there was one man existed, that was all, and he was called God, and all the rest of them, all the rest of us were derived from . . .	
Terence:	Caves, cavemen.	
Joseph:	All the rest of us were derived from him so he must have been a canny bloke. And we're going back to all that.	260
Me:	Why is the bull the mind?	

Joseph: I don't know like. People talk, they say 'he's a
            bull in a china shop' and things like that. I   265
            don't really know like. Something to do with
            the brain probably. You see, you live in this
            environment where your medicines is changed,
            and things like that you know, your state of
            mind changes and everything doesn't it? They   270
            change the gases inside. You see we're living
            under the influence of hypnotic gases and if
            anybody is showing too much activity they
            give them some work to do so they don't go
            outside.   275

Me: I'm struck that over all these months you have
            never talked about domes before; is it some-
            thing you have just thought of?

Joseph: We've always lived where we could under one.
            We must have come from somewhere.   280

Me: No, we may always have *lived* under one, but
            you've never *talked* about it before.

Joseph: No I know, because . . . no I don't know like.
            We also live in special suits don't we, like with
            diving. Everybody has been in a pressure suit   285
            you see and we all talk about deep sea diving
            now. Now we don't talk about domes, we
            talk about diving and submarines and things
            like that. It's under 15s you see, under ward
            15s. The dome's under the sea as well. Why we   290
            are talking about submarines is simply that we
            are in a dome which is under the sea. For the
            simple reason that the sea protects us from any
            flying particles and dissolves them before it
            hits the dome.   295

Terence: You're talking scientifically Joseph about Mars
            and the fact that the spacemen . . .

Joseph: Ay.

Terence: That's why you're talking about.

Me: No, I think Joseph's talking about living in   300
            M15s and living in the hospital. I think he's
            talking about what it's like to live here.

(long silence)

Joseph: We, eh, no what I'm beginning to think is, I
            realize now that I can't exist in the outside

	world. I *must* stay here, and I'm feeling a kind	305
	of revolt against that, of staying in a, of living	
	in an artificial, in an environment like this.	
Me:	Revolt against it?	
Joseph:	Ay, where you have to live with people, and	
	eh, you see you can't go outside at all.	310
Arthur:	You could call a house a dome, if you want	
	to look at it that way.	
Joseph:	It's a pity you couldn't have your own private	
	dome. But you can't you see.	
Me:	Why can't you?	315
Joseph:	Why, it'd be too expensive wouldn't it.	

(A conversation develops in the background between Eric, Arthur and Terence. Eric comments that what Joseph seems to be saying is that 'if you go outside this dome, this hospital, it's either death or you have to come back in again.')

Me:	What was that Eric?	
Joseph:	So what you do is you build private houses	
	inside domes.	
Eric:	The dome is some sort of barrier between us	320
	and the outside world.	
Joseph:	It is, that's what it is, you talk about breaking	
	the . . .	
Me:	No, let Eric speak.	
Eric:	You said it was instant death to go on your	325
	own outside the dome.	
Joseph:	It is, it is. I've been outside. You'll have to go	
	out in a pressure suit. Otherwise you'll be	
	killed instantly.	
Eric:	Some people can't exist outside a mental	330
	hospital.	
Me:	Well, I think Joseph's not just talking about	
	this hospital. He's saying that everybody has	
	their own dome.	
Eric:	Their own problem?	335
Joseph:	Ay, ay, at times you feel a revolt towards this	
	eh, idea of living under this environment, but	
	you realize like that you would be dead if you	
	didn't, you know, there would be nothing left	
	of you, if you went outside.	340
Me:	Outside of where?	
Joseph:	Outside the environment of the hospital and	

the place in the atmosphere in which you live. We're stuck here, aren't we? We must work here. We must clean the place up and 345 keep it tidy. Otherwise any dust accumulating gets into us.

Me: What do you think Arthur, about what Joseph is saying?

Arthur: I feel that . . .   350

Joseph: Why you feel a sort of revolt, you know you think to yourself.

Arthur: I feel that nowadays it's the only thing that I can do.

Me: Which is what?   355

Arthur: To come here like. I could perhaps get an outside job but I'd probably not be fit enough to keep up the pace.

Joseph: That's it you see. Now this is a hospital. This is where people come for treatment who are 360 working in another environment. They come here full of muck and dust you know and things like that. They come here dead, don't they? They come here dead, they come here dead you know.   365

(During these last few moments Arthur has continued to speak, but he cannot be heard above Joseph.)

Arthur: You can only think of one thing at a time. To be efficient like. And yet outside there's so many things to think about.

Joseph: Ay I know, what can you do.

(I ask Joseph to keep quiet for a bit.)

Arthur: I mean that's how it is, isn't it? You can only 370 think of one thing at a time. There's all sorts of things to think about. There's rent to pay, the coalman to pay, the gas to pay.

Joseph: But there's not you see, there's not you see, everything's provided for you.   375

Arthur: You've got to make your bed, wash your clothes, and get your meals. You've got to go out and buy your clothes and buy food. You have to do everything.

Joseph: Ay, that is activity.   380

Arthur: It's a very busy life.

Me:	Yes, I think Joseph has been talking about something a bit similar. We need a dome for protection, at the same time it's a limitation.
Joseph:	Exactly, people want to get out of it and go for a long walk. It'd kill them instantly.
(pause)	
Me:	You're perhaps using different language to say something a bit similar.
Joseph:	Oh ay. We both mean the same thing though don't we? They give you something to do, something to talk about.
Arthur:	You find yourself getting bored if everything's done for you, if you're not putting much into life. This is one of the things I feel about the hospital. But the problem is not being able to cope when you have to do things for yourself. That's what brings people in here.
Joseph:	There used to be a series on television called 'Survival'. That's what it is you know.
Arthur:	Probably another thing that brings people in here is that they think that life is not worth working for.
Eric:	We used to have values once that were worth working for, but nowadays they're open to doubt. If you don't have something to believe in you just don't feel like going out and working.
Me:	What are you thinking of Arthur?
Arthur:	It all depends on how much people value their selves. If they don't think a lot of their selves they won't do much for their selves, but if they think a lot of their selves they'll do a lot for their selves.
Me:	What does that depend on?
Arthur:	I think it's childhood, and the influence of our mothers and fathers and the outside world.
Me:	How's that in your case?
Arthur:	Well, sometimes I was treated all right, sometimes I wasn't. It's not only the people at home, the people I lived with, but those whom I worked with, outside in the garage.
Joseph:	I mean, your childhood is what you might go back to, see.

385

390

395

400

405

410

415

420

Arthur:	They weren't always very nice people. It's not just bad language, it's bad behaviour.	
Me:	How's that?	425
Arthur:	Well, I can give you an instance. I was just walking through a door to the spare shop and without any warning somebody threw a big screwdriver. He threw it from the other end of the shop and it just missed me, and stuck right into the metal door. Well there was no need for him to do that, and if it had hit me I would probably have been seriously injured, for no reason at all. I can't figure out what he did it for, and when people do things like that you don't class them as very important people, as friends, and you think, oh if a lot of people are like that you don't have friends, and its a lonely life isn't it if you don't have friends?	430 435
Me:	Yes, yes it is.	440
Arthur:	I'm not saying everybody's the same. Some people can be very good to you like. But it's just the place that I worked at. And when I lost interest I lost my job. When I lost interest in my job I was sacked.	445
(pause)		
Terence:	It's a hard world outside, we wouldn't be able to manage.	
Arthur:	We've got to do things for ourselves. Think about all the jobs that have got to be done. Like the washing up and that.	450
Eric:	It's a job and it's got to be done.	
Arthur:	It's got to be done. It's not a thing that's easy to forget. A job like washing up isn't so easy to forget.	
Joseph:	Well, the point is, I mean, some people here just watch the messages from the world.	455
Terence:	What would patients do if they had no relatives, nobody to care for them? Things like that. They'd just be lonely. Marriages and things like this and children living in derelict buildings.	460
Me:	Derelict buildings?	
Terence:	Not able to manage, not able to maintain the house.	

Me: Who?

Terence: Why, different people. Spending £7 rent on the   465
house, they'd be in debt all the time, in arrears.
They'd be in arrears all the time wouldn't they?

Me: Who would?

Terence: These people who get married and go off and
leave their parents.   470

Joseph: I think, I think you really want to have a talk
with Jacky Watson. He's more on the psychiatry
side, isn't he, the abstract side like. He sees
gases in the air. (laughs uproariously, rest of
statement incomprehensible) You know what I   475
mean?

Me: What do you mean when you say that he's
more on the psychiatry side?

Joseph: I don't know like. He seems to have some idea
about how it all started this carry on. He thinks   480
(laughs), he's got me thinking in the same way.
I think I've made progress you know. (laughs
again) We need some new people around,
that's what he says.

Arthur: I think that people should be livelier than they   485
are. They should be stronger, fitter, brighter,
have more inspiration you know. I think the
wars have really had a bad influence on it.
I don't think the atmosphere of before the war
has been recovered you know.   490

Joseph: People here are more interested in a peaceful
way of life aren't they. I mean some people just
sit in the chair and watch television. We're not,
are we? We're always looking on the outside.
(laughs)   495

Arthur: I mean people watch television war pictures
sometimes. We're all constantly reminded of
what's been gone before, of the conflict
between each other.

C   Settled for life?

Terence: Nobody can see what we're doing can they?
When you're on your own can no one see you?

Does the spirit of the woman or the man see
you when you're by yourself or we're speaking
here? Are other people watching us? I feel as   5
though people are watching us all the time,
through the door. Can they see through the
door?

Arthur: I've heard other people complain about that,
about being watched.   10

Terence: How do those canteen girls know how the
patients are keeping when they've finished
in the tea room and go back to the wards?
Can they see them or do they know what
they're doing or do they know their actions?   15

Joseph: Oh, they know all right. The opposite sex can
tell what you are doing by looking at you.

Terence: They can tell what you're doing can they?
The opposite sex? But you (turning to me)
said earlier that they can't.   20

Me: Not sure what you have in mind, Joseph.

Joseph: Well, you might get a job as a teacher. How
long you exist as a teacher depends on your
pupils, doesn't it?

Terence: Observation!   25

Me: Well of course, if you're sitting in the tea room,
Terence, the canteen girls can see what you are
doing.

Terence: Is that right? She can see what I am doing?

Me: Well yes, but she can't see inside you, what   30
you're thinking about and so on, inside your
mind.

Terence: Body neither?

Me: Well, she can't see inside your trousers.

Terence: Well, do they know how you feel and all that, 35
women? Can they tell by looking at you? I'm
sitting here but does Joyce know what I'm
doing? If they're in love with you do they
know what you're doing.

Me: I don't follow.   40

Terence: Well, supposing I was courting and I was sitting
here, does this woman that I know know what
I'm doing?

Joseph: Of course she does.

Me:	No!	45
Terence:	They don't?	
Me:	I think, Joseph, that you're . . .	
Arthur:	Unless she was sitting in the same room as you, she wouldn't know.	
Terence:	You sit in the tea room, don't you, well do you take any notice of anyone, are they watching you? Do they know what you're doing?	50
Joseph:	Well this is my point, Terence, that you knock around with this Joyce, I mean, she's your type exactly you know.	55
Terence:	Well, if I went with her would I be looked down upon?	
Joseph:	No. You knock around with Joyce, she's your type, she's built like you. She knocks around with a mini-skirt and all that you know.	60
Terence:	But supposing I courted Joyce, would anybody look down upon me for courting her because she's no good?	
Joseph:	Oh, they wouldn't worry like, they'd just say well Terence if you want.	65
Terence:	That's that. They'd just say that's that, would they?	
Joseph:	Ay, but I don't regard Joyce as . . .	
Terence:	My type?	
Joseph:	I mean, what you've got to find is a good woman, mate, to look after.	70
Terence:	To look after?	
Joseph:	No I mean Joyce to me is your type. If you stick by her.	
Terence:	If she sticks by me.	75
Joseph:	Ay, I mean you go round together and all that you know. But that's not the point. You're not helping anybody else are you?	
Me:	How's that then? How isn't he helping anybody else?	80
Joseph:	Well, he is in a way like. I mean eh, I can't really put me finger on the right word. I mean Joyce has settled for life hasn't she. I mean like you. You can knock around together quite happily.	85
Terence:	For life? Will I be here for life?	

Joseph:	Well, you're both physically fit aren't you, so you might as well knock around together.	
Terence:	Will I be here for life?	
Joseph:	You probably will be.	90
Terence:	We all will?	
Arthur:	That's a thing nobody knows about other people. You can't forecast the future.	

(long silence)

Terence:	Supposing a man's at sea in the navy, and the wife's at home maintaining the house and she writes letters to the husband. How do they make love at so great a distance? They can't.	95
Arthur:	They can't. But they can express their feelings in the letters, you see.	
Terence:	They write it in the letters do they?	100
Arthur:	Ay, they express their feelings for each other.	
Terence:	It's just written down is it?	
Arthur:	Ay, it's just written down, what they've been doing perhaps or . . .	
Eric:	But you don't describe the physical actions of love-making.	105
Arthur:	No.	
Joseph:	What Terence is describing, I mean him and this other woman who knock around together, if it's the same one I'm thinking of, they're good companions, that's all, isn't it?	110
Terence:	Just friends!	
Joseph:	Well what I mean is, how can I describe it, I mean look at Ward 15s. There's something there, everybody in that ward is different. It shouldn't be like that. You should have your own . . . . They're going backwards, aren't they, some of them?	115
Terence:	That's all I wanted to say now.	
Joseph:	We all want to get out of the place and go home.	120
Eric:	But we haven't all got homes to go to.	

5

The chronic schizophrenic as
historical agent

I said, 'No I never starts his self.'
He said, 'Yes they do. You dont start the life in you
thats like a river running in you stil there comes a time
when you push your oan boat out in to the middl of it.'
I said, 'Or you put your self on to the road to the hart
of the wud.'
He said, 'How dyou spel that?'
I said, 'W-u-d!'

Russell Hoban, *Riddley Walker*

Nobody can truthfully say of himself that he is filth.
Because if I do say it, though it can be true in a sense,
this is not a truth by which I myself can be penetrated:
otherwise I should either have to go mad or change
myself.

Ludwig Wittgenstein, *Culture and Value*

For reasons of space, and also because there is more than enough
to be getting along with here, this discussion will to a large extent
concentrate on Joseph: I shall start with some general observations
on these conversations and on Joseph's role in them in particular;
I shall then move to a consideration of the sorts of difficulties
that Joseph presents for other participants in a conversation and
why we should judge them to indicate something more serious
than some local aberration; and finally I shall provide a more
extensive discussion of the narrative enterprise of Joseph's life.

The conversation as dramatic production

As with any other conversation, we can view these conversations
as a set of dramatic productions in which the participants are both

actors and joint authors who in various ways either co-operate, or fail to co-operate, in bringing about and carrying through a dramatic work. The conversation is, as Alasdair MacIntyre remarks, the most familiar context of enactment of the narrative enterprise of human life and it is, typically, by reference to their place in a conversation that we try to make particular utterances, or sets of utterances, intelligible. We render a conversation as a whole, or some segment of it, intelligible by bringing it under a description, or assigning it to a genre, that identifies it as one of the many sorts of dramatic consequence that may ensue when human beings meet and converse together. It does not necessarily follow that we will have fully understood it — we might need to learn a good deal more about the histories of the participants and of the settings in which they live out their lives to achieve that — or even that we are able to render intelligible every utterance or set of utterances in the conversation. To identify an occurrence as an intelligible action is, as MacIntyre describes, 'in the paradigmatic instances to identify it under a type of description which enables us to see that occurrence as flowing intelligibly from a human agent's intentions, motives, passions and purposes'. We thus 'understand an action as something for which someone is accountable, about which it is always appropriate to ask the agent for an intelligible account.'[1] Perhaps, in the case of a seemingly unintelligible episode in a conversation, the agent or agents suffered some sort of momentary lapse, perhaps the episode could only be made intelligible by reference to some other dramatic history that is unavailable to us in the context of the present enactment, and so on. A conversation of any length may, moreover (even, perhaps, is *likely* to) contain digressions, blatant misunderstandings, areas of incoherence and other forms of departure from some rigorous rational norm.

We can make these sorts of allowances, and we are right to do so. None the less, in judging a conversation intelligible we do need to feel assured that we are dealing with a recognizable form of human drama involving human actors and authors as distinct from some sort of natural occurrence, something that appears to be taking place beyond the reach of our conceptions of human agency.

Now in the case of the conversations we are concerned with here we ought, I think — to put it as strongly as that — to judge that there are some episodes where some very serious problems of intelligibility arise. However, we ought I think to judge also that in these dramatic productions Joseph, Arthur, Eric, Terence and Henry draw us into the life of what is recognizably a human community with its multifarious ways of making out, of sharing hopes and grievances, of coping with the wear and tear of lives lived in close proximity, in short of trying to sustain or salvage the value of a human enterprise within a difficult and limiting set of circumstances. The dramatic productions of these people are sometimes comic, on occasions banal or pathetic, but also tragic. Perhaps overall what comes through most strongly are the sufferings of these lives, not as the passive register of a set of pains, but as the collective articulation of particular life histories within a particular social history, of sufferings that are individually felt but also exposed, interpreted and combated within a collaborative enterprise.

And it is apparent also that, among other things that he does, Joseph plays a powerful role as actor and author in establishing a set of perspectives, sometimes on the hospital and sometimes on the wider projects of human lives, that serve alternately to heighten, relieve and enlarge individual preoccupations and perceptions, to bond them into a shared understanding. There are a number of obvious ways in which he does this as, for example, in his direct and poignant statements about life on a locked ward (e.g. A7, B35); in the clever, if somewhat muddled, account of the two-way switch to evoke the erosion of autonomy in the hospital setting, the process of mortification as Goffman terms it, which got everyone in the group laughing; and in the ironic play of his remarks about tablets:

Joseph: They told us psychiatry was dependency on tablets. We didn't quite understand this, we thought surely to God we weren't put on earth to live on tablets all the time. (A82)

But it may be useful to look briefly at an instance where it is, perhaps, less obvious what he is about. In the 'Settled for life?' (C) sequence Terence, we can take it, is looking for advice on how to handle his relationship with Joyce in the way that in an ordinary social situation a young man might turn to those somewhat older and more experienced than him. The best analogy I can think of is with a conversation between a group of men in a pub, with its characteristic combination of repartee, ribaldry and seriousness. Thus in the early stages of the dialogue it is unclear as to how seriously Joseph takes himself or means his fellow discussants to take him. But then at line C76 something rather curious appears to happen:

Joseph: Ay, I mean you go round together and all that you know. But that's not the point. You're not helping anybody else are you?

From this point on through to the end of the sequence Joseph is, I believe, engaged in an attempt to convey a perspective on what is taking place that brings out the tragic dimension in the collective situation of these hospital inmates and identifies a form of suffering that derives from the constraints imposed on agents *qua* agents, on what they can meaningfully do for, or say to, each other. At line C110 he puts the question about Terence and Joyce:

Joseph: They're good companions, that's all, isn't it?

and then immediately he goes on — and we can sense the rising anger — to give voice to a collective experience of rupture:

Joseph: Well what I mean is, how can I describe it, I mean look at Ward 15s. There's something there, everybody in that ward is different. It shouldn't be like that. You should have your own . . . . They're going backwards, aren't they, some of them?

'It shouldn't be like that': not the potential for individuation, for 'difference', but the institutional condition that aggregates lives into a common denominator, that stunts growth and prises individuals away from their proper embodiment as, among other things, men and women in relation. The point, then, is that in this condition Terence and Joyce can *only* be 'good companions', that is *all* they can attain to. There are doubtless a number of things that could be said about Terence's query about the separation between a sailor and his wife, but one of them certainly is that in the hospital environment the separation of men from women is such that it is as if they were separated by a sea. (As Joseph himself put it on another occasion: 'A married man is separated from his wife in hospital, and an unmarried man is separated from his future wife.')

It is, then, as though at a certain point in the conversation it is borne upon Joseph how unlike a conversation in a pub between ordinary agents the present conversation is. The participants have, as it were, been proceeding as if they were ordinary agents free to determine their own lives, and to help others to determine their lives, to the extent that most ordinary agents are — to make plans for marriage, to give meaningful advice to other agents etc. But such are the constraints of the actual setting that advice of the sort that Terence is looking for cannot meaningfully be given from one agent to another just because the setting does not allow scope for that advice to be acted upon. There are, then, serious limits on how one person can 'help' another or on how any one individual can 'help' himself. And hence the need for the affirmation, against the deadweight of what often seems and feels to be the case, that there is still amidst all of this genuinely 'something there'. This then leads Joseph to say (C121):

Joseph: We all want to get out of the place and go home.

and permits Eric's rejoinder, in a form of dramatic conclusion that was often repeated in these discussions:

Eric: But we haven't all got homes to go to.

It was clear to me along the way that other participants in the group had considerable respect and regard for Joseph, both for his capacity to entertain, and to capture and convey difficult areas of feeling, and also for his aptitude for taking matters in hand as circumstances seemed to require. 'A beautiful punch, you should have seen it, right on the nose', Eric remarked to me one day when Joseph had apparently felt more than 'a little frustrated with his lot', as his ward notes put it, and felled an unfortunate charge nurse. But this, needless to say, does not adequately describe either the range of Joseph's actions or the difficulties that some of those actions produced for other participants, including myself, and it is to the sorts of difficulties that called out Arthur's sad but painfully accurate declaration:

Arthur: A lot of people are different, but I think you're a lot different than anybody else here myself. (A168)

that we must now turn.

Convention and the human speech community

I shall now look at the section in sequence B which Joseph
introduces with the question 'Have you been to F. lately?' (B47)
where he goes on to discuss his belief in (among other things)
domes. Let me try to follow through some of the problems that
arise here. In the opening stages it is, of course, unclear whether
we are dealing with some passing conversational remarks or the
prelude to a longer account. It seems, though, that whatever
we are in for the discussion is going to hang around facts and
realistic description. His assertion that his parents don't live in
F. any more is for me therefore (though not I suspect for the
other members of the group) a bit of a puzzle, but his description
of the decay of a once thriving community is for this particular
area none the less credible enough.

By line B71, however, with the remark 'If you buy a house on
dry land like, you find that you're never out of the house' things
take another turn, and the whole matter is made still more
difficult when Joseph asserts (B77) that this state of affairs
applies generally. At this point, then, as my questions indicate,
I am uncertain as to what Joseph is *doing*. To start with he gave
every indication that he was going to engage in description, and
my question (B78) is, in effect, an attempt to retain some
credibility for this mode by restricting its application to a
localized site. But this, as we have seen, Joseph won't allow,
nor does he give us any indications of his intentions in pursuing
this narrative course or provide us with an indication of how we
might properly describe his actions. He makes us work very
hard.

'Most people', Joseph tells us, 'live in communities under
big domes.' (B88) What kind of speech act is this? We are
obliged, I think, in its immediate context to take it as a
declaration or assertion that such and such is the case. We have,
in other words, to assume that Joseph as well as 'saying something'
is also 'doing something' and to recognize that the form of the
statement invites certain assumptions as to the nature of that
'doing'. In more formal terms what concerns us here is the
'illocutionary' as a non-reducible component of speech acts.[2]
'In the case of illocutionary acts', John Searle writes, 'we succeed
in doing what we are trying to do by getting our audience to
recognize what we are trying to do.'[3] In order to carry off an

illocutionary act successfully the speaker must be able to satisfy an account of meaning or understanding that shows the connection 'between one's meaning something by what one says and what that which one says actually means in the language'; the account must, that is, capture 'both the intentional and the conventional aspects and especially the relationship between them.'[4] In the case of the type of illocutionary act that we can take Joseph to be presently engaged in — namely assertions, declarations, statements (that etc.) — we need, for any proposition *p*, to be able to make a number of assumptions. So, for example, that the speaker has evidence for the truth of *p*; that the speaker believes *p*; and that *p* is to be understood as representing an actual state of affairs.

The problem with Joseph's declaration is, of course, that it asserts a state of affairs that is drastically at odds with the world as I know it. In his next utterance he appears to cover himself: 'Now you don't know the dome is there.' (B89) But in effect this only increases my difficulties because he now ventures upon another claim, namely that he has privileged access to a truth which is unavailable to ordinary mortals. And so it goes on. For the rest of this sequence I am engaged in trying to discover evidence for the claim that Joseph makes and to elucidate the state of affairs to which he has introduced me. I proceed, in other words, on the assumption that I have correctly identified what Joseph is trying to do, and that I have in that sense understood his utterances, albeit that I find them sometimes puzzling, sometimes false etc. I assume, that is, a direct linkage between what that which Joseph says actually means in the language and what Joseph means by what he says. And as we can see I have a hard time of it proceeding in this way. At one point I get myself into a regular muddle: 'But in fact the animals are, we are the animals, inside'; and Joseph has to help me out: 'Ay, the animals exist in us you see.' (B247) By line B281 or so I have reached something of a crisis: the conventional schema that I have deployed — namely the assumption that Joseph was telling us something about the state of the world and all that that entailed procedurally for the dialogue that ensued — has broken down. Somehow I have allowed myself to be led into error and deception and I find myself in a state of perplexity, not unlike the kind of epistemological crisis discussed in chapter 2 in which the conventional ways of relating 'seems' to 'is' cease to be effective.

At B296 Terence brings a different schema to bear with the suggestion that Joseph is talking scientifically about Mars. This was doubtless an expedient remedy for the immediate conversational discomfort, but implicitly it thrust Joseph even further outside the conventional human speech community. I then try to reassimilate Joseph into community by ascribing to him a different set of intentions: I suggest that he has been trying to say something about what it is like to live in the hospital etc. My remark is followed by a long silence. Joseph then speaks, and in this and his subsequent utterances he picks up on some of his earlier concerns, but relocates them: not only are they directed to the hospital environment but they are now cast in a locutionary form that identifies them not as propositions about a state of affairs in the world but as declarations of a personal state. The break from the earlier mode is radical: 'We, eh, no what I'm beginning to think is, I realize now that I can't exist in the outside world.' (B303) For the first time we have a change of person.

And Joseph's reworking of his earlier propositions – hastened or invited by my own reinterpretation – has, as we can see, important consequences. Arthur, for example, takes up the theme of the dome and later goes on to enlarge on his own difficulties in making out in the social world beyond the hospital. The members of the group now have an implied set of instructions as to how to behave; the recasting of the earlier discussion that I undertook, and which Joseph then enlarged upon has, that is, provided them with a set of indications as to what has been done, what is being done, and thus also as to what they can now do. In the earlier part of the conversation the other members of the group were, perhaps, less foolhardy than I was and by and large opted out of the discussion. They did not know what to do because they did not know what was being done. Only by clarifying Joseph's intentions, and thus reworking the connections between what Joseph meant by what he said and what he said actually meant in the language, was it possible to re-establish a form of shared communication.

But what does it mean to say that I clarified Joseph's intentions? In ascribing a different set of intentions to Joseph, are we therefore to understand that all along he meant us to bring his utterances under a metaphorical description but that somehow he either felt unable, or didn't recognize the need, to make his purpose plain? Perhaps, one line of argument might run, I misidentified the relevant type of speech act and Joseph was really recounting a folk legend, further contextual evidence for which might be recovered from his local community? Perhaps indeed, but whilst we cannot rule this out as a logical possibility I think we have good grounds for claiming that it is not simply a breakdown on the surface of conversational etiquette that is at issue, a failure to comply with some perhaps rather arbitrary conversational norm, or the kind of misunderstanding that might be engendered by a speaker who was unable to articulate his beliefs clearly, but a much more fundamental breakdown in a human drama, in the enterprise of a human life. We should, that is to say, judge that this was a conversation in which in certain key episodes Joseph's intentions became unavailable to him, and that when therefore I ascribed intentions to him I was pointing to how he *might*, perhaps, have talked, have used the metaphor of the dome etc., had he had an intelligible grasp of himself as an agent (i.e. we would not have expected Joseph to say at this point: 'Ah yes, I should have done it differently, I shouldn't have taken it on trust that my meaning would be plain to you' etc.)

To make this a little clearer we need to enlarge on the problem of conventions on which I remarked in chapter 2. We must make a distinction between conventions in the sense of 'contrived agreements, consciously and deliberately entered into by men', and what we can think of as ' "natural conventions", features of our lives and world which logically might have been otherwise, but which just happen to be this way among all men in all times and places.'[5] Conventions of this last kind are 'fixed' by neither custom nor agreement, but rather by 'the nature of human life itself, the human fix itself'. Someone *may*, for example, be 'bored by an earthquake or by the death of his child or the declaration of martial law, or *may* be angry at a pin or a cloud or a fish, just as someone may quietly (but comfortably?) sit on a chair of nails. That human beings on the whole do not respond in these ways is, therefore, seriously referred to as conventional.' And 'conventions' in this sense are 'not patterns of life which differentiate men from one another but those exigencies of conduct which all men share'.[6]

In this conversation, therefore, we find ourselves pulled beyond the limits of our conceptions of the 'human fix'. For someone to experience the world like *this*, to talk about it in *this* way etc.: this is a form of behaviour that our schemas of human agency, of what it is to carry through a life, cannot accommodate. I am unable to provide the kind of context for these speech acts that would render them fully intelligible just because I find myself drawn into a dramatic work that I cannot locate, into a form of human enactment that defies comprehension as an expression of what human life (and thus human community) could ever viably be like. And it is for this reason that we properly identify an enactment of this sort not as a peculiar way of talking, a breach of some conversational norm, but as a form of suffering, a breakdown in the enterprise of a life, as the expression of a life that has run into deep trouble.

Yet I do, of course, provide a context of a kind in that I recognize (on the basis of my knowledge of him, my wider dealings with chronic schizophrenics etc.) that Joseph might be helped out of this conversational frame into an alternative frame that reconnects him with his fellow men and thus (albeit rather tenuously) re-establishes him in human community. And to the wider question of Joseph's relation to community I now turn.

The narrative enterprise of a schizophrenic life

We must now look more closely at the narrative enterprise of Joseph's life and at the difficulties he encounters in trying to sustain a sense of himself as someone who has a meaningful part to play in a meaningful story, whose life can be envisaged not as a series of disconnected episodes but as a whole and, above all, as an enterprise that possesses value. On meeting Joseph two things are made startlingly plain. One is that not only is he (like any other agent) by definition a story-teller, someone who is constantly engaged in ordering and reordering his life into new dramatic and narrative forms, but also that he is positively drawn to the telling of stories. The second is that, much as he is attracted to story-telling, and *needs* to tell stories, the telling of them often gives rise to a good deal of difficulty and not infrequently anguish, both in his efforts to make different strands of his life intelligible to himself — to construct a form of internal coherence — and, as we have already seen, in his communications with others.

What we find in his narrative productions are a number of narrative histories, some of which are internally coherent but appear to conflict with each other; and others of which are internally perplexing if not incoherent. In some cases what appears to be at issue is the difficulty in trading off the descriptions under which he brings his own actions against the descriptions that are proffered by others. And at other points the difficulty is more fundamental and concerns the complications of the narrative character of selfhood, of what is required of the agent in having to make himself, and thus make his own stories, through making intelligible the story or stories of which he is part.

We may think of Joseph as attempting to steer a course through life and we can distinguish rather roughly between three different forms of passage (roughly, because as is perhaps already apparent, in any single episode of Joseph's journeyings all three, and variations upon them, may appear in sequence). We have first a number of episodes in which Joseph deploys his navigational skills to present himself and his life as part of a meaningful story-in-motion, in which he tries with varying success to establish his bearings, albeit that along the way he has to reconcile inconsistencies between his own accounts of the social landscape that he takes himself to be moving through in time and those that are put forward by other travellers. We can think of these episodes as concerning his social identity: his identity as worker, the identity he can work up in relation to me and that which he is able to negotiate with others, the problem of assimilating his present predicament within the scheme of his life etc. Second, there are experiences of storm, occasions in which his capacity to assimilate the organic continuity of his life into a form of dramatic unity is put in crisis, in which, as it were, the dramatic frame that connects him to the wider human drama grinds to a halt and he finds, in his own words, that he can no longer cope with his 'direction gear'. But breakdown in Joseph's dramatic steering resources or not, the play of life none the less carries on remorselessly, taking him along with it, and thus at points he finds himself utterly bewildered, surrounded and menaced by fragments that he cannot cohere, and left to repair the damage as best he can. And, finally, there are times when, from within the movement of his life, he is able to comment on the under-taking on which he is embarked, to identify the kind of undertaking that life (from his particular historical experience of it) is, the dilemmas and conflicts that it poses for him, and to assess his own strength to go through with it. In what follows I shall illustrate and discuss different aspects of these dynamics.

Joseph's work

One of the most important ways in which Joseph tries to establish a part in a story for himself concerns his social identity as a worker. The institutional setting of the psychiatric hospital provides constant reminders to the individual patient of his social failure and of the extent to which the evaluation of his life turns on his motivation and success as a worker. These reminders are in part brought out in the contrast between the hospital as an environment of failure and exclusion with an envisaged environment of ordinary living and productive efficiency elsewhere. But they emerge also from the internal economy of the hospital, from the provision of work roles — bottle tops, domestic ward duties, garden groups etc. — that transmit the double message that the patient must work, that he ought to work, but also that there is nothing (or almost nothing) for him to do, and that signal the extent of his distance from the site of valued productive effort.

And it is, then, perhaps not altogether surprising that for an individual who over the course of his life has come to set considerable store upon himself as a worker, we should find not merely a desire to appear productive, but a positive affirmation of himself as a worker. A man who does not work, Joseph tells me, is not a proper man. And his discourse with me is filled with avowals of his duties and responsibilities, of the demands on his time, of how much work there is to be done, of the troubles of the working environment, constant assertions of his daily busyness. Sometimes it is writing that he is engaged in, sometimes painting, sometimes building and decorating, sometimes farming — working on the land or looking after the animals — and sometimes a combination of these. But most important of all is his work as builder and decorator, his responsibilities for the renovation and maintenance of different parts of the hospital environment. Much of the hospital, he tells me, is in a bad state of repair. Together with a number of fellow patients he has been working on the reconstruction of some of the buildings, in particular Male 15s:

Joseph: We've put a lot of work into the insides. We're just going to keep on working on the insides all the time. We're working on the roof at the moment to make it watertight.

The walls, he tells me, are in need of papering:

Joseph: The trouble is that there's 40 on the ward. We may have to transfer them over here whilst we paper the walls.

Male 15s, he tells me on another occasion, is home:

Joseph: I've got it the way I want it. The work I've put into the place I wouldn't want to leave. I'd have to start from scratch again on a new building. It takes 40 men to look after a hospital this size and they all come from 15s.

It is, of course, easy to note the inconsistencies in his accounts — thus the other patients are variously coworkers with Joseph in the hospital labour force or patients in contrast to Joseph as supervisor of building operations — and to envisage the conversational difficulties to which these give rise. But we can, none the less, readily enough understand the point of the imaginative recasting of the institutional drama of the hospital, with its highly specified allocation and definition of roles, into a dramatic frame that provides considerably enlarged scope for maneouvre. Thus he can fashion himself sometimes as a self-employed man — in charge of time and of his own decisions about his life — and sometimes as a wage labourer. He can give expression both to his ordinariness — a man with ordinary cares, ordinary ambitions — and to a view of himself not as a solitary individual, locked in the idiosyncrasies of a personal trajectory that sets him apart from his fellow men (though at points he finds himself thrown back to this) but as a participant in a community of endeavour, in a co-operative and shared history. And within the terms of this scenario he can mitigate also other disquieting features of his institutional predicament. Thus his paltry hospital allowance[7] can be attributed to the exactions of the Inland Revenue:

Joseph: We're all on the same wage in 15s, about £35 per week. By the time you pay your tax you have about £1 pocket money.

His involuntary sojourn in hospital, which he senses is likely to harden into permanence, can be presented, albeit somewhat tentatively, as a choice enforced upon him by the requirements of occupational mobility:

Joseph: I think I might stop here. After all I settled in F. (his home town) for 35 years. I only sleep here. I'm out working on the roads all day. I might stay here, provided there's work here. There's always something to do here. I think I'll be here for quite a while. I like these remote areas.

His narrative of 'ordinary life', of a dramatic action played out by 'ordinary actors', is often jeopardized by his experience of some of his fellow patients — and the stories they tell — with whom he lives in the confined space of a locked ward and who seem in certain obvious respects not to fit the parts that the scenario requires of them. Sometimes what he does is to contrive an account that distances both the actors and the form of relation from suggestions of 'pathology'. Thus one morning he says of Tom, a schizophrenic patient some years younger than him, who was painfully bewildered about almost every aspect of his experience:

Joseph: It dawned on him last night that he's only got himself to make his own career. He's on his own, he's got to take his own initiative. I told him: 'I doubt if you'll get very much nursing in the world at all. Choose a course and follow it!' It's up to him to decide what he wants to do in the world. I mean he's only got himself to look after. If he wants to stop here with me he can, if he wants to go to S. he can.

But the dramatic resources of the hospital environment are clearly a bit limited, and Joseph does not always find it easy to maintain a benign view of it. 'It's a rubbish tip', he tells me one day, 'a dirty, scruffy, rotten hole', though he has also heard others, he goes on to remark in a more humorous vein, describe it as 'one of the stately homes of England'. And on occasions his accounts of himself as a worker are woven into narratives in which — sometimes humorously, and sometimes in an active process of reflection upon his situation — he tries to reconnect the closed system of the hospital environment, and thus the closed system of the self as a component of that environment, with other social forms and practices and thus with enlarged forms of participation in social life. So, for example, he would draw me into debates over whether the institution in which we met was a farm, a college, or a hospital:

Joseph: We thought it was a college when we first got here. Next we thought it was a farm. Then we thought it was a hospital. Then we thought it was a farm again.

Now he thinks it is a college, and a college that, in Joseph's characterization of it, seems to resemble one of Foucault's disciplinary or corrective environments:

Joseph: It looks more like a college to me than anything — the OT and the group work and that — it looks more like a college than anything to me, a very old-fashioned college like.

On the view of the institution as a farm Joseph generally works on the land, but sometimes the farm comes to serve a veterinary function:

Joseph: I see this place as working overtime to look after animals, sick animals. The cows are the worst of the lot. Part of my job is to look after the animals.

Where in a narrative history of labour Joseph attempts to establish a meaningful part for himself within a community of endeavour, he also seeks to repair the conflicts and ruptures in a personal history and to find in a narrative history of his relations with his mother and his sisters the means both to protect himself from isolation or from 'getting lost', and to fend against the threat (to use his own words) of 'adverse weather conditions' which might throw him off course. Not long after his final admission to hospital, during a period when he sometimes still went home on leave, he wrote to his consultant to complain that his father

has a terrible temper at times and we wish he would leave home. When my mother and I are together we talk and chat about politics, my sisters' children etc.

(i) He loses his temper

(ii) He is football crazy. Honestly, sitting watching TV showing men kick a bit of leather around for hours!

(iii) When I am listening to records he takes the plug out and insists that the TV is put on.

(iv) He cannot cook and is utterly dependent on mother and I to solve his problems.

(v) He loves slot-machines and saves a fortune to go to Blackpool to play pin-ball etc.

(vi) One cannot seem to have any conversation with him at all. Honestly, at times I am pleased to get back here when I have been on leave.

All I want is for you to bring my mother into here so that she will have to get her tablets taken and to get her back on her diet.

Not unreasonably, the consultant could find no grounds to comply with this request. Three years later when I worked with him, however, he would sometimes announce that the 'weather conditions' were now very bad — it had become 'much too hot' for example — and he had therefore made arrangements for his mother, and sometimes his sister, to be brought into hospital. His mother, so he would tell me, 'makes tea and does a bit of secretarial work, not too much, mostly making the tea all the time for the doctors and things like that'. 'My mother's all right you know', he went on to say on one occasion, 'she used to go to the art classes with me.' It is apparent from what he says that it is now very much for Joseph's protection rather than for the sake of her own health his mother has come into hospital in that: 'One of her jobs is to make sure I don't wander off. Wherever I work she is.' Worries about loss or 'getting lost' seem to have been a constant feature of his passage through life and are never far from his mind. In his childhood, so he told me, his mother was prone to 'wander off' and she therefore had on her finger 'a large ring which wouldn't come off, tied to a mile of guitar string so she could only walk a short way'.

'Adverse weather conditions'

Sometimes, however, the 'adverse weather conditions' prove too severe and Joseph finds himself propelled off course into a solitary and painful engagement with hostile elements. In its most crucial aspects we may think of this as the engagement with the problem of life not as personal or social chronicle but as biology — 'life itself'. Health, whether considered in its 'mental' or its 'physical' aspect, is a psychological phenomenon: selfhood, as Winnicott describes, involves 'psyche-soma continuity of being' where 'psyche' means 'the imaginative elaboration of somatic parts, feelings and functions, that is, of physical aliveness'.[8] In the sorts of predicaments that concern us here, by contrast, the individual comes to experience physical aliveness as a formidable source of threat that is to be imaginatively resisted, and to feel that he has been taken out of his element. As Joseph puts it (B178):

Joseph: We're living on a world where you're not sort of accustomed to living.

The problem of how human beings are to think of themselves as natural beings, and thus return answers to questions of the type 'Of what story or stories do we find ourselves part?' that include reference to their individual natures, and to their part in the drama of nature, has proven historically extremely vexing. Certainly, one way to characterize the history of culture is as the history of a remarkable and persistent set of conflicts in ways of conceiving nature. And a brief digression into some of these inherited vocabularies may, therefore, help us to identify Joseph's meteorological preoccupations more securely.

Within one tradition of usage nature comes to mean the shaping force which directs human lives and within which culture unfolds; in a sharply opposed sense it is the 'state of rude nature' out of which culture has developed and which it has now transcended. In one view, nature is personified as a goddess, 'nature herself', in another it is an arbitrary, capricious and sometimes implacably hostile force that human beings can at best but seek to control. In the latter perspective the world of nature is set outside culture as irretrievably alien, a repository of forms of natural proclivity and expression which culture claims to have banished.

Perhaps the most powerful expression of the conflicts and tensions between these competing ways of conceiving nature is to be found in the conventions of Western dramatic tradition. Thus as Michael Long describes in a lively study, in Shakespeare's drama we find realized a 'tragic psychology of social life seen in its dramatic engagement with nature' in which there is continuous reference to the participation of social action 'in an energetic and manifold drama played out between the capacities of the human mind and the energies of the natural world'. In the festive comedies the interaction between the natural and social worlds serves to enhance social life, and 'social man' shows himself able 'to confront regions of dangerous volatility and then return to the social world nourished by the experience.' In the tragedies, by contrast, the capacity for engagement with the natural has gone awry and we are presented, 'again and again, with minds in fear of flux, chance and change, minds which close and grow brittle round a set of social values, minds for which the volatilities of unstructured experience hold terror, not release'. Such is the 'workaday world's hostility to the kinetic' that men become 'blind or inflexible, shutting off their consciousness from forces which are within and around them, closing their minds in hostility or fear until, at the worst, they are, as Hamlet puts it, "bounded in a nutshell" '. And when the nutshell cracks 'minds which are invaded and inundated by energies which disrupt and knowledge which bewilders sink below the level of their society's "normality" to find a volatile kinetic world of the destructive and the absurd, to which accommodation is nearly impossible.' In the festive comedies we are given the 'journey from law into release', in the tragedies its tragic counterpart in 'the journey from culture into trauma'.[9]

We cannot of course use late sixteenth century enactments of the problem of nature to explain how a late twentieth century psychotic patient such as Joseph comes to be in his present plight, but they can at least help us (and modish 'scientific' prohibitions notwithstanding, we ought not to be ashamed that they can so help us) identify the sort of predicament that it is and enable us to locate what are unequivocally delusionary and hallucinatory experiences against the background of a long-drawn cultural inquiry. For Joseph, in some of what he says, appears to enact a version of the journey into trauma, and to suffer the volatility and violence of a natural world devoid of healing powers not unlike that of *Macbeth* with its 'witches and mousing owls and crows making wing to rooky woods and horses eating one another'.[10] Such is the violence of horses, Joseph asserts, that 'there is only one way you can handle a horse, by putting it in a special cart. You can ride a horse but it's got to be encased in metal. The whole of the armour is the gearbox and you change gear with the sword.' Cows are gentle if rather inadequate creatures but nature treats them roughly: the meadows round about the hospital are lacking in grass and the cows 'can't find enough to fill their stomachs'. They cannot in any case get by in the natural world without tablets to support them, and 'when the tablets wear off they stop eating, sit down in the meadows and starve to death.' Cats, by contrast, are much more potent and a particular source of turbulence:

Joseph: It's a fact that what a cat does breeds cavemen. It roams all over the countryside taking semen from animals, carries them into houses, hypnotizes women and before you know where you're at a caveman is born, a demon from hell.

Cats are indestructible, you can shoot at them 'at point blank range and they'll still live'. 'While you're awake you have hallucinations, while you're asleep you have dreams. Know what causes the dreams? A cat comes into the room and digs its claws into you.' And then abruptly:

Joseph: There's a cat arrived in here. I can smell it, it may be in the kitchen. I know what colour it is as well — black, the worst kind. Cats stink.

Perhaps, a fellow inmate suggests, Joseph is merely *imagining* the cat:

Joseph: Well, I've moved away, I've prisoned myself up, I've done all sorts — there's a black cat followed me all my life. It was somebody who died, somebody had a cat and they died, and ever since it's been following us.

At points like these the powers of nature and the forms of human life have come to be set in irreconcilable conflict. The tolerable world that he had sought to sustain through the histories of labour and kin has now broken down and he finds himself invaded or threatened by alien elements. The interplay between separateness and union can only produce fearsome hybrids and hence he must cut himself off, prison himself up, or move away. Notions of viable human community, and of the co-operative continuity of human lives, come to lack point and the only description under which Joseph can bring his experience is of a condition of unremitting persecution and victimhood, of a relentless struggle against unintelligible dangers. And as we have seen in the 'Going outside' sequence (B), he then finds himself thrown back to those anguished primal questions from which we all set out on our journeys and from which, as Bettelheim described, fairy-tales offer a form of provisional deliverance: 'Some people say: "Where did we originally come from? Why are we here?" We're living on a world where you're not sort of accustomed to living.' (B177) And the answers that he returns to such questions are always in terms of the extreme precariousness of the human predicament. Thus we must perforce. live in an 'artificial environment':

Joseph: Ay, ay, at times you feel a revolt towards this, eh, idea of living under this environment, but you realize like that you would be dead if you didn't, you know, there would be nothing left of you, if you went outside.
Me: Outside of where?
Joseph: Outside the environment of the hospital and the place in the atmosphere in which you live. We're stuck here, aren't we? We must work here. We must clean the place up and keep it tidy. Otherwise any dust accumulating get into us. (B336)

The risk to life takes the form not only of 'muck and dust' but also of hostile objects such as 'bits of aeroplanes' some of which, he ponders, may be inside him.

An agent's capacity to order his life, or an episode in his life, into an intelligible narrative presupposes that he is able to recognize himself as playing a part in a dramatic frame for which the language of human action provides the appropriate form of description. Even a delusionary recognition of a non-existent part is, in this respect, better than no part at all. But suppose now that, from the vantage point of a given agent, the conditions of dramatic participation prove so treacherous that his hold on the dramatic frame in which he takes himself to be playing a part is undercut and that, in consequence, he comes to view such conditions not as a resource on which he can (and must) draw in order to negotiate his passage through life, but as a state of affairs to be repudiated. Such an agent has lost his conviction as to what it is to be part of, or to tell and make sense of, the story of a human life, and in his dealings with his fellow men will find himself in the painfully untenable position of an actor who is unable to leave the stage but can no longer render intelligible the dramatic action of which he is part. Just this appears to happen to Joseph in the 'Going outside' sequence (B) when the world of ordinary social intercourse comes to take on the aspect of 'another world or another planet', penetration into which will result in 'certain death'. At its most devastating there is no longer a story to be told but only a catastrophe to be demonstrated, a series of fragments to be gestured at:

Me: You said earlier on that there were bits of aeroplanes.
Joseph: Well, there is at times. At times you see there's one crashed you know. So you maybe just drive down the motorway ... like that ... that is a dome about that big, and make probably a full-sized aircraft and just stick it somewhere, you see. (B166)

In Joseph's account of domes we have a description not only of a particular set of defensive strategies, and of what it feels like to be in a condition where such strategies have become necessary for survival, but also of the consequences of adopting such a stance within life. For in seeking to rid himself of all that connects him most directly to the human action of which he is part, to sequester himself in an inviolable shelter, he rids himself also of his ability to make sense of his situation. At its most devastating he comes to suffer his experience of life as one might suffer an undifferentiated experience of bad weather. The alternative to devastation is retreat or refuge, but the resources for self-protection always prove inadequate to the task required of them. On an occasion when weather conditions on dry land had taken a sharp turn for the worse, he described how it had become impossible to work in the fields, even with a dome for shelter, and he had therefore moved to the coast to work on a farm under the sea.

Language was for Joseph always a form of unreliable weather and he complained repeatedly about the complications of meaning. The trouble with English, he says, is that there are 'so many misunderstandings'; Spanish, by contrast, is 'definite'.[11] When he was younger the *Concise Oxford Dictionary* had seemed to put meaning on to a secure footing and to promise the answer to everything: 'every word that has ever been written, and six different ways of spelling the same word, the name of every town and every person'. But then he discovered that people 'kept changing their names'. To try to stabilize matters he 'bought a book called *Who's Who*, but to little effect. At its most turbulent, language is felt to be active in a natural process that whilst it is enticing is also dangerous: he had, he once told me, been engaged in 'a very interesting project' that is 'all to do with language':

Joseph: All sorts of new words and phrases, poetry and bits of poetry, written in the ground like. Our farm produced poetry, novels, portraits and things like that. A very interesting project. Unfortunately almost ·everybody was taken ill and it hospitalized us all. I'm compiling a book on what happened! (laughs)

Perhaps the most startling — and shocking, for the suffering it evinced — example of how the story of his life ceased to be available to him as a potentially intelligible narrative (and thus also of his despair at his inability to produce such a narrative) is this:

Joseph: I can't dream. It's just like being in the Arctic. I can go to bed and I don't know a thing. Sometimes it's a week or a fortnight. All I can remember is a room in a hospital.
Me: Remember of what?
Joseph: Of my life. A room with beds in it. I was in this room that was all painted white and there were yellow beds and there was a little lass there. She was a nurse or something. I was in a room like, just sort of standing still.

Then he went on to say:

Joseph: I don't know what happened. I just woke, I just *dreamt* (said very quickly and almost inaudibly) I was in this room with white walls. That's all I can remember of my whole life. It's as if I've lived twice. One part of it I remember was all black and then all of the sudden I finished up in this little room with white walls.

> Somebody was living a terrible life and I don't know what kind of life it was.

The 'little room', it seems, is one of his lives and:

Joseph: The other of my lives is all black. That's the terrible life. It stuck in my memory all this horror, that was my father's life.
Me: Not your life then?
Joseph: It was somebody's life. I don't remember who. Somebody was leading a persecuted life.

Psychoanalysis and the action of the psychotic

To fill out our understanding of the sort of crisis of narrative participation that is involved here, and of how Joseph contends with that crisis, we need help from a more specialized vocabulary, one that has made it its business to identify the vicissitudes and strategems in the underlife of 'becoming'. Historically, the project of psychoanalysis has shown itself epistemologically extremely peculiar, not least in its adherence to those ideas about science (and thus also to mechanistic notions of mind and of selfhood) that we have inherited from the traditions of Descartes and Newton.[12] However, as Roy Schafer among others has argued, we do much better to conceive psychoanalysis as a narrative project that has as its aim the retelling of the tellings and showings of a human life within a co-ordinated account of the beginning, unfolding and ending of the narrative enterprise of lives. So long, therefore, as we do not take notions of mental mechanisms and the like literally, we can recover from psychoanalytic narrations a body of crucial insights into how the process of individuation is either sustained as a durable affair or permitted to fragment.

We may return briefly to our earlier discussion of the emergence of individuation in the writings of Winnicott and Lacan. As I interpreted them, Winnicott and Lacan try to give us a sense of what is involved at a very basic level of experience in moving from a condition of simplicity, in which whatever the extremes there is no story to be told, into the complications of a story, into a dramatic space of excitement and temptation and also of absence and loss, where conflicting desires encroach upon each other. The achievement of integration, or 'unit-status' in Winnicott's term, is one way to describe what happens when

the difficult and interdependent process of individuation works
well. But where there is a world to be found here there is also a
potentially viable form of selfhood to be lost or impinged upon.
So far as the entry into language and into dramatic narrative
produces a form of complication that jeopardizes the achievement
of a viable form of interdependence, the individual may, as we
noted earlier, find himself pushed back into isolation and the
fabrication of 'more and more defensive organization in repudiation
of environmental impingement'.

But what form of 'defensive organization'? At quite an early
stage in his writing Freud set about the task of defining a defence
mechanism specific to psychosis. Where in neurosis the ego
represses the incompatible idea, in the case of psychosis 'the
ego *rejects* (*verwirft*) the incompatible idea together with its
affect and behaves as if the idea had never occurred to the ego
at all.'[13] Thus where the neurotic represses the unacceptable
into the unconscious, the psychotic projects it in 'the form of
a literal and immediate expulsion into the external world'.[14]
There then ensues a form of disavowal (*verleugnung*) or radical
repudiation of reality in the sense that in breaking from an
incompatible idea that is in any case 'inseparably connected
with a piece of reality' and expelling it into the external world
the ego necessarily detaches itself 'wholly or in part from
reality'.[15]

Lacan uses the word 'forclusion' (in English foreclosure or
repudiation) to translate Freud's use of the term *verwerfung*
and to denote the process whereby a fundamental 'signifier'
(e.g. the phallus as signifier of the castration complex) is
expelled from the subject's symbolic universe. As Laplanche
and Pontalis describe in their critical dictionary:

> Foreclosure is deemed to be distinct from repression in
> two senses:
> (a) Foreclosed signifiers are not integrated into the subject's
> unconscious
> (b) They do not return 'from the inside' — they re-emerge
> rather, in 'the Real', particularly through the phenomenon
> of hallucination.

Foreclosure thus 'consists in not symbolizing what ought to
by symbolized (e.g. castration): it is a form of "symbolic
abolition" '.[16]

The psychotic, we may say, does not like what he finds. What he *finds* is an intersubjective human world, a complex psychological field in which, to borrow from various idioms, the subject must make his way and find his 'place' in a pre-established symbolic order; in which the psychological agencies that sustain participation in the human world on the only terms that it viably knows are menaced by dangers on various fronts and all the time engaged in trying to reconcile contradictory demands; and in which, as Joan Riviere describes, 'other persons are in fact parts of ourselves' and 'we ourselves similarly have, and have had, effects and influences, intended or not, on all others who have had an emotional relation to us, have loved us or hated us': a world, in short, in which 'we are members of each other.'[17] In certain kinds of psychotic states we thus find expressed an intolerance (or even hatred) not merely of a particular idea or set of ideas but of the process of 'becoming': a matter of 'not wishing to be' rather than of 'not wishing to know'. From this point of view, therefore, what the psychotic characteristically repudiates — what he *does* in response to what he *finds* — are the terms of participation that the human world ineluctably seems to offer. It is not so much that the psychotic turns *away* from reality, as is sometimes said, as that he turns *on* it. So, for example, the Kleinian psychoanalyst W.R. Bion tries in his writing to get us to understand that entry into the symbolic, into language in Lacan's sense, is painful and to describe both how a psychotic individual sometimes seeks to divest himself of that pain and also the (no less painful) consequences of such divestment.

Bion uses Melanie Klein's term *projective identification* to describe the expression of a violent hatred of internal and external reality: 'projective' in the sense of the 'ejection on to the outside world of something which the subject refuses in himself — the projection of what is bad', and 'identification' because 'it is the subject's self that is projected.'[18] Sometimes it is a matter of projecting into another person feelings and impulses that are too painful for the subject to bear. In these circumstances projective identification can be understood as a method of communication, an attempt by the subject to retain his hold within intersubjective reality. Sometimes, however, the process of repudiation is more drastic and entails the fragmentation, followed by the violent ejection into the outside world, of those parts of the personality — of the ego capacities — that serve to sustain participation in an intersubjectively meaningful human world.

Bion wants us to see that in ejecting particular complications of thought and feeling, the subject ejects also his *capacity* to organize meaning and thus to control the consequences of the original ejection. The expelled fragments of the personality are made to lodge in objects in the external world and in combining with these to engender what Bion terms 'bizarre objects'. The objects are 'bizarre' in the sense that from the standpoint of the subject they are neither features of some recognizable outer world nor identifiably expressions of a 'make-believe'. In other words the subject is painfully confused as to their status. But because the fabrication of these 'bizarre objects' so immediately issues out of emotional complications that are continuously reproduced for the subject within intersubjective reality, he cannot escape his connections with them. The subject thus comes to feel 'imprisoned in the state of mind he has achieved and unable to escape from it', a sense of imprisonment that is 'intensified by the menacing presence of the expelled fragments within whose planetary movements he is contained'.[19]

It is as though in this state of mind in seeking to put away his pain the subject has also put away from him all the resources that he needs for sustaining a viable form of participation in the symbolic. As Anthony Wilden describes, that is why in this dire strait the psychotic only perceives in terms of projection, in terms that is of a *refusal*.[20] But deal with the consequences of that refusal he must, because that is all that is left to him: the subject depends on the expelled particles of ego to try to form thoughts but, because these particles now circulate in an indeterminate space that is neither that of the mind and its creations nor that of real objects and their movements, he comes to lose hold of the distinction between 'ideas' and 'real objects' and to 'feel that words are the actual things they name'. One result is that the subject 'strives to use real objects as ideas and is baffled when they obey the laws of natural science and not those of mental functioning'.[21]

Largely because they are ensnared in the legacy of assumptions about the mind that we have discussed, the writings of psycho-analysts like Bion are less than satisfactory and sometimes downright perplexing, but for all of this they do, I believe, help to illuminate — particularly with regard to Joseph's own account of the fragments by which he feels himself to be menaced and surrounded in the 'dome' sequence — what on occasions (though by no means all of the time) seems to be happening with Joseph.

To put some of this in the terms of our earlier discussion, we can compare the predicament of someone like Joseph with the sort of philosopher or scientist who devotes his life to the unsuccessful search for an external vantage point from which to rebuild the system of beliefs or to conduct observations. Like Descartes, Joseph aspires to an ahistorical, self-endorsed form of consciousness and he asserts a distrust of language that would have impressed Locke and de Tracy. One way to characterize Joseph is as a thwarted cognitivist, a cognitivist who discovers that his theory of the interaction person—world, and of his own detachment from the world, continually breaks down. In the image that Otto Neurath used to describe the predicament of science and philosophy, our situation is akin to that of a sailor who must rebuild his boat at sea. Perhaps in time each part of the boat must be rebuilt, but at each stage enough of the boat must be left to keep it afloat. Joseph, however, in his rage at finding himself tossing in a boat on the sea starts to tear up the planks, and to beat the sea with them, as though somehow he could put an end to the interaction boat—sea and contrive a form of life that did not involve the predicament of boat-tossing-on-the-sea.[22]

Art and science

Yet for all that I have described here, Joseph, like many of his fellow inmates, never ceased to laugh. In these last sections I have discussed the bleak, solitary and — to a considerable extent — incoherent aspect of Joseph's predicament. But what needs to be said as well is that even when recounting the breakdown in the linkages with his fellow men, even when he appeared to suffer his immersion in conditions of community like an experience of bad weather, he none the less took an eager pleasure in the performance itself, in the to and fro of a communicative exchange: as though the linkages that were repeatedly and insistently repudiated and broken in the content of what he said were for ever renewed and repaired in the dramatic interplay of dialogue itself. People come to the hospital, Joseph says, for treatment:

Joseph: They come here full of muck and dust you know and things like that. ... They come here dead, they come here dead you know. (B361)

Listening to him we can never be sure — because he is himself
so unsure — of the difference between living and not-living.
A good deal of the time what he lives out is a struggle between
conflicting ideas (and thus impulses) about the sort of undertaking
that the living of a life can properly be taken to be. Characteristically
he represents the opposing poles about which his life moves in
the terms of *art* and *science*.

Nature, as we have seen, demands mastery and control. Union
can only unleash dreadful hybrids. Mastery and control is the
idiom of science in contrast to art; the life of art is worked out
in the 'interplay between separateness and union', between
'originality and the acceptance of tradition', but here the self is
exposed to possibilities of violation and theft. When he came
into the hospital, Joseph tells me, he threw his pen away. There
was, in his word, too much 'poaching' going on: people taking
ideas from other people and transforming them in their own
style. Much of the time, therefore, he opts for science and
punctuates his discourse with statements about tractors, cars,
aeroplanes, woodwork, metalwork etc. But it is obvious enough
that this is a disguised way of talking about growth, about the
vicissitudes of selfhood. Winnicott, we may recall, distinguished
between the individual who experiences a continuity in the line
of his existence and the individual who finds that he always
has to start again. The best thing for us, Joseph argues:

Joseph: is to start off on something simple, then gradually
           you work out something more complicated like a
           good quality car. I would recommend, if it was
           possible, for us to remain in the stage of tractors.

But even this more primitive stage of development presents
its complications for the last tractor he designed 'went a hundred
yards and dropped to bits':

Joseph: I couldn't believe it. We're right back to square one!
           We sort of get to a point where we could make
           something good and we go backwards you know.

When he first saw a psychiatrist:

Joseph: He said I was turning the whole thing towards science.
           Everything I drew out was really a design, you know,

that could be made. Instead of doing something like poetry or something like that. In other words I was losing me emotions. I was becoming too self-centred, too much science. I feel that now. I'm too much on the scientific side. Everything I draw out is made of metal or wood. It first started when I drew a model aircraft plan. Somebody pinched the plan and built a model aircraft to the plan and it worked!

And then after a pause:

Joseph: I was getting away from the modern idea of art which is more or less spirals, like wallpaper design. I was completely away from that altogether. I got to a point where I was leaving art behind.

Shortly afterwards he drew me a diagram in which ART was placed at the top of the page with the words 'home', 'peace', and 'oil paintings', and SCIENCE at the bottom with the words 'machinery', 'hospital' and 'place of horror'. Between the two domains ran a road on which he put his own name and under it the caption 'drive car myself'. The road thus provides the link between art and science, and travelling along it was once, so he said, a source of pleasure. A few months later he tells me that a journey in a car no longer gives him the sense of pleasure that it used to and that a car is now just a form of transport. So, for example, he could, he said, like me travel to the neighbouring town if he wanted to. But if he did go there he wouldn't know what to do. And if he went home there would only be trouble. Over the time that I knew him the road between home and hospital seemed to be invested with less and less hope. He was much preoccupied with roadbuilding but roads have now become impassable:

Joseph: Any type of practical work has had to be stopped apart from sitting on benches. You can't build a car because to put a vehicle on these roads would crack the roads and completely spoil them. Now the roads have gone and we all seem to be stuck on this desert island here.

'Roads', he goes on to say 'are the lifeline of the country. If you ever lose your roads you can manage like, but its difficult'.

Resisting demoralization

The problem for Joseph, then, is how to forge a viable stance in life within the interdependencies of separateness and union, agent and setting. The whole participative difficulty is perhaps most directly stated at B36 when he says of life on the ward:

Joseph: I don't know, you get to a point where you think 'oh, have I hurt his feelings or has he hurt my feelings?'

And we find it also in the oscillations of his relationship to the 'outside'. In one aspect the 'outside' is the social world of valued identities, in stark contrast to the degradations and constraints of the hospital environment. In this aspect the 'outside' represents the community – perhaps more notional than actual – that he wants to rejoin and he makes a point of distancing himself (and the other members of the group) from those people in the hospital who don't 'look on the outside' and 'just watch the messages from the world'. Yet in another aspect (as in his account of domes) the 'outside' is the life process itself against which he endeavours, unsuccessfully, to construct a carapace and against which the hospital (much though it exacerbates his demoralization in other respects) provides him with a form of material shelter.

We can come at the difficulty in another way and say that what he both enacted and sought to reconcile in his performances were two seemingly conflicting sets of narrative histories: a history of Joseph as a competent and efficient worker versus a history of Joseph as suffering from a severe mental illness; Joseph as a 'carer', someone capable of performing a caring role and making a valued contribution to the lives of others, versus Joseph as desperately in need of care; Joseph as autonomous and able to look after himself versus Joseph in need of help and direction; Joseph as the individual who discards all his tablets versus Joseph in search of a 'group of people who tell everybody else what to do'; and so on.

The conflict as a whole is perhaps most sharply brought out in the opposing conceptions of himself as a 'carer' and as 'cared for'. In the earlier discussion of his affirmation of his work identity we saw how an aspect of it – and it was one that he quite frequently returned to – concerned his responsibilities for the care of sick animals. It would, I think, be quite misleading to regard a 'delusion' such as this in isolation from other features of his situation, for what he most feared was to be totally defined by his illness, to be regarded by others — and to come to feel himself to be — an utterly useless person. Notions of himself as a 'carer' had, therefore, a very necessary function for him both as a means to give expression to his own deep-rooted and genuine concerns for others, but also as a counterbalance to notions of himself as a sick person; as though in striking the alternative he could contrive to sustain a conception of himself as someone who was indeed severely ill (as he recognized himself to be) and yet not wholly defined or taken over by it. Yet to work out such a stance within a single life, to draw these aspects together against the historical pressures — and their enactment in the present in his immediate structural location — that set them apart, was certainly a desperate and perhaps forlorn undertaking. An example of what he was trying to do is brought out in a poignant gesture of reciprocity when he surprised me by saying one morning that he would now like to do something in return for all I had done for him and that if, therefore, I had a sick animal that was in need of care perhaps I would like to bring it to him. On another occasion, at the end of a very long day in which I had come to feel that perhaps the turn of the century psychiatrists, with their beliefs in 'jerry-built brains', had been right after all, and must have looked visibly depressed, Joseph asked me after the meeting was over, and other members of the group had left, if he could write me a message 'to see what you can make of it'. This is what he wrote:

> A DOZEMEZE
> COMMANDANT
> OUR A VOIR
> Espaniola
> VOUS ET LE MOIR
> Joseph

Unhappily I was able to make rather little of it, but Joseph readily translated from what he said was Spanish and the message now read:

> Where are you bound for Commandant?
> Where are you going?
> Good bye.
> You are sick of the job.

It is, then, perhaps in the whole difficulty of working out a viable stance from within these various historical constraints — not only for Joseph but also for the other members of the group, for all of them in different ways were preoccupied, and sometimes perplexed, about the stories of which they found themselves a part — that we can recognize that what we encounter in these lives is always a form of participation in the social, a matter of people having to construct and negotiate their identities as best they can against the weight of a historically still active process of demoralization. In the case of someone like Joseph there is of course no suggestion that we can resolve all that he says and does into a fully coherent narrative history or make him out to be a rational agent when appraised on his own terms, but on the basis of our earlier discussions of human agency we can none the less judge him to be engaged in an enterprise which we recognize and with which we can identify, albeit that he sometimes carries it through in ways which we deem to be inadequate and on occasions irrational. And we can perhaps see also that we must bring schizophrenic people under this kind of account not as a secondary requirement against an account of a primary illness but as a precondition for being able to characterize adequately in what that illness consists.

The last occasion on which I saw Joseph was on a return visit to the hospital about other matters, and we had a brief and stilted conversation which went like this:

Me: So you're still on the locked ward then are you?
Joseph: Well, I use the telephone myself see.
Me: You what?
Joseph: I use the outside telephone.
Me: Well, they let you out do they?
Joseph: Well, I'm not supposed to be out but I use the outside telephone.
Me: Yes, so you can go out on your own for walks and that.
Joseph: Well, I take no notice of them, I just get on with my job.
Me: So that's good. So you're not locked up all the time.
Joseph: No. Officially I am, but I'm not.
Me: So you manage to get about then.
Joseph: I've got my own telephone like, you know.
Me: That's not so bad then.
Joseph: I've got it hidden away though.

Over a very brief interval Joseph's statement that he has access to the outside telephone (from which I took him to mean the public telephone in the hospital forecourt) is transformed into a declaration that he possesses his own telephone which is hidden away. As I understood it, he invoked the telephone in the first place to attempt to convey to me that appearances notwithstanding he managed to sustain some contact with the wider social world. Had I left it at that nothing further about telephones would perhaps have been said. Yet there was, I believe, something about my questioning that suggested to him that the credibility of his account of himself as someone who was able to contrive a relatively autonomous relation to the context of social action that included the public telephone — the telephone is in the forecourt, in order to reach it the patient must be able to leave the ward and walk to it etc. — was open to doubt. In order, therefore, for him to sustain his primary purpose of conveying an account of himself as a viable and socially connected agent, his solution was to remove the telephone from the public, and hence corrigible, context of action and to possess it for himself. But the sad truth of the matter is, of course, that in privatizing his relation to the telephone in discussion with me the telephone continued to figure publicly in another kind of action, the action of a language game, and Joseph therefore laid himself open to being discredited still further. Some years earlier, we will recall, he had predicted that he was 'heading for the life of a recluse, being valued at 7 and ½ pounds per calendar month'. The task of recovering a weightier sense of value for himself now seems to have become still more onerous, and it was on this occasion that he went on to tell me that weather conditions on dry land were intolerably grim and that he had presently therefore taken himself off to work on a farm under the sea.

6

Psychology, social life and the schizophrenic

Separateness and union

The scrutiny of the narrative enterprise of the life of someone like Joseph cannot, of course, tell us all that we should like to know about schizophrenic conditions; least of all can we extract from it an exhaustive theory of that particular form of human 'carry-on' that we have come to term schizophrenia. However, it can perhaps help to underscore the need for an approach to the action of schizophrenic lives that proceeds from a historically grounded understanding of human action. We now need to link the discussion in the previous chapters more directly with some of the questions that were raised in chapter 2 and with some current issues and debates.

Our task has been in one aspect to locate people like Joseph within a conception of the sort of undertaking that human living and understanding can be taken to be, in a second aspect to locate ourselves within that same conception. As we have seen, the sorts of concepts we require are ones that point us towards the interdependencies of action and structure, mind and environment, individual and setting, separateness and union. The most apposite way in which to express these interdependencies is, perhaps, through metaphor: Neurath's image of the sailor who has to repair his boat at sea helps to convey the predicament of someone like Joseph as much as that of science and philosophy. Various other metaphors have also been proposed to identify the same area of complication: so, for example, Norbert Elias uses the image of the 'mobile figurations of independent people on a dance floor'[1] to get us to understand that the object of our analysis is neither 'the individual' nor 'society', but a 'continuously repatterned social dance, the changing figurations of which are nothing but the dancers in action within the relationships of their dance'.[2] The image of the dance can take us so far, but Philip Abrams proposes an alternative to bring out more precisely the predicament of the individual within the historical production of social figurations. 'Dances', Abrams writes, 'after all are rule-governed as to both form and content. It would be only reasonable to say of an individual sitting eating an apple on a dance floor where others were doing the polka that he was not dancing.'[3] Much better, he suggests — and here we are reminded of Joseph once more — is to think of the human situation on the analogy of a game in which the only rule is that everyone is a player and must go on playing.

The boat tossing on the sea, the dancers weaving about on the dance floor, the player conscripted into a game from which he cannot escape: it is a long epistemological haul from all this activity to the traditional concept of the individual as 'encapsulated "inside" himself, severed from everything existing outside'.[4] This image articulates a particular cast on social relations, a particular view of what participation in social life amounts to; yet, as we have seen, scientifically it is deeply flawed. The notion of the mind acting on its own is at best true only for a certain kind of relation to the environment, for a scientific way of looking in which the scientist does self-consciously separate himself from his circumstances and surroundings. Though we celebrate this separation for rhetorical purposes it represents only a partial and occasional stance on life, and once we look closer at the action of lives we are brought to recognize that we need a different vocabulary for mind and consciousness, one that can steer a path between solipsism and subjectivism on the one hand and physicalism on the other — a vocabulary that is both biologically based and socially based, that can describe the relation to the environment not in the terms of physics but in terms that are appropriate to a given type of organism, to the 'moving animal' rather than to the 'metaphysics of presence'.

Cognitivism

The arguments that have been propounded for this way of thinking about the relation to the environment clearly mark off such an approach from the efforts of behaviourism and empiricism, but these same arguments also connect quite closely with some of the criticisms and misgivings that have been raised against the much-vaunted project of cognitivism. This is a matter of some importance, not least because attempts to frame the problem of schizophrenia in the terms of information processing, as a breakdown in the rule-governed interpretative processes acting on information received by the senses, have begun to acquire a good deal of currency. More generally, the attraction of cognitivism, in contrast to behaviourism and empiricism, is that it attempts to dig itself out of crippling notions of what a science of psychology ought to look like and to devote concerted attention to the vexed question of how the 'meaningful' and the 'intentional' are to be dealt with empirically. The concern with meaning notwithstanding, cognitivism none the less remains steeped in traditional assumptions about the separation of mind from environment, and it may be useful to look briefly at how this is so and to consider how these features of the cognitivist project may perhaps set limits on its attempts to arrive at a more precise specification of what is at issue in schizophrenic conditions. I shall begin by singling out a more obviously ideological aspect of the approach and then move to some remarks on a number of formal properties.

The familiar picture of the individual set against the environment and fending off hostile forces is nicely reproduced in the following quotation from an early study of disorders of perception in schizophrenia in this tradition. Perception, the writers tell us, is

> finally stabilized by our capacity to modify the incoming pattern of stimulation to provide a degree of perceptual constancy. .... By such processes we reduce, organize and interpret the otherwise chaotic flow of information reaching consciousness to a limited number of differentiated, stable and meaningful percepts from which our reality is constructed.[5]

More recently Frith (among others) has enlarged upon this line of inquiry and put forward a theory of schizophrenia as a breakdown in the selective capacity of consciousness, as a defect in the filter which controls and limits the contents of consciousness. On Frith's account:

The role of consciousness is that of a high-level executive system. Such an executive system must select one course of action from among many and then carry it out without hesitation or interruption unless the need for change becomes very strong. To achieve this aim there must be an unambiguous representation of the current situation and the desired goal. In addition, the system must have a certain amount of inertia so that a chosen course of action will not be abandoned simply because an alternative action seems momentarily more desirable.

As a precondition for the successful functioning of the corporation, the high-level executives of Consciousness Inc. are extremely intolerant both of ambiguity and of information which is not immediately relevant to the task in hand — indeed, of anything that might undercut the priority of the 'dominant action system' in the 'interpretation of perceptions and the selection of responses'.[6]

Now this is the self conceived on the model of some sort of multinational corporation, busily engaged in the narrow and single-minded task of servicing its expansive interests, scrutinizing the environment from on high for new pickings on which to settle, yet always fearful of usurpation by more cunning competitors. The parentage of this stance upon life we have already encountered in chapter 1 in the form of the promotion of the 'rationally' self-interested individual as the desired type for the advancement of the market system. Yet whilst this sort of thing may perhaps flatter the self-images of a certain breed of contemporary psychiatrists, happily there is, as we have seen, more to life that the definitions of it offered by the terms of the market, and certainly we should not be misled into supposing that this kind of account yields anything that is intrinsic to the enterprise of human lives. Rather than accord it any special scientific status, we perhaps do better to view it as the sort of theory that might be developed by someone who was especially fearful of the interdependency of self and world as a defence or protection against a schizophrenic illness.

We can come at the more formal difficulties by looking at cognitivist assumptions about the nature of human understanding. The preconditions for studying people as information processing systems (IPSs) is that they can justly be assumed to be intentional black boxes (IBBs) who in their attempts to understand the phenomena that the world throws up work through a rule-governed interpretative process. But it is just here that the cognitivist account of the meaningful, and of what understanding amounts to, gets into difficulty; for, as John Haugeland describes in a spirited exposition and critique of the cognitivist project, 'understanding pertains not primarily to symbols or rules for manipulating them, but to the world and to living in it.' Cases in which people do 'explicitly and deliberately work through a rationale' and where understanding is just a matter of manipulating symbols (or where we might be able to claim that it is) are, Haugeland suggests, both peculiar and parasitic:

> Paradigms of understanding are rather our everyday insights into friends and loved ones, our sensitive appreciation of stories and dramas, our intelligent handling of paraphernalia and commerce. It is far from clear that these are governed by fully explicable rules at all. Our talk of them is sensible just because we understand what we are talking about, and not because the talk itself exhibits some formal regularities.[7]

Cognitivism aims to cut through the ambiguity of natural language as to permit an exclusive trade in quasi-linguistic representations of inputs and outputs and its pedigree is in this respect 'coeval with that of clear and distinct ideas': to be intelligent, on this view, 'is to be able to manipulate (according to rational rules) "clear and distinct" quasi-linguistic representations'.[8] Yet as emerged from our earlier discussion, and as a number of contributors to the debate about cognitivism have argued, the irritating ambiguity of natural language is not a dispensable feature but is deeply and irrevocably tied to the 'complexly embedded characteristics of ordinary human life'.[9] The meaning of what people say cannot therefore be recovered from a holistic semantic scheme that assigns interpretations to utterances independently of their specific contexts, no matter how detailed and refined that scheme may be. So, for example, Charles Taylor identifies the problem of context by pointing to the important role in human understanding played by what he terms 'the implicit grasp of a domain', the agent's coming-to-grasp of a situation from within as it is lived. The cognitivist theory of meaning, by contrast, is an external one that presupposes the identification of recognizable patterns, and it is, as Taylor remarks, very much the kind of account of meaning that 'might be developed by an outside observer who never entered into communication with the beings whose language he was trying to map'.[10]

It is, then, doubtful whether cognitivism is conceptually equipped to deal with the complex interpretative burden that is borne uniquely by human agents in living in the world. As MacIntyre describes, in the 'ascription of actions and passions to others' agents always 'in an important way go beyond the evidence provided by the bare observation of behaviour',[11] and thus in consequence 'at the level of characterization which enables us to respond to the actions of others — that is, at the level of characterization which makes all social transactions possible — we are inevitably engaged in a task of theoretical interpretation.'[12]

The notion of the ordinary agent as a 'theorist' is a useful one, but we should not be misled into supposing that a theory (or schema or map) is something that he 'has' in the way that one may be said to possess an object. A theory or a schema may sometimes be taken as an object for reflection, but more generally we need to think of theories and schemata as embedded in the cycle of interaction between agent and social world and thus as subject to modification and development by movement through the world.[13] As we discussed earlier, we can think of 'the individual' as a process of individuation that is thrown up by (and participates within, and acts upon) a pre-existing social world, as in a sense an interpretative process within an interpretative process; and 'where there has to be interpretation, there always arises the possibility of rival, incompatible interpretations', hence 'a good deal of social life is constituted by the coexistence and sometimes the conflict of such interpretations.'[14] From this point of view difficulties of orientation within a social field reside not so much 'in' a mechanism as in a movement, in a structure-in-action. The language of mechanisms, Ulric Neisser has suggested, has generated unhelpful fictions of mind and consciousness not as 'an aspect of activity', but rather as an 'independently definable mechanism' or processing stage, a 'switching center on the intrapsychic railway'.[15] So, for example, in keeping with the concept of the self-possessed individual, fictions of 'filter mechanisms' are related to fictions of the 'singleness of consciousness', the idea that one can only be consciously aware of one thing at a time. But, as Neisser comments, 'the very notion of a "single thing" is far from clear: how many things am I aware of when I listen to an orchestra, watch a ballet, drive a car, make love?'[16]

Cognitivism is perhaps, like behaviourism, another case of an imposter paradigm in psychology, a paradigm that is to say that has been worked up in a non-human sphere of study and only secondarily applied to human beings — a product, as one critic has it, of 'the incoherent dream dictated by the demands of giving a scientific account of meaningful behaviour',[17] of discovering the means to get outside the historical embedding of human lives. The argument is not, of course, that the cognitivist project has nothing to teach us, and the whole question of what it can achieve is far from settled. None the less it may well be that in the case of a disorder like schizophrenia it is unable to give us the sort of specification of what is going on that we need, and that we will do better to think of schizophrenia not so much as a cognitive disorder but as a crisis of interdependency or as a form of panic within the matrix of participation in human life.[18] None of this is of course to suggest that Joseph and others like him are not instances of a biological type which finds the interpretation and understanding of human life peculiarly difficult, but any attempt to develop this line of argument must proceed from an adequate characterization of what such interpretation and understanding involves. Otherwise, as we have seen, we risk isolating the schizophrenic in a sphere of functioning that is wholly disconnected from the enterprise of living that the rest of us are engaged in. As Haugeland rightly remarks, the sorts of capacities for understanding and making out within human life that we have described must all of them be physically instantiated, but we may require a very different account from that which cognitivism offers to grasp how this is so.

But what, in its own terms, we have also to ask, would it be for cognitivism to show us that there is something quirky about how the schizophrenic's mind works, about the way in which he processes information? It is, after all, a very plausible hypothesis; yet, as Rorty argues, we have to defend against the temptation to reproduce in the contemporary project of cognitive psychology the sorts of assumptions and aspirations that informed the Cartesian tradition in philosophy. The Cartesians believed that the 'difference between the man whose beliefs were true and the man whose beliefs were false was a matter of "how their minds worked".' To put this view in contemporary terms would 'amount to the assumption that "truth-generating mental processes" were natural kinds in psychological theory', that knowledge of the internal code, of the internal 'language of thought', would enable us to find truth and falsity, rationality and irrationality or whatever written into the mind.[19] There may indeed be important differences between how people's minds work, and the identification of the processes involved may in a particular instance provide an explanation of how a subject came to hold the beliefs he did. It is quite another thing, however, to proceed from here to use such an explanation in the service of justification of a particular belief or set of beliefs. As Rorty describes:

> Explanation may be private, in the sense that, for all we know or care, psychological quirks might make yellow men or red-haired men process information in quite different languages and by quite different methods than do white men, web-footed men, or whatever. But justification is public, in the sense that dispute between these various people about what to believe will probably make no reference to how their quirky minds work, nor should it.[20]

Now in the case of schizophrenic people we do of course judge that there is that about the way in which they feel and think about the world that marks them off from the sphere of dispute between red-haired and web-footed men or whoever. But following our earlier discussion, the justification for our concern about schizophrenic people neither requires nor entails any assumptions about 'how the schizophrenic's mind works': it partakes rather of judgements that we make about each other (about suffering, for example) from within the narrative enterprise of human lives. We may be able to learn something definitive about how the schizophrenic's mind works, or again we may not. The justification for singling out schizophrenia as a special category of aberration does not depend upon this support; similarly, so far as we are able to acquire it whilst statements of the order 'he is saying this because there is something quirky about how his mind works' may come to play a useful role (e.g. where we cannot cope any longer in any other language), the role they play must always be a contestable one — in need, that is, of justification in terms that do not refer to 'how the schizophrenic's mind works'. Though we may sometimes have recourse to them in this way, we are mistaken if we think that we can legitimately assimilate the schizophrenic person in his several aspects into statements about 'how his mind works' and treat these as a means to escape from the difficult and precarious business of agents trying to understand one another. As that redoubtable philosopher Michael Oakeshott puts it:

> In virtue of an agent being a reflective consciousness, his actions and utterances are the outcomes of what he understands his situation to be, and . . . this understanding cannot be 'reduced' to a component of a genetic, a biochemical, a psychological or any other process, or to a consequence of any causal condition.[21]

The contribution of Manfred Bleuler

Finally, it may be useful to link these arguments about the interdependencies of self and world as they bear upon our understanding of schizophrenia with our discussion of Manfred Bleuler's writings; for, interestingly, an important part of Bleuler's concern is to forge a concept of schizophrenic illness not as a discrete and encapsulated aberration but as 'staged in the same general spheres of life where the neuroses are formed, and in which the human personality is shaped in a constant interplay between hereditary developmental tendencies and environmental experience'.[22]

We should not, Bleuler argues, assume that somatic disorders are the prerequisites of schizophrenic forms of illness. As he makes plain:

> We must reconcile ourselves to the fact that our colloquial speech contains the same expressions for two different concepts about somatic and organic factors: the narrow concept, of calling somatic and organic only that which appears perceptibly as a physiological manifestation, and the other, more extensive concept, that takes its place above the imaginary world of dualism and does not concern itself with the criterion of sensual perceptibility of what is physical.[23]

A very common and dangerous error, he goes on to say, 'lies in the practice of postulating tangible anatomic or physiological changes from mere philosophical deductions, while the philosophical deductions actually apply only to the fundamental identity of the essentials in the nature of the somatic and the psychic'; in other words, 'everything that is schizophrenic, together with everything that is functional, may be somehow identical to somatic processes'. However, we should not assume from this that demonstrable somatic disorders are a necessary prerequisite for the schizophrenias: it may well be the case that their genesis 'manifests itself in processes that, like most of the normal psychological processes, do not perceptibly reveal any somatic correlates'.[24] Research into the somatic basis of schizophrenia is no less urgent than it was in the past, however:

> Today we must learn to count seriously on the other possibility, that somatic correlates of the schizophrenias will never be detected because they escape detection by the senses in a way similar to the way the somatic correlates of mental processes and of the differentiated human emotional processes do.[25]

Further confirmation of the need to think interactively in terms of the embedding of schizophrenic lives within history comes, as we saw earlier, from Bleuler's critiques of the concepts of schizophrenic deterioration and dementia. What even severe schizophrenic states indicate, Bleuler argues, is not an 'internal destructive process'[26] as is to be found in diffuse chronic atrophy of the brain but 'an autistic attitude on the part of the patient, as an aspect of his struggle with his environment'.[27] The essential difference between the two conditions

> lies specifically in the fact that with skilful, indulgent and prolonged association with the schizophrenic dement, one always encounters indications of intact intellectual capacity and normal, healthy emotional impulses; whereas, by contrast, the organic dement has become permanently incapacitated . . . and is forever impoverished in his imaginary world.[28]

Moreover, the old concept of dementia is refuted 'by the findings that the patient's attitude towards his environment is reflected in his dementia, and the conditions of "dements" do, in fact, often improve and are not necessarily always final.' Thus:

> Every clinician who knows and has treated schizophrenics over an extended period of time is fully aware that there

are no completely unchanging 'end states' that last for years. It is one of the most highly emotional, dramatic experiences in the daily routine of a psychiatric clinic, to sense again and again that even the apparently dullest, most rigid, inert schizophrenics are internally alive and somehow developing.[29]

But then against this:

It is also an inherent part of the daily life of the clinician to suffer with disturbing frequency the disappointment of seeing such promising signs of an improvement and inner life vanish. Suddenly the patient begins to revile his doctor again, delusively, incoherently, without motivation, just when it was felt that a personal relationship had been established. Suddenly patients recede again into passive lethargy, just after they had been activated at the cost of monumental effort and patience.[30]

Yet patients learn to accommodate themselves to their illness:

Even though older schizophrenics seldom laugh, they do smile on occasions. After years of illness they can still discuss their symptoms in detail, banter them about as if they were nothing but one of their whimsical ideas, and then adapt themselves in keeping with the effect of all this on the conversational partner. One patient remarked with regard to his symptoms: 'It was partly my own choice, and partly it was repugnant to me.' Schizophrenics learn no longer to live in the world of delusions, but to live with it; they no longer allow themselves to be driven my madness, but they work through it as part of themselves, in shaping their own will and manner of living, by considering and applying normal, healthy traits of human behaviour.[31]

Bleuler's understanding of the absence of activity and personal initiative found amongst some improved schizophrenics whose active psychotic symptoms have disappeared is perhaps brought out most sharply in the contrast he draws between his own conception and that of the Swiss psychiatrist Gert Huber. Huber, he writes, 'is inclined to compare the impoverished personality after a schizophrenic psychosis with the condition after psychosurgery or localized cerebral diseases. I should prefer to compare it with the impoverished personality after long-standing frustration in a concentration camp or after an uneventful, unsatisfactory life during which the person's talents and abilities had no occasion to develop.'[32] And elsewhere he writes:

> Obviously, numerous schizophrenics are passive and give little evidence of activity, particularly little activity that is goal directed and aimed at the successful accomplishment of a meaningful task. But let us not forget that the schizophrenic's activity is artificially inhibited. Years ago he was shackled, strapped to his bed, or isolated. Today, the entire pressure of social therapy and pharmacotherapy with psychotropic drugs and neuroleptics works out towards the same end. For this reason it may be said that the adynamia of the schizophrenic can be interpreted as a result of a partially successful therapeutic effort. Perhaps schizophrenics are not adynamic because their brains are atrophied but because their dynamics are directed towards pathological behaviour and we are able to suppress such behaviour extensively, as we must. At any rate, it is certain that behind the adynamia of the schizophrenic, there is always in evidence a rich, active inner life; behind the adynamia of the demented organic brain patient, however, this is not the case.[33]

Bleuler recognizes clearly that the type of chronic schizophrenic that we inherited from the last century together with the theory of schizophrenia as a progressively deteriorating condition is still with us today. The theory has 'outlived its blossom', yet

> now, as then, it exerts its paralysing influence on therapeutic initiative, and in its own secretive way promotes hopelessness and resignation among doctors, nurses, families and among patients themselves. The theory still holds sway in wide circles of the population and administrative jurisdictions, suggesting the idea that only those funds should be spent on the insane that are left over after facilities for general patients have been adequately equipped. This concept, that the schizophrenias are irrevocable processes that lead to idiocy, does agree rather neatly with the interpretation of schizophrenia as brain processes and chronic metabolic diseases from 'inborn errors of metabolism'. Hypotheses in this vein, however, are most difficult to reconcile with the fact that, on the average, the schizophrenias do not by any means necessarily take a chronic-progressive course, and that in many cases schizophrenics can still change,

improve and occasionally even recover years and decades
after onset.[34]

Bleuler and the social sciences

Bleuler thus helps us to fathom the cultural unwillingness to
allow the credibility of a more intricate and complex interweaving
between schizophrenic and 'normal' forms of life. He has worked
in relative isolation but we can see how, unawares, he arrives at
formulations and conclusions that are in keeping with much of
what theorists of the human sciences have been arguing in recent
years. His intellectual struggle is twofold: first to try to understand
his patients, to fashion a satisfactory language for discussing
these strange and perturbing modes of existence; and second,
and equally important, to contend with the problems of an
intellectual legacy, with the plethora of dogma and mistaken
biases in which the lives of schizophrenic people have become
entangled. At points in his writing he debates with himself
whether he is not half clinician and half scientist, not fully
reconciled to his purposes. But this is a customary idiom, and
we should see in Bleuler's repeated conflicts of adjustment and
presentation not a set of personal foibles but the attempt to
sort out what a scientific assay on this field can achieve. These
are not sundered voices, they are both of them the expressions
and equivocations of a scientist debating with himself and his
material over what is to be said and how, and in his work
Bleuler provides us, through the imaginative effort of a single
scientist, with a conception of what scientific study in this field
ought to look like.

Most of all, perhaps, he succeeds in giving substance to a
conception of the schizophrenic person not as someone 'who
has become unintelligible in his thinking and feeling and in
principle a creature different from ourselves', but 'as a brother
whom we can judge according to our own nature'.[35] The treatment
methods that have 'proved their worth with schizophrenics',
he writes, are those that 'consist of emphasizing the distinction
between "I" and "we", and between "you" and "all-of-you"
in an active communal relationship'.[36] And to the wider questions
of schizophrenia and community, of the difficulties involved in
sustaining schizophrenic people within social life in our type of
society, and of the continuing attraction in this regard of ideologies
of schizophrenic deterioration, we must now turn.

Part III

Schizophrenia, Community and Welfare

7

The problem of community

The formal legal framework of modern democratic societies is the guardian of the abstract individual. It provides for formal equality (before the law) and formal freedom (from illegal or arbitrary treatment). These are critical and indispensable gains but, if we are to take equality and liberty seriously, they must be transcended. And that can only be achieved on the basis of a view of unabstracted individuals in their concrete, social specificity, who in virtue of being persons, all require to be treated and to live in a social order which treats them as possessing dignity, as capable of exercising and increasing their autonomy, of engaging in valued activities within a private space, and of developing their several potentialities.

Stephen Lukes, *Individualism*, pp. 152–53

Inequality in the various aspects of man is inevitable and even welcome; it is the basis of any rich and complex life. The inequality that is evil is inequality which denies the essential equality of being. Such inequality, in any of its forms, in practice rejects, depersonalizes, degrades in grading, other human beings. On such a practice a structure of cruelty, exploitation, and the crippling of human energy is easily raised. . . . A common culture is not, at any level, an equal culture. Yet equality of being is always necessary to it, or common experience will not be valued. [In a common culture an individual who is successful in his work will not] think himself a better human being than a child, an old woman or a cripple, who may lack the criterion (itself inadequate) of useful service. The kind of respect for oneself and one's work, which is necessary to continue at all, is a different matter from a claim to inequality of being, such as would entitle one to deny or dominate the being of another.

Raymond Williams, *Culture and Society*, p. 305

'Community' and community

In entering upon the vexed questions of 'community' and 'community care' in relation to people who suffer (or have suffered) from a severe mental disorder, of one thing we need to be clear at the outset: we will compound the confusion that already obtains around these matters if we persist in framing the central issue in the terms 'mental hospital' versus 'community'. The symbolic hold of the asylum as a site of degradation and exclusion is certainly a very powerful one, but we have only to set the opposition 'mental hospital'—'community' within the context of the opposing conditions of 'exclusion from moral community' versus 'inclusion within moral community' to recognize that community conceived as a mere *site*, without reference to the forms of social relationship that are embodied there and to the constraints on those relationships, certainly offers no guarantee whatsoever of any improvement in the form and quality of our moral relationships with psychiatric patients. We can put this argument more forcefully if we recall that the type of the chronic schizophrenic was prepared for not by the institution of the asylum but under the specific historical conditions in the late nineteenth century of social life dominated by the celebration of the market system. Permanent sequestration in an asylum together with the scientific promotion of schizophrenia as a naturally deteriorating disease did, of course, serve to ratify and confirm the image of a vulnerable class of people as devoid of social value. However, we err if we suppose that administrative changes in the form of the transfer of those people from one category of sites to another necessarily indicate a deeper social change in the terms on which such people are to be regarded and permitted to participate in social life.

On a pessimistic reading of the role of the state in relation to conditions of life dominated by the workings of the market, we can say that what counts is not the transition from a condition of degradation and disregard to a condition of enhanced participation and respect (the state cares not one jot for this in itself), but the transfer from a cost-intensive site to a low-cost site, from an administratively constructed site in which care is provided by specialized personnel under state auspices to sites located within the milieux of everyday life in which, to a greater or lesser extent, individuals (and their families) have, depending on their class positions, to make shift for themselves within the constraints of the subsistence existence available to those deemed 'unemployable'. Within this scheme of things, therefore, social policy will be directed by the essential criterion of economy of location, and whilst under some circumstances this may be mixed with other considerations and perceptions of longer-term gains as to permit a strong (if narrowly conceived) role for official services, such services cannot assume security of tenure within the social order and are always at risk of being judged dispensable.

But if economy of location provides the motive force, the ideological representation of what is being done is likely to borrow from the moral vocabulary of a very different type of society. For as John Dunn astutely remarks, there 'never has been and there never could have been a conception of capitalist society which both acknowledged in their entirety its factual properties in any instance and presented it as a morally rational order.'[1] That is why, despite the historically attested role of the capitalist mode of production in the destruction of moral community, in 'the genesis of modern individualism and the radically instrumental conception of community which this implies' as an incidental convenience to be played for what could be got out of it, 'community' should be proffered as a substitute term of social organization to conjure a communal framework which exists only very partially and residually in social reality.[2] Contrary to what the conditions of life ruled by the workings of the market will permit, the transition from hospital to community is represented as though it involved a transformation not only of location but also of value. For those in whom market moralities combine easily with, in Dunn's phrase, a mood of 'facile eudaemonism', such contradictions provide not grounds for disquiet but plentiful opportunities for exploitation. However to the extent that there exist social groups for whom notions of community are still a genuine focus of moral aspiration, the physical passage from hospital to community may come to be regarded as if in itself it possessed moral significance. Be they psychiatric patients themselves, professional workers or relatives, those groups for whom 'community' functions in this way as a term of anticipation and desire will find themselves deeply bewildered at how their vocabularies and expectations can have let them down so badly when in the historical present they are forced to recognize that they have now arrived at destination 'community' ('Is *this* "the community?" Is this where are are?').

But how accurate a depiction is this of our immediate historical situation? The historical origins of the project of community care in the 1950s are certainly ambiguous but, whatever the extent of the concern to remove the more hideous features of the nineteenth century institutional inheritance, notions of community care recommended themselves readily to a state beset by fiscal crisis, the more so because the recent availability of phenothiazines seemed to promise a technical solution to the problem of maintaining psychiatric patients within social life as a programme that could be carried through without incurring a heavy burden of expenditure or generating undue disturbance in social relationships.[3] What can be said with assurance is that in the intervening period successive governments have shown themselves markedly unwilling to engage seriously with the implications and consequences of community care policies. So, for example, nineteenth century scenarios have been re-enacted in the dereliction in the field of mental illness in particular, and chronic illness in general, of those sorts of conditions which respond only partially to intensive, short-term curative treatment and are instead in need of long-term support to maintain social viability and self-esteem in the sufferer and to prevent the slide from chronic illness into chronic status and chronicity.

At the widest level what is involved here is the assessment of the origins and consequences of the institutions of the welfare state in a society such as our own and the difficulty, amply brought out by the history of post-war reforms in Britain, of establishing, as Ramesh Mishra describes in a riposte to the social-democratic view of the welfare state as constituting a significant modification of capitalism, 'the values and institutions of public welfare even partially in a society whose "core" institutions remain capitalist'.[4] In the more specific case of the project of community psychiatric care we may say that the choice is between on the one hand the transition from an exclusively medical and custodial approach to the problem of mental disorder to the creation of what we may think of as a properly *welfare* approach to the mentally ill, and on the other the promotion of ideologies and policies of community care to erode the limited gains that have been achieved by the institutions of welfare in this field. Is the present period to be regarded as an opportunity to undo the malign consequences of a previous era, and thus to rethink and restructure the practices of welfare on terms that help to reassimilate the socially marginal into a communal framework, or is it to provide the occasion for the reproduction in a new guise of a settled disdain within capitalist society for the proclivities of schizophrenic and associated people, and for efforts to assert and carry through their claims for membership of community?

Whatever degree of scepticism one brings to the subject these questions are still open. However, it needs to be said that the disambiguation of the rhetoric of 'community' has not been helped by its ready assimilation within the terms of an encompassing liberal tradition that celebrates the 'communal' over against the bureaucratic and the institutional, as if formal liberties were themselves a guarantee of the transformation of abstract individuality into personhood, as if the space of 'community' was something other than the space of profound contradictions and conflicts in the justifying theories of Western societies between the ethical and the actual, between as C. B. MacPherson describes 'equal freedom to realize one's human powers and freedom of unlimited appropriation of others' powers, or between the maximization of powers in the ethical sense and the maximization of powers in the descriptive market sense'.[5] The idea that the emancipation of the chronic schizophrenic − a person 'alienated, empty, without initiative, isolated, without any rights'[6] − was to be achieved by the abolition of the asylum, by making the schizophrenic over to a receptive community that would confer upon him none of the noxious consequences that had befallen him under some asylum regimes. It is difficult to believe today that anyone ever supposed this to be a feasible programme and it was always, perhaps, the fantasy of liberal individualists driven by suspicions of structure and by a view of the individual 'as absolute natural proprietor of his own capacities, owing nothing to society for them'.[7]

Yet an idiom of community predicated on notions of self-possession and self-expression is perhaps least qualified to amend that lack of nexus which schizophrenic and other vulnerable people often experience. To view the problem of community critically, by contrast, is to recognize that the crucial issue concerns not only the physical distance between hospital and community, or the formal distance between incarceration and freedom of the subject, but the moral distance between schizophrenic people and the society of which they are part.

Physical separation is not self-evidently a factor in this assessment, and certainly physical proximity offers in itself no assurance that the terms of respect on which such moral assimilation depends will be forthcoming. Once we take the concept of community seriously in its connection with the concept of respect between persons, we can be helped to see that the agenda which is masked by much of the conventional rhetoric of community care is that of the structural and institutional forces which militate against equality of participation and respect for the more vulnerable members of society, and of the sorts of policies and practices that might be constructed in order (minimally) to enhance the terms of participation in social life for such people. Peter Sedgwick puts the requirements forcibly for people who have suffered a severe mental illness: 'how to create the economic means of employment, the material apparatus of housing, the ethical structures of fellowship and solidarity, for those who through various forms of mental disability cannot purchase these benefits as commodities in the marketplace'.[8]

A precondition for putting the hidden agenda of community care to work is that we are able to give an account of what respecting an individual as a *person* involves. As Steven Lake describes, 'the principle of respect for persons requires, among other things, that we regard and act towards individuals in their concrete specificity, that we take full account of their specific aims and purposes and of their own definitions of their (social) situations.'[9] Respecting individuals as persons thus involves understanding them in both their social and their individual aspects:

> For, on the one hand, such respect requires us to take account of them as social selves — moulded and constituted by their societies — whose achievement of, and potential for, autonomy, whose valued activities and involvements and whose potentialities are, in large part, socially determined and specific to their particular social contexts. On the other hand, it requires us to see each of them as an actually or potentially autonomous centre of choice (rather than a bundle composed of a certain range of wants, motives, purposes, interests etc.).[10]

We deny respect to someone when, for example,

> We fail to treat him as an agent and a chooser, as a self

from which actions and choices emanate, when we see him and consequently treat him not as a person but as merely the bearer of a title or the player of a role, or as merely a means of securing a certain end, or, worst of all, as merely an object or when we diminish, or restrict the opportunity to increase, his consciousness of his situation and his activities.

And finally, 'workers — and citizens in political society as a whole — are denied respect to the degree to which they are denied possibilities of real participation in the formulation and taking of major decisions affecting them.'[11]

In contending that the project of community care must adopt a critical bearing on the obstacles to the realization of respect between persons in our type of society, and thus on location not as an end in itself but as a means to the enhancement of value or respect, it may be useful to recall our discussions of Joseph. For, as I constructed it, Joseph's concern was to be helped to find the means to participate in social life on terms that took account of his need both for shelter or retreat (for asylum in the proper sense) and for recognition as a valued person who was as much capable of conferring care and consideration upon others (and of contributing to their well-being more generally) as he was in need of care himself, and whose desire overall was for a context of reciprocity of respect substantial enough to withstand the assaults inflicted upon it by the acknowledgement (from others, together with his own self-acknowledgement) of his tribulation, vulnerability and (on occasions) incapacity. His deepest preoccupation was thus with the sense of his own value, and from what he said it was plain that the question of how he might come to live a valued life (where and on what terms) was not to be settled by any amount of gesturing at 'the community' as he knew it.

The schizophrenic as fellow citizen

A commitment to community care involves us in looking at needs in a particular way, namely within a conception of the subject of care as a social agent or as a member of the community. So, for example, it requires of us that wherever possible the subject of care be taken seriously as an agent who holds views about the nature of his disability and about the forms of provision that benefit him, and who thus has a potential role to play both in his own care and in the determination of forms of care. More particularly, it asks of us that we attend both to the personal and social repercussions of forms of disability and of health problems, and to the interconnections within the action of a life between different components of need. The philosopher Ronald Dworkin expresses the core of these commitments when he tells us that: 'Government must treat those whom it governs with concern, that is as citizens capable of suffering and frustration, and with respect, that is as human beings who are capable of forming and acting on an intelligent conception of how their lives should be lived.'[12]

But what exactly are these rather abstract prescriptions to mean in the case of the schizophrenic person? Quite the strongest case for taking schizophrenic people seriously in their aspect as social beings comes, as we have already seen, from our knowledge of the nature of schizophrenic conditions. Whilst such conditions not infrequently bring with them a number of functional impairments, the course and the extent of social disablement that arises out of them are to a considerable degree amenable to social influence; as Wing describes, 'any idea of inevitable clinical deterioration, i.e. deficit remorselessly increasing over time, must be rejected.'[13] Wing's concept of 'secondary reaction' is of radical importance here in that it points us away from notions of a schizophrenic illness-in-itself and towards an understanding both of the enactment of the illness within a particular life history and of the interaction between life history and social context. An experience of severe illness necessarily involves the sufferer in an act of biographical reconstruction and in the redefinition of his life project, and the way in which he comes to so redefine his life, and his sense of what he is now capable of, will clearly depend very much on how his condition is defined and reacted to by others and on the terms of participation in social life that are available to him in the light of it.[14] Among schizophrenic people, loss of confidence in the viability and value of their life projects, and the reconstruction of themselves as useless, are as much as anything powerful determinants in the transformation of a potentially manageable disability into permanent social disablement and chronicity, and adverse secondary reactions like these are fuelled and aggravated by forms of contextual disadvantage such as unfavourable attitudes and expectations of others, lack of opportunity to practise social skills, isolation from everyday life and enforced pauperism.

Yet if we are now in possession of some extremely promising indications of what a concerted address to schizophrenic people in their aspect as social beings could in principle achieve in terms of maintaining social viability and value, the effort involved in doing so is formidable indeed. Stated in the most immediate terms, people with schizophrenic conditions not infrequently put the frames of everyday life under severe strain. Thus they may show scant regard for conventions of behaviour, exhibit peculiarities in conversational style, and demonstrate serious difficulties both in managing work routines and in forming and sustaining social relationships. Moreover, the manifestations of schizophrenic conditions are often deeply ambiguous and involve sharp breaks between different modes of behaviour: as a consequence the 'status' of the individual as a social agent, and thus the assumptions about the kinds of claims and demands that can be made of him, may be left unresolved or in tension, often over long periods. All these aspects render dealings with such people on the part of unspecialized agents in particular at times painful and perplexing, and efforts to maintain and enhance the participation of the individual within social life, and to prevent chronicity, are thus inevitably hazardous and painstaking.

Furthermore, we have to reckon with the awkward fact that, in attempting to shift the emphasis in our dealings with people who have been disadvantaged by schizophrenic illness from conceiving them primarily as patients to conceiving them primarily as social beings who, in common with other people, may for certain purposes need to be viewed in their 'patient' aspects, we have at the same time to recognize — not as a secondary matter but as part of what taking such people seriously as social beings involves — a spectrum of functioning ranging from severe mental disabilities at one extreme to independence within the context of an underlying vulnerability to further episodes of illness at the other. Whilst we should not think of any particular position on the spectrum as determinate, there are none the less, as Douglas Bennett and others have described, a body of people for whom long-term dependence on the institutions of welfare is — and is likely to continue to be — a dominant feature of their lives. But it is essential that, in recognizing as we must the constraints that are imposed by particular forms of disability, we do not then capitulate once more to the language of 'patienthood'; for it is perhaps precisely these most severely disabled — and not infrequently despondent — schizophrenic people who stand most in need of recognition and understanding in their aspect as social beings. As is apparent from what we now know about the role of secondary reactions, it is in respect of strategies that seek to enhance value — that fortify the individual's 'feeling of being trusted, esteemed and linked in a social nexus' — and social competence, and that build upon positive capacities, that effort is badly needed.

But what has then to be said is that our knowledge of the actions of schizophrenic lives in community as distinct from hospital settings, and thus of the difficulties that disadvantaged people of this type encounter in negotiating an existence within social life, is extremely limited. There has perhaps been a tendency to order thinking and practice in terms of the preparation of 'patients' for social agency frames at some point in the future, to the relative neglect of conceptions and practices that connect more directly with the difficulties and dilemmas of the actions of lives in community settings in the present. The promotion of various forms of self-care is a key component of community care policies and, the complexities notwithstanding, we need to learn much more about the extent to which people with severe mental disabilities might be involved more directly in their own care. Wing has in this respect made small but crucial beginnings in the elaboration of the sorts of strategies of self-help and personal control that people with schizophrenic conditions might be encouraged to develop,[15] but we still lack knowledge about the way in which the transmission of formal doctrines about 'schizophrenia' come to be incorporated into agents' self-understandings and to interact upon agents' own theories as to the nature of their conditions.

Yet the real difficulties in moving in this direction do perhaps run still deeper. For what we have also to contend with is the language (and thus a whole way of thinking and feeling) in which — formally and informally — we talk *about* the schizophrenic and speak *to* him, the space of a language that is necessarily also the space of a relationship, and the question then of our willingness to accommodate (where, and on what terms) the words of the schizophrenic person himself. 'The discovery of the independence and legitimacy of the client's point of view',

Abrams writes, 'may well prove the most revolutionary development in the whole field of social care since 1950.' In the field of mental illness, he goes on to say, 'it is clear that clients' views of the objects of care can differ drastically from those of therapists', yet 'the tendency of policy has been to accept therapists' accounts of need very easily', and we have therefore still to learn how to 'take into account, and assign a meaningful value to, the subjects' own views of what benefits them as well as those of various caring agents'.[16] We may think of the schizophrenic person as someone who has come back amongst us after a long absence to reclaim what formally we may agree to be his equal place in the community, but for whose return, and the claims it may make on us, we are in actuality not at all well prepared. He is still hedged about in the formal language of bureaucracy and, even by those who should know better, schizophrenic people in the large (and in particular working-class schizophrenics) are still represented as 'inarticulate', as if all the difficulties over meaning resided in the schizophrenic speaker and not in the historical field, and the terms of relationship it offers, in which schizophrenic and non-schizophrenic come to meet each other. The vocabularies and forms of knowledge we derive from the medical sciences are useful for certain purposes but not for others, and so far as we want not only to predict and control schizophrenic conditions in their clinical aspects but also to 'sympathize and associate with' schizophrenic people, 'to view them as fellow citizens', then we need to develop vocabularies and forms of knowledge that are suited to these tasks.[17] More is at stake here than the values of community care: to a considerable extent the successful realization of community care policies turns on our capacity to help clients with disabilities sustain their self-respect as social beings and play a role as agents in the management of their own disabilities.

The view from the relatives

If we are to take the schizophrenic person seriously, however, and endeavour to treat him with concern and respect, then it falls on us to accord just the same measure of concern and respect to the other members of the social field which he inhabits. In the early 1970s a new set of voices joined the

debate about the care of schizophrenic people in the community
— the relatives of people who had suffered a schizophrenic
illness. Previously kept from the door, or allowed only — usually
in ones and twos — into the doctor's surgery, they have forced
their way into the arena of public debate and influence and now
stand firmly in its midst, making their case with increasing
coherence and demanding to be heard.

Unlike other maladies, schizophrenia had never had a specialist
society of its own. From nineteenth century records we learn
of instances of pressure put by families on the medical profession:
pressure to incarcerate a relative or to seek redress for the
abysmal conditions in an asylum. But none of these adds up to
a collective effort. The site of meaningful public articulation
around madness was over a long period the hospital itself; the
hospital was a repository of these meanings as much as of
patients themselves, and to have lived at close quarters with
madness in the community was to be disconnected from
communal symbols. The family of the schizophrenic was, of
course, not unknown to those who maintained and serviced
the institutions of psychiatry, but the terms of the relationship
were hardly of the family's making. It had been talked about
and written about, but it had not been allowed to speak; or,
at least, so far as it did speak it was, wittingly or unwittingly,
to elaborate on the constellation of pathology around the
individual patient. At worst it was a representative of a form
of pathology. At best it was a nuisance, an administrative
hazard, upsetting the smooth running of the hospital, hovering
in a form of servitude on the whims and decisions of doctors
and other professionals, a moment here and a moment there;
with its plaintive, emotionally laden questions a threat, perhaps,
to the delicate balance between ignorance and the profession of
expertise. Never were the relatives treated as meaningful social
actors, with a claim to significant authority.

In May 1970 the father of a young chronic schizophrenic
wrote an article for *The Times* in which he described his son's
collapse:

My son succumbed to an alleged 'depression of adolescence'
in his second year at Oxbridge where he had gone with a
major open scholarship. He began cutting lectures and
tutorials, shutting himself off in his rooms, and avoiding
his friends. It did not occur to the college authorities that

his behaviour could be due to anything other than idleness. They neither sent him to a doctor nor told us, the parents, but first took his scholarship away; then, as that had no effect, sent him down — with 24 hours notice to us. They admitted afterwards that suicide notes had been found.

Ejected from the sphere of influence and achievement by the operation of a powerful set of categories, it is the family that must take the burden of the expulsion and thereby put itself at risk:

> A family suddenly faced with this situation has, in my experience, two problems, and it is hard to say which is worst. The first is how best to cope with the strange new member of the household whose moods alternate impossibly between sullen lying on his bed in the dark to wild fits of aggression, with social manners regressed to an almost animal level. The second problem is how to penetrate the obfuscating fog of hospital vagueness and evasiveness to obtain intelligible guidance on the first set of problems.

The articulations of specialized institutions provide little or no guidance as to how life is to be conducted within this area of proximate practicality:

> On almost any specific point on which advice was desperately needed — should he be persuaded to get up, dress, keep himself clean, encouraged to work or study or just be left alone, which course was best for him? — we grew used to receiving from the doctor weary platitudes about showing 'patience', or from the hospital 'welfare' side surprised counter-questions: 'Didn't you ask the doctor that?' Failure in co-ordination and communication seem to hang about the administrative management of schizophrenia almost like a grim parody of the condition itself.[18]

The writer's purpose in the original article was 'simply to ventilate some of the ways in which public understanding of the conditions and provision for it were lagging behind'. Such, however, was the response from other *Times* readers that it was decided to establish an association, the National Schizophrenia Fellowship (NSF) as it subsequently came to be known. The writer's account clearly enabled the elevation and transformation of a set of intractable private troubles into a public issue: 'How marvellous to hear of the formation of the Schizophrenia Fellow-ship', wrote one recruit, 'I want to jump on to my rooftop and shout out that I have schizophrenia in my family after 20 years' isolation.' From small beginnings the Fellowship has burgeoned: it now has groups in several parts of the country, has published a number of reports, sponsored research and forced itself upon the attention of government.

The field of concern to which they speak does, of course, reach across class boundaries, but for the most part these are vulnerable and articulate middle-class voices. Pushed by the pressure of day-to-day worry about a schizophrenic member of the household and by the conflicting and ambiguous responses that they receive from members of the community, the caring professions and govern-ment bodies alike, these relatives find themselves dragged from their settled and articulate positions within the social structure into a situation of guilt-ridden isolation and despair. The isolation is of course the dark underside of the family's structual position; what considered in one aspect is the successful entrepreneur freed from the bondage of structured contexts of social relations and able to make his way within industrial society as he pleases, looked at in another aspect is the loneliness of the destitute schizophrenic, severed from all contexts of communal obligation and support. The slide from Oxbridge into chronic schizophrenia and destitution: here we have a measure of the insecurity of the unpropertied middle classes themselves. In the following account a mother writes about the strains and dilemmas that she and her husband have had to face in relation to their schizophrenic daughter:

My husband is a scientist of — I suppose one can say — national eminence. He feels that the central question is: Does one sacrifice oneself and one's wife for the sake of the schizophrenic son or daughter? Looking after the patient or ex-patient at home will stop any work of a creative sort. We both feel that the end result for parents of our type and temperament would be our own breakdown. He thinks that ordinary life has severe enough strains for most people, and an additional strain of a schizophrenic child is almost more than one can take. . . . Whenever Ruth is at home he feels continually irritated by her lack of purpose and idleness, and has to hold himself in check. He says she is not the sort of person he would choose to spend time with, or make a friend of. He thinks a fundamental instinct is involved which causes both animals and human beings to peck the oddity, to rid themselves of the one who does not conform. He resents the effects this situation has had on me, the mother, and says that every time I visit Ruth or she comes home, you can scrub 2 or 3 days out of our lives, since it takes time to recover and time to prepare, all like being under a heavy cloud.[19]

If we look closely at the literature which the Fellowship has produced we notice that — largely in response to cultural pressures to assume the burden of responsibility for contortions of relationship within the family — it is the voices of the mothers of schizophrenic people which come through most strongly and strive to work out from a long history from which they were excluded but talked and written about by others, both directly in the imagery of the 'schizophrenogenic' mother and more obliquely in the imagery of schizophrenic families.

The achievement of the NSF over the past decade is indeed considerable. I suggested earlier that the transition to a policy of community care provides us with both the conditions and the requirements for new kinds of knowledge. And a new kind of knowledge is what the NSF has amply given us. Both in the accounts that they have produced of relatives' own experiences, and in the work that they have invited others to do on their behalf, we now have a rich documentation of the sorts of difficulties and dilemmas experienced by unspecialized agents in caring for and supporting people who have suffered a schizophrenic illness.[20] Most of all, perhaps, they have helped us to see that the dispersal of psychiatric patients into the community has not been matched by a dispersal of the burden of care, and that in many instances the burden of care has merely been transferred from a point of concentration in the psychiatric hospital to a point of concentration in the family. Community, as Philip Abrams has described, may variously be viewed as a *site* in which care is provided by specialized agents or as a *resource* in the provision of care by unspecialized agents. The achievement of the NSF has been to bring out the unwarranted and sometimes detrimental (both for schizophrenic people themselves *and* for those who live with them) pressures on a single site in which the resources of unspecialized agents have to a large extent been taken for granted. As Abrams remarks, in community care 'the care of some is the need of others.'[21] In one aspect, therefore, we are directed inward to ask what can be done to alleviate the pressures within the family; and in a second, outward to inquire into the scope for alternative care and support.

Looking on the outside

Some people in the hospital, Joseph recounted, 'just watch the messages from the world' by sitting in their chairs and gazing at the television; others like himself, in contrast, are 'always looking on the outside'. To understand just how difficult it is for people like Joseph to sustain a stance of 'looking on the outside' in settings in the community, and of the conflicting meanings that are attached to the 'outside', we may turn to some disquieting evidence produced by Jan Carter from a national inquiry into the operation of day services for the mentally ill and other client groups. In a graphic account Carter shows how problems of loss of self-respect, and of the marginalization of people with severe mental disabilities, may be reproduced ever as forcefully in day centres — though of course not only in day centres — located squarely in urban settings as they were in the distant psychiatric hospitals.

Thus only about one-third of users in units for the mentally ill sampled by the study had any plans, however vague, to occupy themselves after leaving the unit, and only an equally small proportion considered that 'anyone on the staff had talked to them at any time at all' about their future plans. Moreover only about one user in 20 considered that the unit had been of value in helping them in the conduct of their lives outside the temporal span of the unit. In respect of staff aims, 'internal' aims (where participation in the unit is to a large extent an end in itself) tended to predominate over 'external' aims (where the emphasis is on directing the user towards participation in the outside world). Sometimes the day unit itself was perceived as the 'outside world' by contrast with the psychiatric hospital, and images of the 'ideal user' were for the most part informed by notions of client docility. The semantics of 'external' aims like rehabilitation were found to be diffuse and perplexing: so, for example, rehabilitation was sometimes used as a synonym for chronic to characterize activities that have the function of 'filling in time'. In the case of 'outcome' the most common meaning was a return to 'a normal way of life', but 'normality as such was never defined nor was it refined by class, subculture or regional differences.'[22]

Carter aptly distinguishes between *time-bound* and *time-less* day units. In time-bound units the user is expected to adapt himself to the application of a burst of effort over a predetermined period and to gear himself for departure when his time is up. In time-less units, by contrast, routines are pursued for their own sake, the clock is disregarded and no plans are made for the user's future. Time-bound units, as Carter describes, 'mirror an attitude to time found in the marketplace. Time is inflexible, valuable and regulated entirely by the clock.' Practices of this sort are likely to entertain vague ideas of 'returning a mass of users to "normality", or to a mythical world where "work" will be available'.[23] The time-bound embodies the notion of labour power as a commodity, as the 'objectification of a given amount of labour time'.[24] 'Time', Marx wrote, 'is everything, man is nothing; he is at most the in-carnation of time. Quantity alone decides everything: hour for hour, day for day.'[25] The time-less, on the other hand, has as Carter remarks a good deal in common with the characteristics of bureaucracy. Thus 'inefficiency, lack of urgency and devotion to routine ensures the survival of the unit itself, not the users.'[26] Characteristic of both types of regime, however, is that they take for granted the definitions of value and 'useful service' that are set by the working of the market, and personalize the failings of those who either cannot or will not (the historical ambiguity between these two assessments persists) remedy their conditions through selling their labour on the market — in the one case in the promise of work roles for those prepared to give up their wayward habits and apply themselves hard enough, in the other in the diurnal storage (whilst the rest of society gets on with the main business) of the socially useless.

Wing and others have helped us to see that in understimulating or depressed environments schizophrenic people with severe disabilities tend very easily to lapse into withdrawal and inactivity. Thus patients in hospitals characterized by 'social poverty', and unemployed people at home, were found to spend hours of the day 'doing absolutely nothing' and (in the case of the patients living at home) 'even those who had some activity tended to adopt some ritual way of spending the time, for example, by brewing tea continuously or chain smoking.'[27] The problem of achieving an appropriate balance between social withdrawal and social over-involvement assumes a very specific form among schizophrenic people. However, if we are to avoid isolating the difficulties that such people experience simply as a function of their conditions, it is important at the same time that notions of 'doing nothing' or 'doing absolutely nothing' versus 'doing something', together with the question of chronic boredom, be viewed in a broader cultural context.

So, for example, John, a young working-class unemployed schizophrenic, recently discharged from hospital, sat at home all day, brewing tea and smoking, and playing records, and proving himself a great aggravation to his mother. He had two brothers, Duncan and Albert, a couple of years younger than him, both of them also unemployed, and it puzzled me that on the occasions when I visited John they were rarely to be seen about the house. According to sociologist Paul Corrigan they were to be found 'on the wet pavements of Wigan, Shepherds Bush and Sunderland'. The main activity in these venues is, in fact, 'doing nothing'. Thus:

What sort of things do you do with your mates?
Duncan: Just stand about talking about footy. About things.
Do you do anything else?
Duncan: Joke, lark about, carry on. Just what we feel like really.
What's that?
Duncan: Just doing things. Last Saturday someone started throwing bottles and we all got in.
What happened?
Duncan: Nothing really.

As Corrigan points out, 'doing nothing on the streets must be compared with the alternatives: for example knowing that nothing will happen with Mum and Dad in the front room; being almost certain that the youth club will be full of boredom.' John, in the meantime, sat at home in the front room, and one of the things that proved particularly perplexing and irritating to his parents is that he was given to uttering 'weird ideas'. However, it would appear that Duncan and Albert were given to something rather similar:

Do you ever go out and knock around with the lads?
Albert: Sometimes when I feel like it.
What do you do?
Albert: Sometimes we get into mischief.
Mischief?

Albert: Well, somebody gets a weird idea into their head and
           they start to carry it out and others join in.

'The weird ideas', Corrigan continues, 'are born out of boredom
and the expectation of future and continuing boredom, and this
affects the sort of weird ideas that they are.'[28] John, Duncan and
Albert are, then, all engaged in 'doing nothing' and throwing out
'weird ideas' in 'some ritual way of spending the time', with the
difference that one of them lives out his sense of futility in the
front room and the others on the street. There are of course other
differences between their behaviour that lead us to allocate them
to separate compartments of contemporary aberration, but it is
the differences between them that are usually stressed, and we
need to recognize the extent to which in their collective stance
upon life they all entertain a comparably bleak assessment of their
prospects of ever being permitted to 'do something'.

Dependants, casualties or participants?

The problem for the community care of those who have suffered a
severe mental illness resides, of course, not so much in any dearth
of good intentions among practitioners as in the obstacles that
stand in the way of their implementation.[29] Above all, perhaps,
efforts to enhance the terms on which the mentally ill are permitted
to participate in social life, and to take the problem of 'looking on
the outside' seriously, must reach beyond the perspectives and
procedures of the casualty model of welfare that is now on offer.
The rationale for this model is brought out in a recent discussion
by Raymond Illsley in which he recycles the historically soiled
vocabulary of 'dependency groups' and provides us with a listing
that includes the elderly; the mentally ill and handicapped;
patients suffering from strokes, heart conditions, rheumatoid
arthritis, diabetes, chronic bronchitis, alcoholism and any chronic
disabling handicap or disease; together with a number of non-
medical categories such as children in care, maladjusted and
delinquent young people, criminals, the chronically unemployed
and 'that wide category of individuals and families constantly
needing support or "correction" and known classically as problem
families'. The 'conditions' of these people do, of course, differ
but, so Illsley argues, they have a number of characteristics in
common. Thus they are both 'relatively resistant to curative treat-

ment' and 'potentially costly as long-term users of medical and social services'; they have multiple needs and they are therefore not 'the clear responsibility of a single profession or service organization'; and finally their 'condition or situation makes them economically unproductive and hence economically and socially dependent.' Such a proliferation of 'dependency groups' — and it is really this that binds all these unfortunates together — is to be explained against the background of the 'increasing complexity of existence in a highly urbanized and industrialized environment' which

> requires of individuals more sophisticated levels, as well as more varied repertoires, of competencies in occupational and social roles. Individuals with impaired abilities to function independently in these social spheres, or who are believed to be such, are at increased risk, then, of social dependency and of requiring various degrees or forms of social assistance.[30]

It is, of course, easy to take arguments from modernity theory ('the increasing complexity of existence') as a form of common sense because that certainly is what life in our society often feels like. However, in its characteristic usage the word 'complexity' serves not only to describe but also to naturalize the effects of a particular kind of social order and to bring the discussion to a close at the point where the real questions have still to be asked. And against this background it is hardly surprising to note that 'deterioration' theorists of schizophrenia should recently have witnessed a new lease of life.[31] Peter Townsend helps us to envisage the problem of dependency in the terms of a different order of complication when he argues that:

> A large part of any explanation of the scale and severity of problems identified as such by the personal social services are attributable to the forms of distribution of wealth, the institutions of property, and the origins and control of the wage system. They are also attributable to the definition of eligibility for employment, partly by society and partly through the market. 'Dependency' is, in an important sense, the obverse of the process of defining who are to be the economically active and what are to be the conditions and privileges of their roles.[32]

That is one kind of challenge to the rationalizations of the sullen obduracy of the market system. Unless we are prepared to follow this line of argument where it may take us the project of releasing (in a reversal of the project celebrated by Edgar Sheppard) the 'loose and scattered madness of the country' from the conditions of observation and confinement under which over a long period they have been brought, and finding for them 'fitting homes and refuges' in the community, is likely to issue in the reproduction and perpetuation of just those states of chronicity and demoralization within social life to which Sheppard and others contributed so ably more than a century ago.

Afterword:
The edge of the common

The schizophrenic, it may be said, resides at the edge of the common. *Common* refers in one form of usage to the life that we may think of ourselves as holding in common, to (as is sometimes said) the common conditions of our lives; yet also in an opposing sense 'the common' is the effect of a history of division and enclosure, the residue of a common estate over which we all of us have rights but that is at the same time 'wasteland'; and common finally is seen as the low and the vulgar, as the converse of the civilised. The *edge* of the common is stipulated not only because, in the various senses of common, that is where the schizophrenic has so often been put, but also because he focuses sharply the whole question of the bounds of community. The *edge of the common*, then, compacts in a single image the conflictual history of a relationship that is not only a history of ideas but equally a material history, a history of where within an altering social structure schizophrenic people as we now know them have been allowed to live and settle, and thus of the settlements and accommodations that have been made with them.

Those who take the road of structures of power and those who take the road of structures of culture differ, Richard Rorty has suggested, not over theoretical issues but over what we may hope.[1] The commitment of those who take this second road is to find ways to extend the bounds of community, and certainly as far as schizophrenic people are concerned the provocative question put to us by Luc Ciompi on the basis of his own rigorous inquiries as to 'whether the whole chronic schizophrenia could not be predominantly a social artefact' does hold out a great deal of hope.[2] But as to whether there are unsuperstitious reasons for thinking that this kind of hope could possibly be grounded in the social conditions of our period is quite another question, and there are some rather cogent arguments to be put for thinking that it could not. Yet we have at the very least to face the issue squarely on these terms and not refer it back to features intrinsic to schizophrenic conditions. In the estimation of Arthur and Joseph matters were, at the very least, unlikely to improve for people in their predicament, and we have some way to go before we can answer them in more positive terms. It is, perhaps, in any case fitting that they should have the last word (well, almost):

Joseph: How do you find this hospital?
Me: Well, um . . .
Joseph: People keep coming and going. They leave instead of sticking it out and getting into a routine. Even Billy Jones wants to go home. I mean, if he goes home — he depends on me. I mean if Billy Jones goes home what's the good of me stopping here? I mean, they just seem to sign themselves out and go home. And we stop here all the time.
Arthur: Are you informal like?
Joseph: No. (said very softly)
Arthur: Are you on a section?
Joseph: Why, I was, I had a house like which I lived in.
Arthur: I mean, could you get out of here if you wanted?
Joseph: (very softly) I don't know. I sort of . . . . (pause) I've sort of settled down now like but eh. . . . (pause)
Arthur: Yes.
(pause)
Arthur: It's so difficult to find things to talk about in here. I mean all we can talk about is the hospital. The only life we're practising is this hospital, aren't we? I mean, some of us don't even go out of the ward to be interested in anything.
(pause)
Joseph: At one time I used to play the guitar. Never bother now. I've repaired it and repaired it. Finally it's all finished now, all bust up. I used to play the guitar like.
(pause)
(shouts and clatter of trolleys from corridor)
Me: Well, that's it for today then. Time for lunch now.

Notes

Introduction: The labours of schizophrenia

1   In contrast, then, to Foucault's notion of madness as a 'permanent, unchanging, "singular experience"' characterized by *une absence d'oeuvre*, 'an unproductive idleness, outside human achievement', outside the real labours of history (Sheridan 1980: 209, 15). (See Foucault 1967.)
2   Kraepelin 1919.
3   Abrams 1982: 238. See also Elias 1978, Giddens 1979, MacIntyre 1981.
4   On the historical origins of schizophrenic conditions see Cooper and Sartorius 1977.
5   Sacks 1982. On general question of genetics see Midgley 1979, 1981.

The best book on the historical project of schizophrenia, and on the life histories of schizophrenics, is undoubtedly Bleuler 1978a. Zubin and Spring 1977 is an interesting (but in the terms of my argument none the less flawed) attempt to grapple with the vicissitudes of a history of scientific effort and to reconceptualize the problem of schizophrenia. Within the British psychiatric literature the writings of J.K. Wing are a reliable and stimulating source of guidance on schizo-phrenic individuals in their social aspects. For discussion of notions of 'mental illness' and critique of some of the wider political debates on this whole subject, see Sedgwick 1982. On this last aspect see also Pearson 1975.

6   Freeman et al. 1958: 46–7.
7   Mayer-Gross et al. 1960.
8   For what little discussion there is, see Al-Issa 1980.
9   Flor-Henry 1974.

Chapter 1: The making of the chronic schizophrenic

1   Canguilhem 1980: 38.
2   Hirst and Woolley 1982: 98, 167.

3 All the quotations that follow are from Maudsley 1871a.

4 Arlidge 1859: 102, quoted in Scull 1979: 220.

5 Bucknill 1880: 114, quoted in Scull 1977: 111.

6 Maudsley 1871b: 427, quoted in Scull 1977: 108.

7 Ibid.: 431.

8 Ibid.: 427.

9 All the quotations are from Sheppard 1872.

10 For documentation and discussion of the increase in pauper lunacy see Scull 1979, chapter 7; also Skultans 1979, chapter 7.

11 Scull 1977: 24.

12 Corrigan and Corrigan 1979: 8.

13 Scull 1977: 26—7.

14 Scull 1981a: 113; 1977: 27.

15 Beales 1948: 315, quoted in Corrigan and Corrigan 1979: 12.

16 Scull 1977: 30.

17 Scull 1981a: 111, 115.

18 Thompson 1974: 66.

19 Ibid.: 58.

20 Scull 1977: 30.

21 See discussion in Johnstone 1909.

22 All the quotations that follow are from S.W.D. Williams 1871.

23 Scull 1977: 129.

24 Thane 1978: 42.

25 Scull 1977: 130.

26 Arnold 1966: 80.

27 Gaskell 1970: 59, 102.

28 Dunn 1980: 218.

29 Granville 1877 vol. 2: 194, quoted in Scull 1977: 128.

30 Locke 1975: 395.

31 Spencer 1940: 79.

32 Bucknill 1880: 3—4, quoted in Scull 1979: 253.

33 Quoted in Scull 1979: 242.

34 Scull 1979: 190.

35 See the entries for *work* and *unemployment* in R. Williams 1976.

36 See the discussion in Johnstone 1909.

37 Figlio 1978.

38 Clark 1981: 284. On the intellectual context of late Victorian psychology and psychiatry, see in particular Young 1970.

39 Ibid.: 284—5.

40 Ibid.: 285.

41 Ibid.: 286.

42 All the quotations that follow are from the record of the debate in Johnstone 1909.

43 The strictures of Jones and Clouston are cast within the same evolutionary frame of reference as is espoused by the defenders of Kraepelin, and it is partly for this reason that they lack intellectual force. Thus in

giving expression to his liberal concerns for the welfare of the mentally ill at the annual meeting of the After-Care Association in 1909 Jones put forward a version of the 'drift' thesis that is still in common currency:

> In work such as ours in the large asylums one cannot but be struck with the greater number of men, women and younger persons who have drifted hither, often through no fault of their own, and whose ruined lives are paying the penalty for our civilization, for is not evolution and progress not infrequently at the expense of those who cannot keep the pace forced upon them? . . . Many for this reason must necessarily drift into ill health and poverty, and it is the opportunity of this Society to lend as such as these a helping hand to prop them up, to reinstate them, and to prevent their being left as failures upon the path of progress.

Our 'boasted civilization', he goes on to say, 'is manufacturing insane persons in London at the rate of 6 or 7 per day.' (Jones 1909) For Clouston see e.g. 1904: 287–8 and 1911: 26.

44   Kraepelin 1919: 37.
The classic account of crowd behaviour as a form of collective irrationality and of the connections between psychosis, the mob and revolution is Gustave Le Bon's *Psychologie des Foules* (1895). The 'social counterpart of the nightmare', W. H. Rivers asserts, 'is the revolution' (1923: 72). Interestingly Jones felt obliged to defend the cause of the After-Care Association with the claim that 'the help afforded by such a Society as ours encourages the self-respect and self-control of honest people who do not demand help as a right, nor do they regard its refusal as a slight caused by the envy and hatred of one class towards another, or possibly even as a further argument for the re-distribution of wealth and capital.' (Jones 1909) For the identification in the early years of the century of state aid for the insane and other groups with socialism, see Harrison 1976.

45   War Office 1922: 131–2, emphasis added. For discussion see E. Miller 1940.
46   Bleuler 1978a: 417, emphasis added.
47   Brower and Bannister 1902: 15, 303, 305.
48   Cole 1913: 12.
49   Knowles-Stansfield 1914.
50   Craig and Beaton 1926: 117, 134, 128.
51   Rivers 1923: 165, 114.
52   C. S. Myers, in Rivers 1923: 174. For discussion of the wider contours of the worries about a physical and moral deterioration among the British people in this era, see Pearson 1983, especially pp. 55–8.
53   Gaskell 1973: chapter XVII.
54   Orwell 1937: 142–3.

Chapter 2: Schizophrenia and history

1   Sacks 1982: 267.
2   Ciompi 1980b; Ciompi and Müller 1976.
3   Brown 1960.
4   For example, Wing 1978d. For a cross-cultural comparison of the course of schizophrenia in industrialized societies and societies of the Third World which suggests that chronic outcomes are much more common in the former, see World Health Organization 1979.
5   MacIntyre 1980.
6   Manfred Bleuler is the son of Eugen Bleuler, who coined the term schizophrenia. Like his father, Manfred Bleuler served as director of the Burghölzli clinic in Zurich. On the Burghölzli tradition see Bleuler 1979. One way of characterizing Manfred Bleuler's project over almost half a century is to say that he has tried to make amends for the inadequacies in his father's very partial critique of Kraepelin's theory of dementia praecox. On the confusing heritage of Eugen Bleuler see Stierlin 1967.
7   Bleuler 1978a.
8   Ibid.: 447.
9   Ibid.: 448.
10 Ibid.: 417.
11 Ibid.: 61.
12 Ibid.
13 Ciompi 1980b: 420; Cromwell in Wynne et al. 1978: 646.
14 Rorty 1982: 194.
15 For a useful discussion of some of the interpretative issues by a geneticist, see Kidd 1978.
16 MacIntyre 1981: 78.
17 Rorty 1982: 194.
18 Ibid.
19 Rorty 1980: 248–9.
20 Lukes 1973:79.
21 Quoted in Billig 1982: 17–18.
22 Ibid.
23 Popper 1963: 30.
24 Ibid.: 127–8.
25 MacIntyre 1977: 454.
26 Ibid.: 455.
27 Ibid.
28 MacIntyre 1981: 201.
29 MacIntyre 1977: 455.
30 Ibid.: 457.
31 Ibid.: 458.
32 Ibid.: 459.
33 Ibid.: 460.

34   Ibid.: 464.
35   Hume, *Treatise*, in MacIntyre 1977: 462.
36   Rorty 1980.
37   MacIntyre 1977: 470.
38   Ibid.: 471.
39   MacIntyre 1973a.
40   Ibid.
41   Ibid.
42   Ibid.
43   Dunn 1979: 103.
44   Dunn 1983: 120–1.
45   Salzinger et al. 1964.
46   Chapman and Chapman 1973: 6.
47   Rutter 1977, emphasis added. I do not have the space in which to discuss them in greater depth here, but the histories of inquiry into (for example) class, culture and the family in their relation to schizophrenia can be shown to be as much implicated in these strictures as is that of language. For a wide-ranging discussion of methodological shortcomings in the study of schizophrenia, see Coulter 1973. For an attempt to situate the project of psychology within the intellectual history I have described, see Marková 1982. For a spirited critique of traditional conceptions of the distinction between scientific and primitive thought, and between rational and irrational thought, see Douglas 1981, especially chapter 2.
48   Rorty 1982: 81, 203–4.
49   Cameron 1939: 265.
50   From Maurice Blanchot's *La Folie du Jour*, quoted in Derrida 1981: 65.
51   On some of these questions see Rorty 1982, in particular chapters 7 ('Is there a problem about fictional discourse?') and 11 ('Method, social science and social hope'). Fullinwider provides an engaging discussion of the construction of the schizophrenic in late Victorian and twentieth century American thought that in a number of respects complements my own arguments, yet because he interests himself in the problem of community only in its manipulative aspect he is left with this: 'The definition of a schizophrenic: someone who throws the observer into the non-Cartesian perceptual orientation. The definition of psychiatry: a defense against the non-Cartesian perceptual orientation.' (Fullinwider 1982: 152)
52   Rorty 1980: chapter VIII.
53   Sacks 1982: 314–5.
54   Ibid.: 241, 206.
55   Ibid.: 208, 219.
56   For example, 'Mental symptoms and public order' in Goffman 1972.
57   Bleuler 1978a: 116.
58   Ibid.: 115.
59   Hare 1979.

60   Bleuler 1978a: xix, 412.
61   Ibid.: 500, 218.
62   Bleuler 1978b: 633.
63   Bleuler 1978a: 226.
64   Ibid.: 187—8.
65   Ibid.
66   For example, Wing 1978d.
67   In this and other aspects of my discussion I have been helped by an unpublished paper by Stant 1974.

Chapter 3: Selfhood, identity and narrative

1   MacIntyre 1981: 197.
2   Ibid.: 192.
3   Ibid.: 194.
4   Ibid.: 190—1.
5   Ibid.: 199.
6   Ibid.: 203.
7   Pitkin 1972: 113.
8   MacIntyre 1981: 201.
9   Bettelheim 1978: 47.
10   Ibid.: 75.
11   Giddens 1979: 38.
12   Winnicott 1952: 221—2.
13   Ibid.: 225.
14   Winnicott 1971: 41.
15   Ibid.: 2.
16   Ibid.: 100.
17   Ibid.: 106.
18   Ibid.: 107.
19   Ibid.: 2.
20   Ibid.: 96.
21   Ibid.: 96—7.
22   Ibid.: 97—8.
23   Eliot 1967: 791.
24   Winnicott 1971: 99.
25   Winnicott 1952: 226.
26   Winnicott 1971: 103.
27   Winnicott 1952: 222.
28   Winnicott 1971: 98.
29   Eagleton 1983: 173—4. In a similar vein Rom Harré (J. Miller 1983: 168—9) has built upon some of Bruner's theories to suggest that

> Mothers have theories about how human beings should be, and what they are trying to do is to fulfil the theory in the person of their

infant. The way to do this is to anticipate the full panoply of social and psychological competence. . . . They do not talk *about* their infants' intentions; they provide them with them, and then they react to the infant as if it had them. What the infant does . . . is to appropriate slowly from out of that conversational matrix those ways of talking for its own purposes, so gradually it learns to do intention-ascribing talk for itself, of itself.

30   Ibid.: 185.
31   MacIntyre 1981: 202.
32   MacIntyre 1973a: 327.
33   Ibid.
34   Abrams 1982: 227.
35   Ibid.: 297.

Chapter 4: Chronic schizophrenics: Joseph and fellows

1   Goffman 1968: 143–4.
2   For discussion of Goffman and 'contingencies' in the context of an historical sociology, See Abrams 1982: chapter 9. In an otherwise incisive account of what the project of historical sociology might mean, Abrams claims rather too much for Goffman. By dint of the radical separateness in his writing of self and society, Goffman on my reading is not really a historical sociologist at all.
3   The transcripts are 'literary' renderings of the occasions to the extent that I have eliminated some pauses, hesitations etc., but I have reproduced all the words (and only the words) that were spoken.

Chapter 5: The chronic schizophrenic as historical agent

1   MacIntyre 1981: 195.
2   The classic text here is, of course, Austin 1962.
3   Searle 1969: 47.
4   Ibid.: 45.
5   Pitkin 1972: 133.
6   S. Cavell, quoted in Pitkin 1972. See also Coulter 1973: chapter 4.
7   See MIND 1983b.
8   Winnicott 1949: 244.
9   Long 1976: 21, 7–8.
10   Ibid.: 188.
11   For elaboration of the idea that schizophrenics may sometimes communicate more easily in a second language to which they do not have such close emotional and historical ties, and that the learning of such a lanuguage may prove therapeutic, see Matulis 1977.
12   As Roy Schafer elegantly summarizes it, Freud used two primary

narrative structures; one begins with the infant and young child as a beast, and the other, based on Newtonian physics, present psycho-analysis as the study of the mind conceived as a machine or a 'mental apparatus':

> In the beginning, the forces that move the machine are primarily the brute organism's instinctual drives. Here the tale of the mental apparatus borrows from the tale of the brute organism and consequently becomes narratively incoherent: the mechanical mind is now said to behave like a creature with a soul — seeking, reacting and developing. The tale continues with increasing incoherence. (Schafer 1981: 28)

See also Schafer 1978.

13 Freud 1894.
14 Laplanche and Pontalis 1973: 167.
15 Freud 1984.
16 Laplanche and Pontalis 1973: 167—9.
17 Riviere 1955: 358.
18 Laplanche and Pontalis 1973: 356.
19 Bion 1967: 39.
20 Wilden 1972: 152.
21 Bion 1967: 40.
22 For a recent discussion of the pertinence of Neurath's image, see Glover 1984: 174—7. This conception may perhaps help to throw some light on why schizophrenics sometimes resort to inflicting such devastating injuries on themselves. Thus we can perhaps comprehend the schizophrenic male who cuts off his penis as attempting to get outside the interaction, to fashion himself as wholly separate. It is relevant to remark here also on the high suicide rate among schizophrenics.

Chapter 6: Psychology, social life and the schizophrenic

1   Elias 1978: 262, quoted in Abrams 1982: 233.
2   Abrams 1982: 233 in a discussion of Elias.
3   Ibid.: 234.
4   Elias 1978: 258, quoted in Abrams 1982: 237.
5   McGhie and Chapman 1961: 114.
6   Frith 1979: 228.
7   Haugeland 1978: 259.
8   Ibid.
9   Neisser 1976: 58.
10 Contribution to open peer commentary in Haugeland 1978: 250—1.
11 MacIntyre 1983: 21.
12 Ibid.: 23.
13 See Neisser 1976 for discussion along these lines. These formulations

can perhaps help us identify the weaknesses of personal construct theory in its application to the problem of schizophrenia. For what personal construct theory offers is a humanized and personalized version of Clear and Distinct Ideas: one's very own Clear and Distinct Ideas. The trouble to which this frame of reference can lead when put to work as a practical strategy is evident from a reading of Bannister et al. 1975.

14 MacIntyre 1983: 23. The notorious 'double-bind' theory of schizophrenia can perhaps be reconstructed as an attempt to talk about the sorts of problems of agency that MacIntyre identifies. That, at least, is what Gregory Bateson seemed to suggest in the last years of his life. But in its original formulation the theory was of course tied, in Bateson's words, to an 'older, realistic, "thingish" epistemology', and gave rise to all sorts of misunderstandings, not least the idea that double-binds were things that could be identified and counted. To reconstruct it in the sort of theoretical context that MacIntyre proposes may be intellectually more honest, but it means of course that the theory loses the explanatory specificity which lent it its immense cultural power and attraction. See Sluzki and Ransom 1976, in particular the foreword and chapter 16 by Bateson.

15 Neisser 1976: 104—5.

16 Ibid.

17 H. L. Dreyfus, contribution to open peer commentary in Haugeland 1978: 233—4.

18 Harry Stack Sullivan (1974: 199) claims that in the histories of schizophrenics there is generally to be found a 'point at which there had occurred what might well be called a disaster to self-esteem', an event that 'is attended subjectively by the state which we identify by the term *panic*'. Where panic 'passes over into a chronic feeling of insecurity or inadequacy',

> there has occurred a grave break in the solidarity or dependability of the frames of reference which the individual possessed concerning the synthesis or complex of his self and the world (especially other people). Such a break or failure takes the form of a vaguely formulated but clearly felt uncertainty in the cosmos. The individual is no longer able to proceed in the elaboration of his life with the same unthinking directness which was previously the case. A number of typical chronic maladjustments in interpersonal relations may be referred to such an event. Such events stand apparently in a necessary relation in the series which culminates in schizophrenia. In other words, there is always such a collapse of that cosmic security which is perhaps our heritage from an exceedingly early developmental period, to be found in the history of a schizophrenic.

19 Rorty 1980: 248.

20 Ibid.: 254.

21 Oakeshott 1975: 38.
22 Bleuler 1978a: 457.
23 Ibid.: 456.
24 Ibid.
25 Ibid.: 457.
26 Ibid.: 418.
27 Ibid.: 480.
28 Ibid.: 419.
29 Ibid.: 215.
30 Ibid.: 216.
31 Ibid.: 216–17.
32 Bleuler 1978b: 633–4.
33 Bleuler 1978a: 217–18.
34 Ibid.: 413.
35 Bleuler 1963: 952.
36 Bleuler 1978a: 470.

Chapter 7: The problem of community

1 Dunn 1979: 116.
2 Ibid.: 20–1.
3 See Scull 1977.
4 Mishra 1977: 80.
5 MacPherson 1973: 23.
6 L. van Londen in MIND 1980.
7 MacPherson 1973: 199.
8 Sedgwick 1982: 241.
9 Lukes 1973: 148.
10 Ibid.: 149.
11 Ibid.: 133–5.
12 Dworkin 1977. Bleuler (1978a) criticizes the traditional view that, because they were incapable of suffering, older (i.e. demented) schizophrenics did not commit suicide, and presents some contrary evidence.
13 Wing 1978d: 607.
14 On secondary reactions, secondary handicaps etc. see Wing 1978a–e. On biographical reconstruction in chronic illness see Bury 1982.
15 Wing 1978d.
16 Abrams 1978. See also the arguments put forward in the Downing seminar on social care, to which Abrams's paper was a contribution on the need to undertake research directed to audiences that include clients themselves (Barnes and Connelly 1978: 141). One attempt to canvas the views of schizophrenics themselves is Wing 1975.
17 Rorty 1982: 198.
18 Reprinted as an NSF leaflet, no date.

19   National Schizophrenia Fellowship 1974: 8. On the slide from Oxbridge to destitution see also Jones 1909.

20   See here Michel Foucault on the 'insurrection of subjugated knowledges'. Foucault argues that it is through the

> re-emergence of these low-ranking knowledges, these unqualified, even directly disqualified knowledges (such as that of the psychiatric patient, of the ill person, of the nurse, of the doctor — parallel and marginal as they are to the knowledge of medicine — that of the delinquent etc.) and which involve what I would call a popular knowledge (*le savoir des gens*) . . . that criticism performs its work. (Gordon 1980: 79—84)

21   Abrams 1978. For attempts to sustain the viability of households with a schizophrenic member see, most recently, Leff et al. 1982.

22   Carter 1981: 204—17. See also Edwards and Carter 1979.

23   Ibid.

24   Marx 1973: 140. For discussion of the commodification of time see Giddens 1981.

25   Marx 1971: 54.

26   Carter 1981: 215.

27   Wing 1978b.

28   Corrigan 1975. See also Corrigan 1979.

29   Discussions of new requirements for service are: King's Fund 1983, MIND 1983a, Richmond Fellowship 1983. On problems of procuring care in the community, and of generating and sustaining patterns of support, see Abrams 1978, 1979, 1984. Martin Bulmer is presently completing a study of Philip Abrams's work under the provisional title *Neighbours: the work of Philip Abrams*. An informative discussion of support networks in the context of schizophrenia is Gibbons 1983.

30   Illsley 1981.

31   See e.g. Crow and Johnstone 1980 and Crow 1983b. Crow 1983a has also advanced a hypothesis of schizophrenia as an infectious disease with the 'possibility that most cases of schizophrenia result from contact with an overt case of the disease'. Needless to say reconstructed contamination theories of this sort do not augur very well for community care. On schizophrenic deterioration see also Morgan 1979.

32   Townsend 1981.

Afterword: The edge of the common

1   Rorty 1982: 204.

2   Ciompi 1981. See also Ciompi 1980a.

Bibliography

I have included a number of items here which I have drawn upon but not referred to directly in the text

Abrahamson, D. and Brenner, D. (1979) *A Study of the 'Old Long-Stay' patients in Goodmayes Hospital* Goodmayes Hospital

Abrams, P. (1978) Community care: some research problems and priorities, in Barnes J. and Connelly, N. (eds) *Social Care Research* London: Policy Studies Institute and Bedford Square Press (also in *Policy and Politics* 6 (1977), 125–51)

Abrams, P. (1979) *Policy, Values* and *Neighbourhood Care: Some Problems of Definition* Volunteer Centre seminar papers (unpublished)

Abrams, P. (1982) *Historical Sociology* Shepton Mallet: Open Books

Abrams, P. (1984) Realities of neighbourhood care: the interactions between statutory, voluntary, and informal social care, *Policy and Politics* October (forthcoming)

Al-Issa, A. (1980) *The Psychopathology of Women* New Jersey: Prentice-Hall

Arlidge, J.T. (1859) *On the State of Lunacy and the Legal Provision for the Insane* London: Churchill

Arnold, M. (1966) *Culture and Anarchy* Cambridge: Cambridge University Press (first published 1869)

Austin, J.L. (1962) *How to do Things with Words* Oxford: Oxford University Press

Bannister, D., Adams-Webber, J.R., Penn, W.I. and Radley, A.R. (1975) Reversing the process of thought disorder: a serial validation experiment, *Br. J. Soc. Clin. Psychol.* 14, 169–80

Barnes, J. and Connelly, N. (eds) (1978) *Social Care Research* London: Policy Studies Institute and Bedford Square Press

Beales, H.L. (1948) The Passing of the Poor Law, *Political Quarterly* 9

Bennett, D. (1980) Rehabilitation for chronic mentally ill people, in *Alternatives to Mental Hospitals* London: MIND

Bennett, D. (1981a) The Camberwell district rehabilitation service, in Wing, J.K. and Morris, B (eds) *Handbook of Psychiatric Rehabilitation Practice* Oxford: Oxford University Press

Bennett, D. (1981b) What direction for psychiatric day services?, in *The Mental Health Year Book* London: MIND

Bennett, D. (1983) The practical problems of establishing a district service, in King's Fund *Creating Local Psychiatric Services: Papers from the Long-term and Community Care Team* London: King's Fund Centre

Bettelheim, B. (1978) *The Uses of Enchantment* Harmondsworth: Penguin

Bhaskar, R. (1979) *The Possibility of Naturalism* Brighton: Harvester

Billig, M. (1982) *Ideology and Social Psychology* Oxford: Basil Blackwell

Bion, W.R. (1967) *Second Thoughts* London: Heinemann Medical Books

Bleuler, M. (1943) Die spatschizophrenen Krankheitsbilder, *Fortschr. Neurol. Psychiat.* 15, 259–90 (abbreviated version reprinted in Bleuler, M. (ed.) 1979)

Bleuler, M. (1963) Conceptions of schizophrenia within the last fifty years and today, *Proc. R. Soc. Med.* 56, 945–52

Bleuler, M. (1978a) *The Schizophrenic Disorders: Long-term Patient and Family Studies* New Haven: Yale University Press (first published in 1972 as *Die Schizophrenen.Geistesstörungen im Lichte Langjahriger Kranken und Familiengeschichten* Stuttgart: Georg Thieme)

Bleuler, M. (1978b) The long-term course of schizophrenic psychoses, in Wynne, L.C., Cromwell, R.L. and Matthysse, S. (eds) *The Nature of Schizophrenia*, New York: Wiley

Bleuler, M. (ed.) (1979) *Beitrage zur Schizophrenielehre der Zürcher Psychiatrischen Universitätsklinik Burghölzli (1902–1971)* Darmstadt: Wissenschaftliche Buchgesselschaft

Bleuler, M. (1982a) Prognosis of schizophrenic psychoses: a summary of life-long personal research compared with the research of other psychiatrists, lesson 31 in Flach, F.F. (ed.) *Directions in Psychiatry* New York: Hatherleigh

Bleuler, M. (1982b) Theoretical basis of research into the course, outcome and prognosis of schizophrenic psychoses, lesson 32 in Flach, F.F. (ed.) *Directions in Psychiatry* New York: Hatherleigh

Bleuler, M. (1983a) Contribution to discussion panel on schizophrenic deterioration, *Brit. J. Psychiat.* 143, 78–9

Bleuler, M. (1983b) Das alte und das neue Bild des schizophrenen (paper delivered at the annual conference of the Schweizerischen Gesellschaft für Psychiatrie, 22–24 Sept. 1983: to be published in *Schweizer Archiv für Neurologie, Psychochirurgie und Psychiatrie*).

Bolton, N. (ed.) (1979) *Philosophical Problems in Psychology* London: Methuen

Brower, D. and Bannister, H. (1902) *A Practical Manual of Insanity* London: W.B. Saunders

Brown, G.W. (1960) Length of hospital stay and schizophrenia, *Acta. Psychiat. Neurol. Scand* 35, 414–30

Bucknill, J.C. (1880) *The Care of the Insane and their Legal Control* London: Macmillan

Bury, M. (1982) Chronic illness as biographical disruption, *Sociology of*

Health and Illness 4, 167—82

Cameron, N. (1939) Deterioration and regression in schizophrenic thinking, *Journ. Abnorm. & Soc. Psychol.* 34, 265—70

Canguilhem, G. (1980) What is psychology, *I & C* 7, 37—50 (first published in *Revue de Metaphysique et de Morale* 1 (1958))

Carter, J. (1981) *Day Services for Adults* London: Allen and Unwin

Chapman, L.J. and Chapman, J.P. (1973) *Disordered Thought in Schizophrenia* New York: Appleton Century Crofts

Ciompi, L. (1980a) Ist die chronische Schizophrenie ein Artefakt? Argumente und Gegenargumente, *Fortschr. Neurol. Psychiat.* 48, 237—48

Ciompi, L. (1980b) The natural history of schizophrenia in the long term, *Brit. J. Psychiat.* 136, 413—20

Ciompi, L. (1981) The social outcome of schizophrenia, in Wing, J.K., Kielholz, P. and Zinn, W.M. (eds) *Rehabilitation of Patients with Schizophrenia and Depressions* Bern: Hans Huber

Ciompi, L. (1983) Research implications of recent trends in the treatment of schizophrenia (unpublished paper)

Ciompi, L. and Müller, C.H. (1976) *Lebensweg und Alter der Schizophrenen* Berlin: Springer

Clare, A. (1976) *Psychiatry in Dissent* London: Tavistock

Clark, M. (1981) The rejection of psychological approaches to mental disorder in late nineteenth-century British psychiatry, in Scull, A.T. (ed.) *Madhouses, Mad-Doctors and Madmen* London: Athlone

Clouston, T.S. (1904) *Clinical Lectures on Mental Diseases* 6th edn) London: Churchill

Clouston, T.S. (1911) *Unsoundness of Mind* London: Methuen

Cole, R. (1913) *Mental diseases* London: University of London Press

Cooper, J. and Sartorius, N. (1977) Cultural and temporal variations in schizophrenia: a speculation on the importance of industrialization, *Brit. J. Psychiat.* 130, 50—5

Corrigan, P. (1975) 'Doing nothing', *Working Papers in Cultural Studies* 7/8, 103—5

Corrigan, P. (1979) *Schooling the Smash Street Kids* London: Macmillan

Corrigan, P. and Corrigan, V. (1979) State formation and social policy until 1871, in Parry, N., Rustin, M. and Satyamurti, C. (eds) *Social Work, Welfare and the State* London: Edward Arnold

Coulter, J. (1973) *Approaches to Insanity* London: Martin Robertson

Craig, M. and Beaton, T. (1926) *Psychological medicine* London: Churchill

Creer, C. and Wing, J.K. (1974) *Schizophrenia at Home* National Schizophrenia Fellowship, 79 Victoria Road, Surbiton, Surrey KT6 4NS

Crow, T.J. (1983a) Is schizophrenia an infectious disease?, *Lancet* 22 Jan., 173—5

Crow, T.J. (1983b) Contribution to discussion on schizophrenic deterioration, in Cutting, J. (ed.) *Brit. J. Psychiat.* 143, 77—84

Crow, T.J. and Johnstone, E.C. (1980) Dementia praecox and schizophrenia: was Bleuler wrong?, *J. Roy. Coll. Phys. of Lond.* 14 (4)

Cutting, J. (ed.) (1983) Discussion on schizophrenic deterioration, *Brit. J. Psychiat.* 143, 77—84

Derrida, J. (1981) The law of genre, in Mitchell, W.J.T. (ed.) *On Narrative* Chicago: University of Chicago Press

Doucet, P. and Laurin, C. (eds) (1971) *Problems of Psychosis* Amersterdam: Excerpta Medica

Douglas, M. (1981) *Evans-Pritchard* London: Fontana

Dunn, J. (1979) *Western Political Theory in the Face of the Future* Cambridge: Cambridge University Press

Dunn, J. (1980) *Political Obligation in its Historical Context* Cambridge: Cambridge University Press

Dunn, J. (1983) Social theory, social understanding and political action, in Lloyd, C. (ed.) *Social Theory and Political Practice* Oxford: Oxford University Press

Dworkin, R. (1977) *Taking Rights Seriously* London: Duckworth

Eagleton, T. (1983) *Literary Theory* Oxford: Basil Blackwell

Early, E.A. (1982) The logic of well-being: therapeutic narratives in Cairo, Egypt, *Soc. Sci. & Med.* 16, 1491—7

Edwards, C. and Carter, J. (1979) Day services and the mentally ill, in Wing, J.K. and Olsen, R. *Community Care for the Mentally Disabled* Oxford: Oxford University Press

Elias, N. (1978) *The Civilizing Process* Oxford: Basil Blackwell

Eliot, George (1967) *Daniel Deronda* Harmondsworth: Penguin (first published 1876)

Figlio, K. (1978) Chlorosis and chronic disease in nineteenth-century Britain: the social constitution of somatic illness in a capitalist society, *Social History* 3, 167—97

Flor-Henry, F. (1974) Psychosis, neurosis and epilepsy: developmental and gender-related effects and their aetiological contribution, *Brit. J. Psychiat.* 124, 144—50

Foucault, M. (1967) *Madness and Civilization* London: Tavistock

Foucault, M. (1971) *L'Ordre du Discours* Paris: Gallimard (translated as Orders of discourse, *Soc. Sci. & Inform.* 10, 7—30)

Foucault, M. (1977) *Discipline and Punish* London: Allen Lane

Freeman, T., Cameron, J.L. and McGhie, A. (1958) *Chronic Schizophrenia* London: Tavistock

Freud, S. (1894) The neuro-psychoses of defense, in *S.E. III* London: Hogarth, 1953—73

Frith, C.D. (1979) Consciousness, information processing and schizophrenia, *Brit. J. Psychiat.* 134, 225—35

Fullinwider, S.P. (1982) *Technicians of the Finite: The Rise and Decline of the Schizophrenic in American Thought 1840—1960* Westport, Connecticut: Greenwood Press

Gaskell, Elizabeth (1970) *Mary Barton* Harmondsworth: Penguin (first published 1848)

Gaskell, Elizabeth (1973) *North and South* Oxford: Oxford University Press

(first published 1855)

Gibbons, J. (1983) *Care of Schizophrenic Patients in the Community 1981–3*, third annual report, Department of Psychiatry, University of Southampton

Giddens, A. (1979) *Central Problems in Social Theory* London: Macmillan

Giddens, A. (1981) *A Contemporary Critique of Historical Materialism* London: Macmillan

Glover, J. (1984) *What Sort of People Should There Be?* Harmondsworth: Penguin

Goffman, E. (1968) *Asylums* Harmondsworth: Penguin

Goffman, E. (1971) The insanity of place, in his *Relations in Public* London: Allen Lane

Goffman, E. (1972) Mental symptoms and public order, in his *Interaction Ritual,* London: Allen Lane

Gordon, C. (ed.) (1980) *Foucault: Power/knowledge* Brighton: Harvester

Granville, J.M. (1877) *The Care and Cure of the Insane* (2 vols) London: Hardwicke and Bogue

Grinberg, L., Sor, D. and de Bianchedi, E. (1975) *Introduction to the Work of Bion* Perthshire: Clunie Press

Hamilton, M. (ed.) (1976) *Fish's Schizophrenia* Bristol: John Wright (second edition of *Schizophrenia* by F.J. Fish first published 1962)

Hare, E. (1979) Review of *The Schizophrenic Disorders: Long-term Patient and Family Studies* by Manfred Bleuler, *Brit. J. Psychiat.* 135, 474–80

Harrison, E. (1976) The changing meaning of social work, in Halsey, A.H. (ed.) *Traditions of Social Policy* Oxford: Basil Blackwell

Haugeland, J. (1978) The nature and plausibility of cognitivism, *Behav. & Brain Sciences* 2, 215–60

Haugeland, J. (ed.) (1981) *Mind Design* Vermont: Bradford Books

Hirst, P. and Woolley, P. (1982) *Social Relations and Human Attributes* London: Tavistock

Illsley, R. (1981) Problems of dependency groups: the care of the elderly, the handicapped and the chronically ill, *Soc. Sci. Med.* 15A, 327–32

Johnstone, T. (1909) The case for dementia praecox, *J. Mental Sci.* 55, 64–91

Jones, R. (1909) The urgent necessity of helping mental convalescents, *J. Mental Sci.* 55, 410–18

Kidd, K.K. (1978) A genetic perspective on schizophrenia, in Wynne, L.C., Cromwell, R.L. and Matthysse, S. (eds) *The Nature of Schizophrenia* New York: Wiley

King's Fund (1983) *Creating Local Psychiatric Services: Papers from the Long-term and Community Care Team* London: King's Fund Centre

Knowles-Stansfield, T.E. (1914) The villa or colony system for the care and treatment of cases of mental disease, *J. Ment. Sci. 1914* 60, 30–9

Kraepelin, E. (1919) *Dementia Praecox and Paraphrenia* (translated Barclay, R.M.) Edinburgh: Livingstone

Kuhn, T. (1962) *The Structure of Scientific Revolutions* Chicago: University of Chicago Press

Laplanche, J. and Pontalis, J.-B. (1973) *The Language of Psychoanalysis* London: Hogarth Press

LeBon, G. (1895) *Psychologie des Foules* Paris: Presses Universitaires de France

Leff, J., Kuipers, L., Berkowitz, R., Eberlein-Fries, R. and Sturgeon, D. (1982) A controlled trial of social intervention in the families of schizophrenic patients, *Brit. J. Psychiat.* 141, 121–34

Locke, J. (1975) *An Essay concerning Human Understanding* Oxford: Oxford University Press

Long, M. (1976) *The Unnatural Scene* London: Methuen

Lukes, S. (1973) *Individualism* Oxford: Basil Blackwell

McGhie, A. and Chapman, J. (1961) Disorders of attention and perception in early schizophrenia, *Br. J. Med. Psychol.* 34, 103–16

MacIntyre, A. (1967) *A Short History of Ethics* London: Routledge

MacIntyre, A. (1973a) Ideology, social science and revolution, *Comparative Politics* 5(3), 321–42

MacIntyre, A. (1973b) The essential contestability of some social concepts, *Ethics* 84(1), 1–9

MacIntyre, A. (1977) Epistemological crises, dramatic narrative and the philosophy of science, *The Monist* 60, 453–72

MacIntyre, A. (1980) Review of *Philosophy and the Mirror of Nature* by Richard Rorty, *London Review of Books* 5–18 June, 15–16

MacIntyre, A. (1981) *After Virtue* London: Duckworth

MacIntyre, A. (1983) The indispensability of political theory, in Miller, D. and Seidentop, L. (eds) *The Nature of Political Theory* Oxford: Oxford University Press

MacPherson, C.B. (1973) *Democratic Theory* Oxford: Oxford University Press

Markova, I. (1982) *Paradigms, Thought and Language* Chichester: Wiley

Marx, K. (1971) *The Poverty of Philosophy* New York: International Publishers

Marx, K. (1973) *Grundrisse* Harmondsworth: Penguin

Matulis, A.C. (1977) *Language ... a Hope* Detroit: National Research Institute for Psychoanalysis and Psychology

Maudsley, H. (1871a) Insanity and its treatment, *J. Mental Sci.* 17, 311–34

Maudsley, H. (1871b) *The Physiology and Pathology of the Mind* New York: Appleton (first published 1867)

Mayer-Gross, W., Slater, E. and Roth, M. (1960) *Clinical Psychiatry* London: Cassell

Midgley, M. (1979) *Beast and Man* Brighton: Harvester Press

Midgley, M. (1981) *Heart and Mind* London: Methuen

Miller, E. (ed.) (1940) *Neurosis in War* London: Macmillan

Miller, J. (ed.) (1983) *States of Mind* London: BBC Publications

Milner, M. (1969) *The Hands of the Living God* London: Hogarth

MIND (1980) *Alternatives to Mental Hospitals* London: MIND Publications

MIND (1983a) *Common Concern* London: MIND Publications
MIND (1983b) *Money in Hospital* London: MIND Publications
Mishra, R. (1977) *Society and Social Policy* London: Macmillan
Morgan, R. (1977) Three weeks in isolation with two chronic schizophrenic patients, *Brit. J. Psychiat.* 131, 504–13
Morgan, R. (1979) Conversations with chronic schizophrenic patients, *Brit. J. Psychiat.* 134, 187–94
National Schizophrenia Fellowship (1974) *Living with Schizophrenia – by the Relatives*, National Schizophrenia Fellowship, 79 Victoria Road, Surbiton, Surrey KT6 4NS
National Schizophrenia Fellowship (1979) *Home Sweet Home* National Schizophrenia Fellowship, 79 Victoria Road, Surbiton, Surrey KT6 4NS
Neisser, U. (1976) *Cognition and Reality* San Francisco: W.H. Freeman
Oakeshott, M. (1975) *On Human Conduct* Oxford: Oxford University Press
Oltmanns, T.F. and Neale, J.M. (1982) Psychological deficits in schizophrenia: information processing and communication problems, in Wing, J.K. and Wing, L. (eds) *Psychoses of Uncertain Aetiology: Handbook of Psychiatry 3* Cambridge: Cambridge University Press
Orwell, G. (1937) *The Road to Wigan Pier* London: Gollancz
Pearson, G. (1975) *The Deviant Imagination* London: Macmillan
Pearson, G. (1983) *Hooligan* London: Macmillan
Peroni, F. (1981) The status of chronic illness, *Social Policy & Admin.* 15(1), 43–53
Pitkin, H.F. (1972) *Wittgenstein and Justice* Berkeley: University of California Press
Popper, K.R. (1963) *Conjectures and Refutations* London: Routledge
Priestley, D. (1979) *Tied Together with String* National Schizophrenia Fellowship, 79 Victoria Road, Surbiton, Surrey KY6 4NS
Richmond Fellowship (1983) *Mental Health and the Community* London: Richmond Fellowship Press
Rivers, W.H. (1923) *Psychology and Politics* London: Kegan Paul
Riviere, J. (1955) The unconscious phantasy of an inner world reflected in examples from literature, in Klein, M., Heimann, F. and Money-Kyrle, R. (eds) *New Directions in Psychoanalysis* London: Tavistock
Rochester, S.R. (1978) Are language disorders in acute schizophrenia actually information-processing disorders? in Wynne, L.C., Cromwell, R.L. and Mattysse, S. (eds) *The Nature of Schizophrenia* New York: Wiley
Rollin, H. (ed.) (1980) *Coping with Schizophrenia* London: Andre Deutch
Rorty, R. (1980) *Philosophy and the Mirror of Nature* Oxford: Basil Blackwell
Rorty, R. (1982) *Consequences of Pragmatism* Brighton: Harvester
Rutter, D.R. (1977) Speech patterning in recently admitted and chronic long-stay schizophrenic patients, *Br. J. Soc. Clin. Psychol.* 16, 47–55
Sacks, O. (1982) *Awakenings* London: Picador (first published by Gerald Duckworth, 1973)
Salzinger, K. Portnoy, S. and Feldman, R. (1964) Experimental manipula-

tions of continuous speech in schizophrenic patients, *J. Abnorm. Soc. Psychol.* 68, 508—16

Schafer, R. (1976) *A New Language for Psychoanalysis* New Haven: Yale University Press

Schafer, R. (1981) Narration in the psychoanalytic dialogue, in Mitchell, W.J.T. (ed.) *On Narrative* Chicago: University of Chicago Press

Schwartz, S. (ed.) (1978) *Language and Cognition in Schizophrenia* New Jersey: Hillsdale

Scull, A.T. (1977) *Decarceration* New Jersey: Prentice-Hall

Scull, A.T. (1979) *Museums of Madness* London: Allen Lane

Scull, A.T. (1981a) Moral treatment reconsidered: some sociological comments on an episode in the history of British psychiatry, in Scull, A.T. (ed.) *Madhouses, Mad-Doctors, and Madmen* London: Athlone

Scull, A.T. (ed.) (1981b) *Madhouses, Mad-Doctors, and Madmen* London: Athlone

Searle, J. (1969) *Speech Acts* Cambridge: Cambridge University Press

Sedgwick, P. (1982) *Psycho Politics* London: Pluto

Sheppard, E. (1872) On some of the modern teachings of insanity, *J. Mental Sci.* 17, 499—514

Sheridan, A. (1980) *Michel Foucault: The Will to Truth* London: Tavistock

Skultans, V. (1979) *English Madness* London: Routledge

Sluzki, C.E. and Ransom, D.C. (eds) (1976) *Double Bind: the Foundation of the Communicational Approach to the Family* New York: Grune and Stratton

Spencer, H. (1940) *The Man versus the State* London: Watts (first published 1884)

Stant, M. (1974) Problems of proof and method in Goffman's *Asylums*, unpublished paper, Department of Sociology and Social Administration, University of Durham

Stierlin, H. (1967) Bleuler's concept of schizophrenia: a confusing heritage, *Amer. J. Psychiat.* 123, 996—1001

Still, A.W. (1979) Perception and representation, in Bolton, N. (ed.) *Philosophical Problems in Psychology* London: Methuen

Sullivan, H.S. (1974) *Schizophrenia as a Human Process* New York: Norton

Thane, P. (1978) Women and the Poor Law in Victorian and Edwardian England, *History Workshop* 6, 29—51

Thompson, E.P. (1974) Time, work discipline and industrial capitalism, in Flinn, M.W. and Smout, T.C. (eds) *Essays in Social History* Oxford: Oxford University Press (first published in *Past and Present*, vol. 38, 1967)

Townsend, P. (1981) Imprisoned in a casualty model of welfare, *Community Care* 3 Sept., 22—5

War Office (1922) *Report of the War Office Committee of Enquiry on Shell Shock* London: HMSO

Wilden, A. (1972) *System and Structure* London: Tavistock

Williams, R. (1971) *Orwell* London: Fontana

Williams, R. (1976) *Keywords* London: Fontana

Williams, S.W.D. (1871) Our over-crowded lunatic asylums, *J. Ment. Sci.* 17. 515—18

Wing, J.K. (ed.) (1975) *Schizophrenia from Within* National Schizophrenia Fellowship, 79 Victoria Road, Surbiton, Surrey KT6 4NS

Wing, J.K. (1978a) *Reasoning About Madness* Oxford: Oxford University Press

Wing, J.K. (1978b) *Schizophrenia and its Management in the Community* National Schizophrenia Fellowship, 79 Victoria Road, Surbiton, Surrey KT6 4NS

Wing, J.K. (ed.) (1978c) *Schizophrenia: Towards a New Synthesis* London: Academic Press

Wing, J.K. (1978d) Social influence on the course of schizophrenia in Wynne, L.C., Cromwell, R.L. and Matthysse, S. (eds) *The Nature of Schizophrenia* New York: Wiley

Wing, J.K. (1978e) Medical and social science, and medical and social care, in Barnes, J. and Connelly, N. (eds) *Social Care Research* London: Policy Studies Institute and Bedford Square Press

Wing, J.K. (1984) Long-term adaptation in schizophrenia, in Miller, N. and Cohen, G. (eds) *Schizophrenia and Ageing* Washington: Guilford Press

Wing, J.K. and Brown, G.W. (1970) *Institutionalism and Schizophrenia* Cambridge: Cambridge University Press

Wing, J.K. and Morris, B. (eds) (1981) *Handbook of Psychiatric Rehabilitation Practice* Oxford: Oxford University Press

Wing, J.K. and Olsen, R. (eds) (1979) *Community Care for the Mentally Disabled* Oxford: Oxford University Press

Winnicott, D.W. (1949) Mind and its relation to the psyche-soma, in Winnicott, D.W. (1958) *Collected Papers* London: Tavistock

Winnicott, D.W. (1952) Psychoses and child care, in Winnicott, D.W. (1958) *Collected Papers* London: Tavistock

Winnicott, D.W. (1971) *Playing and Reality* London: Tavistock

World Health Organization (1979) *Schizophrenia: An International Follow-Up Study* London: Wiley

Wynne, L.C., Cromwell, R.L. and Matthysse, S. (eds) (1978) *The Nature of Schizophrenia* New York: Wiley

Young, R.M. (1970) *Mind, Brain and Adaptation* Oxford: Oxford University Press

Zubin, J. and Spring, B. (1977) Vulnerability: a new view of schizophrenia, *J. Abnorm. Psychol.* 86, 103—26

Index